Skorzeny's Secret Missions

Skorzeny's Secret Missions

The Incredible Exploits of Hitler's Commando

Otto Skorzeny

Foreword by Charles Messenger
Introduction by Dan Raviv

Skyhorse Publishing

CONTENTS

LIST OF ILLUSTRATIONS

pages 91 to 98

FOREWORD

Otto Skorzeny was one of the more colourful characters of the Third Reich and became a darling of the Nazi propaganda machine. He is best known for the part he played in the dramatic rescue of Mussolini from incarceration in a hotel in the Abruzzi mountains, but he also took part in a number of other daring special forces operations. Originally published in 1957, this is an account of his war.

Austrian-born like Hitler, Skorzeny experienced the turbulence in that country of the early 1930s. A believer in *Anschluss*, he joined the Nazi Party in 1930, but says nothing about the assassination of Chancellor Dollfuss as a result of an abortive Nazi plot to bring about union with Germany four years later, although it is difficult to believe that he was not in some way involved. When *Anschluss* did occur in March 1938, Skorzeny's role in helping to prevent bloodshed came to the attention of Arthur Seyss-Inquart, the newly appointed German governor of Austria. But, when war came, he was turned down by the Luftwaffe as being too old to become a pilot and had to content himself as a trainee Waffen-SS engineer officer instead. Skorzeny saw service with the SS Das Reich Division in France, the Balkans and the invasion of Russia before being evacuated sick with colic at the end of 1941.

It was not until spring 1943, after a period of home service, that Skorzeny entered the field that would make him famous. He joined Section 6 of the RSHA, which was its foreign department, covering not just intelligence, but special operations as well. Here he experienced the bureaucratic frustrations and jealousy which characterised so much of the Nazi government system. In the midst of this he turned to studying British special operations, notably those employing commandos, and the activities of SOE, and began to formulate his own concepts. This was helped in that he was allowed to form his own special forces unit, thanks to an extent to the head of the RSHA, Ernst Kaltenbrunner, whom Skorzeny had known in Vienna. It was, however, the order to report to Hitler's field headquarters at Rastenburg, East Prussia, on 26 July 1943, which radically changed his life.

Skorzeny's account of the problems in tracking down Mussolini in the aftermath of his arrest and the operation to spring him from the Albergo Campo Imperatore Hotel is fascinating and it was undoubtedly one of the most spectacular feats of the war. While he states that he was able to obtain decorations for all his men, Skorzeny does not allude to the bitterness that General Kurt Student and his paratroopers, who played a vital part, felt at being ignored in the aftermath. Notwithstanding, Skorzeny was now famous in Germany and personally known to Hitler. He did not, however, ignore his engineering background and became involved in special-weapons developments for all three services, including a piloted V1, which brought him into contact with that renowned aviatrix Hanna Reitsch. Few of these projects came to fruition, an indication of the increasing muddle surrounding German weapons procurement.

Skorzeny's role in the immediate aftermath of the failed attempt on Hitler's life on 20 July 1944 did him no harm in the eyes of the authorities. It is interesting to note his ambivalent attitude towards the plotters, although it is possible to read between the lines that he did consider that they were betraying the fighting man at the front. He was then summoned by Hitler once more to undertake an operation as equally audacious as the rescue of Mussolini. This was to keep Hungary in the war. Skorzeny first kidnapped Admiral Horthy's son and brought him back to Berlin. When this did not work, Skorzeny then stormed the Budapest citadel in which the Hungarian Regent was residing. Hungary was therefore forced to remain on the German side until overrun by the Russians. No sooner had he completed this than he was given another task, one which was to be his most controversial operation of the war.

Operation *Greif*, the attempt by Skorzeny's 150 Panzer Brigade to seize the bridges over the Meuse during the December 1944 Ardennes counter-offensive, has been related many times. His use of men dressed in US Army uniforms was strictly against the laws of war and it was this that caused his appearance as a defendant in a war crimes trial in 1947. Conviction seemed certain until his defence produced an unusual witness, Wing Commander Yeo-Thomas, one of SOE's most highly decorated agents. Although he had suffered at the hands of the Gestapo and in Buchenwald, Yeo-Thomas stated that the Allies had used similar tactics during the war. On the strength of his testimony, Skorzeny and his fellow defendants were acquitted. Yet, he remained a prisoner while other nations investigated possible war crimes against him.

The last part of Skorzeny's life, apart from his escape from Darmstadt internment camp in July 1948, which is still the matter of some debate as to whether the Americans or former SS men arranged it, is not covered by this book and is shrouded in a certain amount of mystery. It is known that he spent time in Argentina advising President Peron (some say he became Eva Peron's lover) and in Egypt, and that he settled in Franco's Spain, a haven for many former Nazis, where he ran an import-export business. It is, however, generally accepted that he was the prime mover, if not the founder, of ODESSA, the secret organisation dedicated to spiriting those wanted by the Allies for war crimes to South America. Post-war life for Otto Skorzeny was still therefore packed with excitement. Even so, he died peacefully in his bed in Madrid from cancer of the spine on 7 July 1975.

Skorzeny was a larger-than-life if controversial character, who clearly had a zest for life and was a man of much charm. Luck was always on his side and he took full advantage of this. Whatever one might think of him – audacious commando or ruthless and fanatical criminal – his memoirs provide a most entertaining account of a man of action.

CHARLES MESSENGER

INTRODUCTION

Otto Skorzeny—a man of great confidence and ability who became Adolf Hitler's favorite soldier—was a man with a deep scar, and not only the fencing slash on the left side of his face that became a memorable badge of honor. He must have had a far deeper flaw. How else could Skorzeny remain an unapologetic supporter of the vicious, murderous Nazi regime, even when writing this book a dozen years after the Second World War ended?

It is well known, in world affairs and specifically after a war, that the winner gets to write the history. But Skorzeny—who constantly violated routine norms in combat and innovative special missions—also shatters the rule about the winner dictating the story.

His side lost. The nation he served, Germany, was smashed to bits and divided in two. Yet, with supreme confidence and not an iota of regret, this Obersturmbannführer (Lieutenant Colonel) in the Waffen-SS—the uniformed and heavily armed fighting force of the Nazi Party—takes command by telling the story his way.

He was such a wartime and post-war celebrity that publishers clamored for him to write a memoir, which was then translated into many languages, and clearly it was his decision to be highly selective in what he chose to reveal in this work. It is, to be sure, a good read. The author takes us from his birth in Vienna to Hitler's takeover of Austria, when Skorzeny was almost thirty. You may perceive the wave of Nazi pride as a hypnotic, vile perfume from neighboring Germany. You will go to war with Skorzeny—and suffer the hardships of the Russian front, and then the pain of being wounded and transferred to Vienna for treatment.

You will also learn the details of his most celebrated feat: leading commando soldiers who flew gliders to a mountaintop in Italy and rescued Hitler's ally—dictator Benito Mussolini. Germany's Führer honored Skorzeny with the country's highest military medal, the Iron Cross.

Whenever the Waffen-SS colonel tells of his meetings with Hitler, it is clear that Skorzeny was infatuated. He declares that the more he heard his supreme commander's "deep voice . . . the more I could feel his influence upon me." In these pages he has nothing but praise for the man who would become the most hated person of the twentieth century.

By failing to condemn or reject, Skorzeny is siding with Hitler's mad ambitions of conquering the world, butchering entire races, and committing crimes against humanity on a grandiose scale.

This book does mention the only deed that led to his being tried by the Allies for alleged war crimes. That occurred late in the war, in the Battle of the Bulge, when Skorzeny put his commando soldiers in US Army uniforms so they could get behind the American lines. Because that violated the rules of war, Skorzeny was jailed for three years after Germany's 1945 surrender. One tribunal acquitted him, and he escaped before further charges could be brought.

Was he also involved in anything ugly, horrible, and unjustifiably brutal during the war? Most experts say he certainly was. The SS, or Schutzstaffel (meaning "Protection Squad"), was comprised of men who were especially strong in their Nazi beliefs, and the Waffen-SS (meaning "the Armed SS") was the highly regimented military-style wing of Hitler's noxious political party.

SS leaders such as Skorzeny knew that the chief targets were the Jewish people, relentlessly condemned by the flood of vile Nazi propaganda. They were blamed for all the ills of Germany, Europe, and the world. Hitler's Final Solution, devised by his senior Party and military officials, represented a plan to kill all the Jews. The Nazis did manage to murder six million.

Yet this book does not contain the word "Jew," and Skorzeny makes no mention of the known SS role in wiping out entire communities, shooting and burning innocents, and loading Jews onto trains that took them to their deaths in concentration camps.

After the war, the famed Vienna-based hunter of Nazis, Simon Wiesenthal, had Skorzeny on his painstakingly researched list of war criminals: men known to have participated in atrocities against Jews and other civilians. Israeli and Jewish sources knowledgeable about one of Skorzeny's deepest secrets have confirmed that he was anxious to get his name off that list, believing that it meant he was marked for assassination. He was so anxious, in fact, that he made a deal with the Israelis.

He agreed to work as an agent of the Israeli spy agency Mossad, starting in 1962, and he even killed at least one Nazi whom Israel was pursuing.

Skorzeny's astonishing deal with the Israelis occurred five years after this book was originally published, and these pages certainly contain no hint that Skorzeny was thinking of helping the Jewish people who had survived his hero Hitler's genocide!

By then Skorzeny was residing in Spain's capital, Madrid, and he also owned a large farm in Ireland. Both of those countries had the reputation of offering shelter to Nazis, whose travel was often arranged by the Vatican.

He was interviewed by international reporters and seemed to enjoy being in the limelight. Yet his personal papers, some of which were sold by memorabilia dealers after he died in 1975, showed that Skorzeny also had a secret and darker side: as an arms dealer and guerrilla warfare advisor. He constantly suggested to the American government that Hitler's former top officers could be the ideal leaders of a multinational anti-Communist army that should be readied to push back the Soviet Union.

Skorzeny's autobiography makes it apparent that he was adventurous, innovative, and conceited. He was also manipulative, opportunistic, and duplicitous, and he weaves half-truths and conceals even more than he reveals in this book. Even more troublesome is the fact that he never expresses regrets or remorse about his and his nation's horrific past.

While his tale is interesting and significant, Skorzeny's life is not a story to be admired.

—Dan Raviv, CBS News correspondent and coauthor of
Spies Against Armageddon: Inside Israel's Secret Wars

CHAPTER I

O N T H E 12th June, 1908, the streets of Vienna were enlivened
by a gay and splendid procession as all the citizens of the ancient
imperial city proudly celebrated the diamond jubilee of the reign of
the Emperor Francis Joseph I. In the early part of the afternoon of
that day my mother, who had been watching the procession in the
morning, gave birth to a child. I was that child.

No outstanding events of my schooldays remain in my memory, but
I recall that I found realistic subjects like mathematics, geometry,
physics and chemistry quite easy, while I had to struggle with the
foreign languages, French and English. I liked any kind of sporting activity and never missed the so-called " Fresh-Air Afternoons "
as I found bodily exercise of all sorts a physical necessity. We
specialized in various ball games and I figured regularly in one of the
teams from our school which competed in the High School Tourna-
ment every summer.

The choice of a profession was already settled. I wanted to be
an engineer, like my father and brother, so in the autumn of 1926
I began to attend classes in the Technical University in Vienna. In
the winter of 1928-9, I passed the first state examination. The opening stage, to all intents and purposes theoretical only, was behind
me, and I could turn to the practical side of engineering.

When I went to the University I became a member of an active
students' association which trained us to become men prepared and
equipped to fight the hard battle of life. We learned that we must
be prepared to back words and deeds with everything we had—
physical force if necessary—and on many occasions in after life I
was very grateful for the self-discipline I learned in this school.

The only political activity in which I participated during my
schooldays was the official demonstration in favour of union with
Germany (the national protest against the refusal of the Entente to
permit the incorporation in Germany of the German-Austrian
Republic) which took place every September in the Heldenplatz and
was entirely non-partisan.

The country's economy was still suffering severely from the effects

1

of the First World War, when inflation on an inconceivable scale came to inflict further damage. Social tensions, provoked by various political parties, became greater and greater. They found their first overt expression in the disorders of July, 1927, which have passed into the history of my home town as the "burning of the Vienna Palace of Justice". One of the reactions to this outrage was the founding of the so-called "Academic Legion" in our universities. Its sole purpose was to assist in the defence of public order and authority. I joined this association, which was soon afterwards transferred to the "Student Volunteers" which in turn was ultimately absorbed in the previously existing *Heimwehr*. At that time the *Heimwehr* resolutely refused to become a political body. Unfortunately, it subsequently struck out on the path, a tragic path in my opinion, which seems inevitable if influence is to be gained. By slow degrees it became a political party and started to call itself *Heimatblock*. As this transformation became clear by 1930, I and most of my comrades regarded it as a signal to sever our connection with the "Student Volunteers". We were determined to have nothing to do with party politics and not allow ourselves to be the tools of party politicians.

In the winter of 1931, I took my final examination at the Technical University and succeeded beyond my best hopes. Unfortunately, qualifying for employment and finding it were two different things, for both Austria and Germany were in the throes of a terrible economic crisis which was at its worst at that moment. However, after some search I had a slice of luck and became manager of a small building business which in a few years I was able to expand into a very considerable concern, despite adverse conditions.

The first political meeting I ever attended was to prove decisive for the evolution of my ideas. In the summer of 1932 Dr. Goebbels spoke to a packed assembly of the NSDAP[1] in the Engelmann Arena in Vienna. The social ideas which he advocated and the promise to put an end to the unprofitable squabbles of the political parties were decisive in my eyes. I became a member at once. But my membership only lasted for a year. I was not required to do anything. I went to several meetings and paid my subscription. In June, 1933, my political activities, if one can call them such, came to an end. The NSDAP was banned by the Dollfuss government.

[1] The German Nazi Party.

Shortly after I was married and spent my honeymoon in Italy, in the course of which I visited the wild and mountainous Abruzzi region, destined to be the scene of one of my better-known exploits, I returned to Vienna and the humdrum of everyday life. Despite economic difficulties, I managed to keep my business going and even increased it. I was able to get together a sound and solid labour force and, even though most of the men came from the "red" camp, I was on excellent terms with them.

The events of February and March, 1938, came as a complete surprise to me no less than the general public. The newspapers gave us but a vague idea of what was really happening, though it was destined to restore normal relations between Germany and Austria and genuine domestic peace in my tortured country. But, even in our wildest dreams, we had never thought that the two nations would be united. When the Chancellor, Schuschnigg, paid his visit to Berchtesgaden on the 12th February, one thing seemed certain—a favourable solution of the problem would be at hand. Everyone in Vienna was consumed with the fever of this political crisis. Then came the Chancellor's speech to the officials of the Fatherland Front at Innsbruck, in which he announced that there would be a referendum on the following Sunday. On the 10th and 11th March, the excitement in Vienna was at its height.

The German Gymnastic Association, which I had joined in 1935, had long since organized so-called defence units, of which I was a member. In view of the threatening situation in Vienna on the 12th March, we were ordered in the afternoon to assemble at our gymnasium. I had arrived and was just about to change when the news of the resignation of Schuschnigg's government came over the radio. It took us completely by surprise.

An order came from the leaders of the German Gymnastic Association that all the defence units were to assemble at the Chancery in the inner town. I invited some friends to join me in my car, drove to the inner town and left it in the vicinity of the Ballhausplatz. All the streets were crammed with crowds making their way towards the Chancery. As both spectators and participants, we took up our stations in a side street behind the building in which we supposed that the destinies of our country were being decided.

Suddenly the Vienna police drove up from the Minoritenplatz in motor lorries. We could hardly believe our eyes when we noticed that they all wore swastika armbands. At length a chorus of cheers greeted the appearance on the balcony of the new Chancellor, Seyss-Inquart, and he made a short speech. Soon afterwards, a number of men rushed into the street where we were. Among them was Bruno Weiss, the President of the German Gymnastic Association, who came up to me and said: "Thank goodness, I've found a sensible man! I've an important job for you, Skorzeny! Did you see a big black limousine leave just now?" I nodded, and he continued: "President Miklas was in that car. We in the Chancery are extremely worried! We've just heard that a biggish detachment of the Guard Battalion is stationed at the Presidential Palace, but a small group of Florisdorf SS men have also been told off to mount guard there and we're afraid that there may be some unfortunate incident when the two forces meet. Will you help us? Have you a car handy?"

I gladly offered my services and he resumed: "You have the new Chancellor's orders to go to the Presidential Palace as fast as you can and take any action you think necessary to prevent any stupidity by anyone."

Weiss shook hands and while stressing the necessity to remain calm and collected insisted that not a moment was to be lost. I swept my friend Gerhard along with me and ran to where I had left my car. "Let's hope this is going to be all right," I said. Driving at breakneck speed I found it difficult to avoid an accident as the streets were full. When I turned into the Landstrasse Hauptstrasse I saw a small column of cars ahead. Was the President's among them? I caught up with the last car and passed it on the right. I thought I was bound to arrive immediately behind the President. When I had successfully overtaken two more cars, the car at the head turned into the Palace and I reached it at the same moment as the second car. A single individual had just got out of the limousine and was hastening with short, swift steps to the gate. Behind him the four occupants of the second car shot through the entrance.

What followed happened so quickly that I had no time to think and could only act on instinct. I thrust my way through the four men and found myself in a small hall. Ahead of me was a staircase sweeping round to the first floor. President Miklas was running up the steps. Some soldiers appeared on the landing and came towards the President. I leaped up the steps myself. A lieutenant of the Guard Battalion and some of his men barred my way. I could see that the officer was being urged on by his men. He suddenly gave the order: "Arms at the ready!" Some of his men raised their weapons and pointed them at me. Glancing down the stairs I saw that some of the men in the hall were also drawing their revolvers. If anyone loses his nerve now anything can happen, I thought to myself.

"You fools! You fools!" I shouted. Turning to the lieutenant I added: "You'll be responsible if anything happens. I've been sent by the new Government to see that no disorders occur."

"Who are you? What do you want?" asked the President, who had so far remained silent. Despite a situation which was half tense and half comical, I introduced myself: "Engineer Skorzeny, Herr President. May I suggest that we ring up the Chancellor together. He will confirm on whose orders I am here."

The soldiers moved aside and we went upstairs together, followed by the lieutenant. Then I heard an imperious knock on the door. One of the men below looked out and a police officer was visible. He greeted me and said: "The Federal Chancellor has ordered me to report to you with my company. Am I needed?"

I was very glad to see him, as his arrival showed that Dr. Seyss-Inquart not only knew of my existence and mission, but was keeping us in mind. I raised my voice and said to the President: "Mr. President, a police company has just arrived at the palace for your protection. We must get in touch with the Chancellery at once so that the lieutenant can hear that there's to be no shooting here!"

We soon got through and I was able to report the situation to Dr. Seyss-Inquart. Then I handed the receiver to Dr. Miklas, who seemed to be in agreement with what the Chancellor said to him. I took the lieutenant aside: "You must tell your men to drop their weapons at once! You can see there's no reason for shooting." He walked away and I heard him give the order. Then Dr. Miklas handed me the receiver. Dr. Seyss-Inquart said that he understood that the credit of preventing bloodshed was mine. He asked me to remain in attendance on the President. I was to assume command of the SS men and be responsible for internal security at the palace. The unit from the Guard Battalion could take charge outside.

Compulsory military service was introduced immediately after the incorporation of Austria in Germany, so I voluntarily reported for recruit training at any time in order to make certain of being called up for the Luftwaffe. In view of my experience as an engineer I

could expect to be enrolled as candidate for a commission. I knew
that I must expect to be called up in the autumn of 1939.

In the last week of August, I took a vacation on Lake Worth with
my wife. Nothing could have been more peaceful than the scene
there, but the news of the actual outbreak of war between Germany
and Poland burst like thunder on our holiday mood. I returned
immediately to Vienna to put my business affairs in order and found
in my mail a not wholly unexpected call-up to a Luftwaffe Communications unit which I had previously expressed a wish to join. So my
military career was to begin at a critical moment!

I was to receive my recruit training in the Trost Barracks in
Vienna, and reported punctually on the 3rd September. Next day
our company commander told us that for the moment no instructors
were available as they had all gone to the Polish front. We should
all receive special technical training and subsequently be employed
as front-line engineers. A course of lectures had been arranged
which we must attend once a week. Our class would comprise a
hundred recruits. We could go home for the time being and our
final call-up would follow later.

This announcement was a great and not altogether unwelcome
surprise to most of us, but I was not so easily satisfied, stood to attention and said: "Sir, may I be permitted to ask whether I can be
transferred to the flying service? I originally applied for service
in the Luftwaffe and have had some experience in flying." "What
year?" was the immediate question. "1908, Sir!" The captain
rapped out: "Much too old!" and obviously considered the question settled.

A gnawing doubt assailed me. Was I really too old for flying?

Our education in the motorization of the army soon commenced
and in the middle of December we were informed that twenty of
us were to be posted as engineer officer-cadets to the Waffen SS (that
part of the SS organized to fight with the army). Only twelve, of
whom I was the oldest, proved sufficiently proficient for that corps.
Some time elapsed before the actual transfer took place.

I was eventually posted to the second reserve battalion of the SS
division "Adolf Hitler" Leibstandarte, in Berlin-Lichterfelde.
Once again I found myself in a room with the older recruits. I had
doctors, chemists and engineers for my new companions. We were
faced with a new and short, but correspondingly intensive course
of training before we joined our specialist unit.

The regulation six weeks passed very swiftly and I became a passable soldier in the highly critical eyes of the Leibstandarte officers. Then I spent a few weeks with the "Germania" reserve battalion in Hamburg-Langenhorn, where I was initiated into my future specialization as a technical officer.

On the 9th May, 1940, we were instructed to take transport and personnel reinforcements to our "Germania" regiment which was in line on the hitherto inactive western front. The same day, much to my disappointment, I received an order to report at the head-quarters of the Waffen SS in Berlin. The western campaign was beginning, and there was I being sent a monstrous distance from the front!

In a few days I had to take quite a number of examinations. I got my military driver's certificate for all classes in addition to an instructor's ticket, but what pleased me most was the expert mechanic's certificate which was issued to "Unteroffizier" Skorzeny.

A few days later I was sent for by Major Hoffman, the senior Motor Transport Officer of the SS. He introduced me to Major Rees, who listened to my pleas for action. "All right!" he said, "I'll take you into my battalion as a technical officer. I can give you your first job straight away. We are taking over eighty trucks which are in your old Lichterfelde barracks. Take them to Hamm early to-morrow morning. Our heavy artillery battalion will then be ready to move. We are part of the 1st SS Division and must lose no time, or the war will be over without us."

I was in Hamm by three a.m., but as I was short of twenty-six trucks I wondered what sort of reception I should get from my new CO. There was only one thing to be done—go back for more! After two hours I fortunately scraped up thirteen from various sources and returned to the barracks by seven o'clock. But when I reported to the CO later on and, somewhat tremulously, gave him the number I had brought, he astonished me by being not too pleased. I was briefly informed that by that evening at the latest the full number must be made up, as the column would be leaving next morning. So *that* was how I was to be initiated!

We were cheered on our way as we rolled through Aix-la-Chapelle, the old "coronation" city, and were soon at the frontier, with enemy country ahead. But would it still be enemy country? At the speed we were travelling we hardly noticed the broken frontier posts. We were busily chasing the war!

Givet, Chinay and Hirson were soon behind us. Formations of our own aircraft frequently passed overhead. They always returned at a low altitude and in the same rigid formation, though many a time there were gaps. At last we stopped for a halt and heard the guns in the distance. We looked at each other. We had really run the war to earth.

Columns of prisoners passed us, endless files of tired, dust-covered faces. I saw many a hunk of bread tossed over to them. My driver offered his flask to a thirsty captive. The youth of Europe do not hate each other!

We eventually crossed the Somme by a temporary bridge, and in the valley of the Oise we found some units of our division in action. But already there was no such thing as a "Front". The French army had been reduced to individual bodies of varying size putting up resistance here and there, so my heavy battalion of the artillery regiment found itself being moved about all over the place. We took Roye, Montdidier and Cuilly in our stride.

We were naturally wondering whether we should go straight to Paris, but soon learned that our commanders had other ideas. We made a great sweep round the city. The rest of our advance through Chaumy, Soissons, Villers-Cotterets, Château-Thierry, Éperny, Châlons-sur-Marne, St. Dizier, Châtillon-sur-Seine, Coulmier-le-Sec, Précy, Pouilly and Autun was little more than the pursuit of an almost invisible enemy. The war seemed decided and the only remaining task was to reach Le Creusot, France's arsenal. On the 10th June our formation went into rest billets near Marmagne.

On the 14th fresh orders were issued to our division to sweep round to the Spanish frontier by forced marches. Passing through Rouvray we reached the Seine at Troyes. Here we could appreciate the accuracy and effect of mass bombing. The bridges had apparently been defended and in order to break resistance our aircraft had been thrown into the battle and bombed the houses on both sides of the streets on the western bank, where they were channelled into the bridges. For a distance of about 200 metres the houses were a mass of rubble, but in the side streets there was practically no sign of damage. Here again there had been no sign of hostile reaction by the civil population towards German soldiers.

On the 20th June, a Saturday, the news reached us that an armistice had been concluded. Germany's sole continental enemy had been forced out of the war. Then followed for me a pleasant but short interval in the south of France, my division was sent to Holland as part of the occupation forces, and I was granted leave. On my return to duty I noticed various indications that the attack on England was now being planned and prepared. An urgent order reached our division one day. It was disclosed that we were to practise embarking our vehicles on land in preparation for the exercises which would shortly be taking place at the coast.

Our division carried out the exercises at the Dutch port of Den Helder. The Rhine barges looked very odd with their bows cut off, nor did they seem particularly suitable for a considerable sea voyage. A single English air attack resulted in the loss of two boats and several men. Our fellows called these boats cockleshells, but without losing confidence in them. But we learned from our exercises that even a little wind or swell would make a landing a dangerous and venturesome operation.

Others have already given reasons why the invasion, which everyone then expected, never materialized, but it is of interest to record here a version which I was given years later by certain people in Adolf Hitler's immediate entourage:

"Hitler had a very high regard for the English nation, which he considered akin to the German. He considered the preservation of the British Empire a condition precedent to stabilization of the world. In spite of the known difficulties and inadequate preparation, the Führer believed in the success of Operation 'Sea Lion', to use the code name adopted for the invasion. But he did not underestimate the English power of resistance or the toughness of the island power and its government. He appreciated that even if the country were completely occupied, it would carry on the war from Canada and South Africa. The German Reich would merely have another 35 million Europeans to look after. Previous sources of supply would be cut off and the provision of food, which would be Germany's responsibility alone, would be hampered by war operations of all kinds. Adolf Hitler was not prepared to take on such a responsibility for a 35-million nation. . . ."

Long afterwards Hitler said something of the kind to me himself, though in connection with other matters.

On the 18th December, our division, known as "Das Reich", left Holland for France in response to a sudden summons, and I was assigned to it as an engineer officer. During the last days of March, after a long period of inactivity in France, we received orders to proceed to a concentration area near the Yugoslav border in south-west Rumania. Late one evening Captain Rumohr sent for me and read me a regimental order which he had just received: "Sergeant Skorzeny is commissioned as second-lieutenant (Reserve) with effect from the 30th January, 1941." Wine was produced and the glasses clinked merrily.

The accumulation of munitions and supplies now showed us that serious business was about to begin and on the night of the 5th April, 1941, we concentrated at the frontier. The weather was as favourable as possible for the concealment of our movements. It rained in streams! Unfortunately, the roads were not adapted for such a deluge. In a short time the mud was a foot deep. What made matters worse was that we had to leave the so-called main road at the frontier village. Our few cross-country vehicles had a very hard job.

We were all on edge, as it would be our new battalion's baptism of fire—and my own first experience of direct contact with the enemy. The minutes passed terribly slowly. For the n-th time the ranges were measured on the map and the directions for the guns calculated and checked. Anyone with a field-glass used it from cover to scan the enemy's positions. The moment came for Captain Neugebauer to send back the signal to open fire at 5.45 a.m. on April 6th, 1941. There was a crash, and the shells roared overhead. Within two hours it was all over and the enemy position was taken. We were given orders to have everything ready to continue the advance, and by ten o'clock we were back on the road and slowly pressing forward. Using an emergency bridge built by the engineers, we crossed the trenches which were about five metres wide.

We passed a group of prisoners, who, with almost oriental fatalism, were either squatting on the ground, smoking or chewing a hunk of bread, or lying on their backs staring at the grey sky. They hardly looked at us when we went up to them. One old soldier could speak German. He was a native of Bosnia and had learned German as an Austrian soldier long, long ago. "No, our losses have not been particularly heavy. We could not hold out against you. The war's over for us now. When shall I see my farm again?" He seemed to be interested in nothing but the answer to this last question. A longing to get home is always the predominant sentiment with men who live close to the soil.

We took every precaution as we approached any village known to be occupied by the Serbians. For some reason or other, I made one gun-carrier use a parallel track about half a kilometre south of me. We arranged to continue thus until we reached the foot of the slopes and then join up again. If necessary we could cross the fields and come to each other's help. We kept in sight of each other, though every now and then the other tractor disappeared behind a rise or a group of trees. Before long both vehicles reached the beginning of the rise. We dismounted because thick scrub prevented our seeing ahead. The tractors followed us slowly.

Suddenly, I heard shots from the other group and bullets began to whistle past. My men and I took cover at once and I got my two machine-guns into position. Then a crowd of enemy soldiers came running towards us from behind. I told my men to hold their fire. When the nearest Serbian was about 80 metres away, I yelled out: "Stoi!" (halt). The men stopped, looked bewildered and turned round. A few more shots were heard. That settled it! They threw down their arms. I was in such a position that I could have immediately taken cover behind a rise, but there was no shooting.

A few weeks later we were employed as occupation troops in the vicinity of Pancevo. We all had our hands full with work to get our formation up to full operational standard again. All our equipment had to be overhauled. It was difficult to believe that a short and easy campaign should have been responsible for such losses and deficiencies. My own special concern, motor transport, thoroughly alarmed me. Our division had not been formed until after the Polish campaign and yet we had to make good the loss of hundreds of our original vehicles from the booty captured in the west.

German industry was continuing to produce vehicles turned out by several separate concerns. There had often been talk of standardization and Hitler had appointed his deputy to see that it was carried out; but the effects were not visible at troop level. Was the importance of this question overlooked? In this war the function of motorization was not merely to promote mobility, but more particularly to guarantee supply, on the swift and smooth functioning of which depends the success of all operations, whether offensive or defensive. A multiplicity of types made the proper provision of spare parts much more difficult. Repairs and replacements took much longer and available transport space was appreciably reduced.

CHAPTER II

In the middle of June our division was transferred to Poland and we established our headquarters in a village about fifty kilometres from the frontier at the river Bug and south of the Russian city of Brest-Litovsk. To our complete astonishment preparatory orders indicated an attack in the immediate future. So the quarry could only be the Soviet Union!

The die was cast one day at the Führer's headquarters (FHQ). D-day for the commencement of the attack was announced. It was to be the 22nd June, 1941! At midnight the guns were brought forward to the prepared sites and at 5 a.m. they thundered at the same moment along the whole front. For a quarter of an hour shells of every calibre roared overhead on their way towards the enemy.

The Russian troops could not withstand the impetus of the first onset. Fighting a desperate rearguard action, they slowly retired to a region of forests and swamps. Our guns had limbered up and my section forged ahead by any practicable track. At Koden, a few kilometres to the north, our engineers had constructed a pontoon bridge. Next morning we slowly advanced and reached Brest-Litovsk by the right bank of the Bug.

Some Russians in the central fortress of the city still resisted desperately. The outer defences had been captured, but I had to crawl, for the enemy sharp-shooters missed nothing. Every summons to surrender and cease the futile resistance had been rejected and several attempts to creep up to the fortress and carry it by storm had failed. The dead soldiers in field-grey uniforms, which were lying about, were sufficient witness. It was to be several days before the last refugees had been cleared out, as the Russians fought to the last round and the last man.

Most of the villages we passed through as we advanced were deserted, the inhabitants having been evacuated further east by the Russian authorities. After only a few days there was nothing that could be called a front. The German divisions swept eastwards and it was often quite difficult to keep them supplied. The whole front had dissolved into separate actions fought by comparatively small bodies. My own division was widely scattered. The advance guard had nearly reached the Beresina, and a little river was the only obstacle. Then a critical situation arose. The reconnaissance unit and a battalion of infantry, supported by a battery of our artillery battalion II, found itself held up by strong enemy resistance.

General Hausser sent for my CO for a talk. When he arrived he described the position. Our leading troops and we ourselves had gone ahead too fast, and it was not certain whether the road behind us had been cleared of the enemy. Our wireless had not sufficient range to call up reinforcements sixty kilometres away. The rest of my artillery battalion must be got up as soon as possible.

I volunteered to go back and was given a big cable carrier and five men! This sort of trip through an area certainly not clear of the enemy, and in a very small party, was most unnerving. We did not find our battalion until seven hours later, when night had fallen.

My return trip was even slower. The landscape looks very different at night. I was with the leading file and was set many a puzzle. Had we come from the left or should we turn right? We only allowed ourselves short stops for refuelling. Many sandy and marshy places gave us a lot of trouble. Every now and then a vehicle got stuck and had to be physically lifted out. We reached regimental HQ about midday and found the staff very thankful to get the guns.

South of Bosinok was the Beresina crossing. It took us three days to force the river barrier, for the Russians had concentrated in strength and defended the position very stoutly.

In the fortnight the campaign had lasted we had learned the importance of digging-in. It was seldom that we could set up a command post above ground and we had to dig small, but deep holes. For sleeping we excavated narrow trenches and tried to disappear underground. The air was too full of metal and the Russian gunners fired too often and too accurately for our taste.

After a short struggle the crossing of the Dnieper was forced south of Shklov. But the road selected for the further advance was found to be impossible and the bulk of our division crossed further north by a hastily constructed pontoon bridge. Then we received the unpleasant news that the pioneer company, which had been left to guard the lower bridge single-handed, had been attacked at night by scattered Russian troops. Two men alone escaped the massacre to tell us about what had been a one-sided fight. The sight that met our eyes at the scene of the tragedy spoke for itself. Now we knew how pitiless the war in the east was going to be!

We met with practically no opposition in our further advance through Sukari to Czernikov, which was the first considerable town we had passed through since Brest-Litovsk. Apart from a few stone buildings in the centre of the settlement—which was just big enough to be called a town—there was nothing to see but the typical Russian wooden houses. The streets were paved, but only in a medieval fashion almost unknown elsewhere. It was a novelty to us to see the loudspeakers attached to posts and pillar-boxes only a few hundred metres apart. When, quite exceptionally, a very old electromagnetic loudspeaker was found in a house, it was certain that the latter had been a community centre. Short of Moscow I never saw a radio in a private house.

In the middle of July, after barely three weeks, we took the little town of Yelna, passed through it and formed a bridgehead about eight kilometres in radius. My battalion was allotted a sector in the centre, at the furthest point east. The main body of the other German formations was still a long way behind.

One day the artillery fire against our "hedgehog" reached unprecedented intensity. We must have been facing the guns of a heavy artillery corps. They gave us no rest and all we could do was to dig further and further down. We had put our motor transport on the reverse side of a slope near the gun positions. We burrowed two metres down into the ground and lived and slept there. Almost everywhere we roofed our holes with several layers of tree trunks laid crosswise, filling in the spaces with earth.

Then came a fresh surprise. The Russians attacked with a type of tank they had not used before. It was to become familiar as the T34. Our anti-tank guns proved ineffectual against this monster. With great efforts we managed to beat off the escorting infantry but the tanks got through. Fortunately, at that time tanks were not employed in masses, but even twenty to thirty of them were quite enough for us to cope with. So tank alarms behind the lines were a common occurrence.

An "unknown soldier" had invented the Molotoff cocktail, a glass bottle containing petrol, with a cork perforated to allow a piece of cotton waste to pass through. The waste was ignited before the missile was thrown. When the bottle broke against the hot armour covering the engine, the flames spread over the whole vehicle. There were some ferocious scenes when our fellows, in their shirt sleeves and clutching these bottles, went tank hunting, and even though it sometimes took hours they never failed to finish off the monsters. Hand grenades and explosives were also useful. A hand grenade detonated in the barrel of the gun, or a charge blown on the turret, forced the crew to surrender.

A fortnight later, at the beginning of August, the losses of our division were so high that we had to be taken out of the line to recuperate and make up our numbers. Our relief by two fresh divisions took place at night and we marched off westwards looking forward to our well-deserved rest. But we had not got far before a new order arrived; the division must immediately take over the protection of the northern flank of the autobahn leading to Yelna. Heavy enemy attacks from the north were expected and must be contained.

So that was the end of our "rest"! The area of our new position was far more difficult to defend. Great forests covered the hills and here the Russians produced something new in the way of tactics in night attacks. Small bodies continuously infiltrated into our position, concentrated far behind and then fell on our men while they were asleep.

At the beginning the Russians had great success with these nerve-racking tactics and caused us heavy losses. But we introduced a system of special patrols and held substantial reserves concentrated at suitable points so that they could intervene when the alarm was given, and this proved the answer to these night attacks.

We learned quite a lot from the Russians, and in one captured position I got my first look at the round, one-man "foxhole". It was about eighty centimetres across and two metres deep. Every trace of the excavated earth had been removed so that one almost fell into the hole before it was seen. The amount of digging involved in producing this little hole was quite considerable. Yet I heard from prisoners afterwards that it did not take them much more than an hour. But it was in camouflage that the Russians were past masters. It was easy to see that they were much nearer to nature than ourselves.

After about a week we were sent to rest billets in the vicinity of Roslavl. This was the very moment I chose for a violent attack of dysentery, but several days later was cheered by the award of the Iron Cross, 2nd Class.

On my return to active service I found that my repair staff had found among the Russian prisoners six motor mechanics who were willing to come with us and help with the maintenance side. We had a pleasant surprise in finding out how expert and inventive these boys were.

The finest and most resourceful of our Russian assistants was Ivan, a short, thick-set, ash-blond youth with bright, intelligent eyes. Like all Russian soldiers, he had his hair cut extremely short and it stood out like bristles from his skull. One day I could not see him anywhere, and when I asked my sergeant foreman about him he was most confused. "I have given him leave for twenty-four hours," he said. "He lives in a village near Smolensk, about forty-five kilometres away. He wanted to see his family and promised to come back at once." I was rather annoyed and started to dress my sergeant down: "He'll certainly never come back. Your stupidity has lost us our best man." I was quite convinced that we had seen the last of Ivan, but he was back the very next morning! All that we could gather from his long rigmarole was that he had found his family in good health and successfully surviving all their experiences. I am sure that what really brought Ivan back was the attraction of our field kitchen.

We were now rushed four hundred kilometres south to close the great ring which had been forged round the Russian armies east of Kiev. The weather was appalling and raging torrents turned the whole area we were traversing into a mixture of mud baths and swamps.

There was fierce fighting at the crossing of the river Desna. South of us, downstream, the Russians maintained a strong bridgehead on our bank. It gave us a great deal of trouble. One of the mysteries was how the enemy got his supplies across the river. The Luftwaffe searched in vain for a bridge. It was not until we had established ourselves on the far side that we found the explanation. It was a surprise. The Russians had constructed an emergency bridge—invisible to us, of course—about thirty centimetres below the surface of the water, and used it for supply purposes at night. It was an excellent idea and the engineering part of it had been carried out to perfection.

At Romny we reached our most southerly point. There the great ring was finally closed on the south side. The number of prisoners must have reached several hundred thousand.

We found a Russian military hospital in the little town where we were quartered. The medical organization was nothing like as modern as ours. We were amazed at the stoicism with which the Russian soldier bore his injuries. He could stand far more pain than a west European. I myself saw a soldier, both of whose arms had been amputated a few hours earlier, get up from his mattress and walk unaided to the latrine in the yard. I believe that he considered it perfectly natural that none of the hospital staff offered him any assistance.

On the 1st October, 1941, we opened our last great offensive of the year. Our target was Moscow and the Volga beyond. We thrust east from Roslavl to Yuknov and then turned north to Gjatsk, reaching the far-famed Smolensk-Moscow autobahn a few days later. In so doing we closed the great Vyasma ring. Even greater hordes of prisoners trooped westwards than after the Kiev affair. At night the road was lit up for miles by the fires kindled by the prisoners. There could be no question of guarding them. I should imagine that there was one German to every five hundred Russian, and am sure that thousands of prisoners took advantage of the situation and escaped.

Later on we suffered severely from the fact that the forests inside the ring were not thoroughly cleared and we did not secure the vast masses of war material which the enemy left behind. During the following winter the Russians got a large number of technical specialists into the area and they had all this material fit for use again in an incredibly short space of time.

The Russian troops caught in the Vyasma ring made desperate efforts to break out from the west while new formations from the east strove hard to smash the ring and free their comrades. It was the tank attacks from the east that gave us most trouble and the immediate vicinity of the road junction was simply ploughed up by the heavy wide tracks of the Russian T34s.

One morning when we woke up the ground was lightly covered with snow. The Russian winter had arrived! The sudden arrival of this terrible weather had a most dispiriting effect on the German Army, and it may well be that here and there doubts arose about the final result of the October offensive. Just at the psychological moment a new theme was broadcast from Rome. The men crowded round the few service wireless sets, when it came over the loud-speaker: "Everything comes to an end sometime; every December is followed by May!" Banal as it sounds, this sentiment restored hope and fighting spirit. The song became incredibly popular.

The little town of Istra, though desperately defended, was captured by us after a few days. Next we reached a village only fifteen kilometres north-west of Moscow, which we could see from the church tower on clear days. Our batteries actually shelled the suburbs of the city. Yet our offensive came to an end at this point. Our neighbour, the 10th Armoured Division, had only a dozen battleworthy tanks left and most of our guns were without tractors to draw them, and had to be towed by lorries over the ice-bound fields. But we had a pretty good idea that the enemy also was nearly at the end of his strength.

The realization that the limit of our advance had been reached was even more depressing than a defeat or the weather. Our goal was within reach and we could not seize it!

Meanwhile, about thirty centimetres of snow had fallen without any diminution of the biting cold. Whenever possible we sheltered in the few remaining houses. The sentries in their foxholes had to be relieved every two hours.

Our neighbour on the right, the 257th Infantry Division, was a weak point on our front, and the Russian generals found it out. The Russians attacked it every day at dusk and eventually resistance collapsed and our right flank was exposed. Russian troops infiltrated into our position almost regularly at dawn and the resulting street and house fighting became reveille for us. We snatched our rifles or machine-pistols and crept through the door. This fighting among the houses in a temperature of minus thirty degrees could have been called our morning physical training.

With the ground frozen solid it was, of course, impossible to bury the dead. We had to collect the bodies in the church. They made a gruesome sight. Arms and legs, which had been oddly twisted in the course of the death struggle, were held fast in the same position by the cold. We would have had to break the joints to give the dead the posture which is supposed to be natural. Glazed eyes stared up at a frozen sky. Later on we blew great holes in the ground and deposited the victims of each day or two's fighting in them.

We came across further examples of Russian indifference in matters of life and death which often gave us a shock. On entering one village we found a Russian soldier sleeping in front of the stove in one of the houses. When we roused him somewhat roughly, his face did not show the slightest sign of fear. On the contrary, he merely stretched himself, raised his arms when we searched him for weapons, and then walked out of the house and stood against the wall, still with his arms above his head.

When we asked him, through the interpreter, what all this was for, he told us that he had been assured that all prisoners were immediately shot by the Germans. He could not bear the idea of being removed even further from his family in White Russia, and had, therefore, decided to wait for our arrival, even if it meant his own death. This mixture of sentimentality and unlimited fatalism is only possible to Russian mentality.

On the 11th December, 1941, Germany and Italy, meeting their obligations as allies of Japan, declared war on the United States of America. We had no time to reflect on the immense importance of this event as the order to retreat arrived somewhere about the 12th. We were to retire approximately to the Volokolamsk-Mozhaisk line. It meant that a great deal of our wheeled transport had to be left behind. Winter, Russia's frigid tyrant, never released his grip. We could not even get all our guns away. The 6th battery had to blow up quite a number, as no tractors were available.

About this time I had a serious attack of colic, and it was decided that I should be sent back to hospital. My request to be sent to one in Vienna was granted. My first experiences in Russia were at an end.

CHAPTER III

I spent the next six months in my old post as engineer officer with a reserve regiment in Berlin. Barrack routine is the same all the world over and never particularly enjoyable, especially to someone like myself, who neither was nor wished to be a professional soldier.

It was in the autumn of 1942, and our Waffen SS divisions were about to be converted into armoured divisions. This seemed to me an opportunity to get away from Berlin. I " forgot " my classification as " fit for garrison service at home " and applied for transfer to armour. After certain courses and examinations I achieved my object and was transferred as regimental engineer to the armoured regiment of the 3rd SS Armoured Division.

The allied conference at Casablanca made the greatest impression on all thinking men in the Axis countries. Our enemies made "unconditional surrender" their declared war aim. Now we knew where we were. I absolutely refused to consider the possibility of anything but a German victory. Both as men and soldiers, we had no other alternative.

I was not long with the 3rd Armoured Division. One day in April, 1943, I was summoned to Waffen SS headquarters, where I was informed that an officer with technical training was required in connection with the establishment of a special formation.

Then I was initiated by an expert into the mysteries of a business about which I knew nothing at all except from hearsay. I was given a broad idea of the functions of two German services about which I must enlighten my readers.

The so-called "Auslands-Abwehr" Department (Army Secret Service) was responsible to the *Oberkommando der Wermacht,* (OKW), the Supreme Command of the German Forces. This department had three sections. Section I was concerned with military espionage, a word which to the uninitiated suggests, quite mistakenly, something sinister and perhaps even sordid. Even the smaller nations, not to mention the big ones, have their own espionage services in these days. Section II had the task of organizing sabotage and propaganda in enemy countries in war time. It was, of course, extremely busy. This organization also has its counterparts elsewhere. The function of Section III was to discover and frustrate enemy espionage and propaganda. Here again every nation has the same institution or something similar.

The three sections together formed what is popularly understood as "Military Secret Service".

Like all other outsiders, at that time I had very little idea of the workings of the organization and the immense possibilities open to it.

The "Reichssicherheitshauptamt" (RSHA), or State Security Department of the SS, established in 1938 the so-called Section VI, which was concerned with the organization of "political Intelligence". Its work was to keep the government in touch with the internal ramifications of the policies of foreign countries and so enable it to adapt its own policy accordingly. "Political Intelligence" and "Military Intelligence" were equally important. A single, "summit" organization should have co-ordinated the activities of both with a view to maximum efficiency.

At the beginning of the war the "Brandenburg" z.b.V. (for special service) battalion was placed at the disposal of Auslands-Abwehr. By 1943 this unit had developed into the Brandenburg Division. Its function was to carry out such military special assignments as Auslands-Abwehr should indicate. Even the existence of this formation was hardly known to anyone in Germany.

In the previous year, Section VI had established the "Oranienburg" Special Training Course for similar tasks. This military unit was to be expanded and vitalized, and a Waffen SS officer, with the widest possible range of military and technical knowledge, was required to take on the task.

The appointment was offered to me. I fully appreciated all it meant if I accepted. I should say good-bye to normal soldiering and enter on specialized employment not open to all soldiers. Nietzsche's words came to mind: "Live dangerously!" I should have the chance to render my country service of an unusual kind in her hour of need. That thought determined my decision. I accepted the offer, reserving the right to resign if I proved unsuitable.

On the 18th April, 1943, I was promoted to Captain (Reserve) for service with Section VI.

As usual, I had to report to the head of the Section, Obersturm-bannführer Schellenberg. A short, dapper, rather young looking man stepped forward. He was very amiable. At first I did not understand much of what he told me about his department. It was a new world to me. He said I must beg, borrow or steal all the information I could get and then go full steam ahead. In addition to my special unit I was to establish, as part of Section VI, a school for espionage and sabotage agents, who could be available for employment by other sections of the department.

I spent the next fortnight "begging, borrowing or stealing" information. What I learned from the individual group leaders was extremely interesting. The importance of this particular type of activity to the war effort was much greater than I had thought. Naturally I was interested most in the development and production of the technical apparatus and equipment required. I found much that was new.

I also learned that the unit I was to take over was already preparing an operation which would be carried out almost at once.

Soon after the war started the oil region in the south of Irak was occupied by British troops. Russian divisions had established themselves in the north of the country. The railways were busily forwarding allied military supplies for Russia, the bulk of which came from America, an active belligerent since the 11th December, 1941. American war material had made a vital contribution to the stiffening of the eastern front. I had never realized its immense importance until I was given the relevant figures. In the fire and fury of the crisis at the front we had not appreciated the full significance of America's entry into the war.

The idea of the projected operation was to interrupt the supply lines far behind the enemy front and for that purpose foment revolts among the restless mountain tribes in Iran. Comparatively small parties of Germans were to supply them with arms and above all give then the necessary training and instruction. The orders of the German High Command would be transmitted to the instructors and the most important targets indicated.

For several months twenty men of the "Special Course" (as my future command was styled) had been learning Persian from a native. To each group was attached a Persian, who was to take part in the operation. The equipment was also ready, and all they were waiting for was a signal from a German officer, who was in hiding in Teheran.

Wireless communication was the province of Group VIf, another department of Section VI. I attached no importance to the fact, as at that time I took the smooth interworking of all German organizations for granted. Later on I was to be repeatedly undeceived. Business at home was not like the front, where our lives were at stake and everyone tried to help each other. Personal jealousies were far stronger than in the field. *Sacro egoismo* and St. Bureaucracy reigned supreme. If I had known what I was in for I doubt whether I should have accepted the job!

The Iran enterprise was given the name of "Operation Franz". A large salt lake south-east of Teheran was selected as the dropping area of the first German group. Two officers of my Special Course and three NCO's and a Persian were quite ready to leave. After much negotiation, Squadron 200 of the Luftwaffe placed at our disposal a Junkers 290, which had the necessary range. The weight of the equipment and petrol to be carried had to be calculated most accurately. Only those who have actually planned such an expedition can appreciate how often we had to reconsider and revise the list of equipment, from weapons to food, clothes to ammunition, explosives to presents for the tribal chiefs. I remember all the trouble we had to procure sporting rifles with silver inlay and Walther pistols decorated in gold, much coveted gifts.

An aerodrome in the Crimea was selected as the starting point, but the runway was so short that the load had to be cut down, of course at the expense of the military equipment. Then there was the waiting for favourable weather, with the darkest possible nights for the flight over Russian territory. When everything was set for the start it was discovered that the load was still excessive as rain had softened up the runway. Another portion of our equipment had to be discarded. It must come on later with a supply aircraft.

At last the party got away. It was fourteen hours before we got any wireless news from the group.

As the revolts we hoped to provoke raised political questions, the further direction of the operation was unfortunately taken out of our hands and transferred to the political department of Group VI, the chief of which was Dr. Graefe. We were referred to only when more material and equipment, or another " dropping ", was required. I found myself in a painful position, having to let men who had been specially trained by myself pass under someone else's orders. I felt still responsible for them, although it was only in exceptional cases that I could intervene to give them any help.

Meanwhile the summer of 1943 had arrived. The prospects on the various fronts were far from rosy, a fact brought home to me by the resistance I met with in trying to build up my organization. No one displayed any enthusiasm to place the men and material I required at my disposal.

The parties we dropped in Iran met with varying success. They actually established contact with the rebellious tribes and did what was possible to achieve the object for which they were sent. Of course we were not in a position to let them have the men and material they required, because we were short of the appropriate transport aircraft, the long-range Ju 290.

We trained another unit of six men and an officer to lead them from the Special Course. Their start was delayed—very fortunately as it turned out—by damage to the Ju 290. An active German sympathizer in Teheran had escaped to Turkey after an exciting journey. He told us, just in time, that our central organization in

Teheran had been broken up and all its members arrested. He alone had had the luck to get away.

The result was that the unit, which was all ready to leave, had no ground organization waiting to receive it and there was no option but to cancel the enterprise for the time being. A few weeks later, the rebellious tribes had no more stomach for a fight. They released all our men who were with them, so that they could escape, but there was no prospect of people with an inadequate knowledge of the language getting away to the nearest neutral country, Turkey. The tribes were soon compelled to hand over their Germans to the English troops. In these circumstances one of the officers decided on suicide. The others passed many years in captivity in the Near East, and only returned to Germany in 1948.

I then turned to much more interesting projects. VIf, the technical department of Section VI, showed me a mass of data about the industrial set-up of the Soviet Union, particularly the Ural region. As none of this information was to be found in books or newspapers, I was extremely impressed with the collection of plans put at my disposal. A scheme had already been worked out under the code name "Operation Ulm", to attack some of the industrial establishments and put them out of action. It occurred to me that a single well-directed attack could do enormous damage to the enemy's war potential.

Before I made my final decision to take on this new job, I studied all the available reports on sabotage operations. I had found out in Russia that, if one kept one's eyes open, much could be learned from the enemy. Why should not that be the case now? I was amazed at what I read about the various enterprises of the English "Commando Troops", which were under the command of Lord Louis Mountbatten. There was no limit to new features. The English "Secret Service" was shrouded in mystery and hardly any publicity was given to it. Its activity in all parts of the world was a complete novelty to me.

Simultaneously I studied the reports of the achievements of the German Brandenburg Division. It appeared that in comparison with England, the resources at our disposal were greatly inferior, although remarkable results had been obtained on many occasions.

I spent a bare two weeks on the study of the material submitted to me, but was able to draw the conclusion that there were great possibilities of contributing to the victory of Germany by an intensification of these special enterprises. Even our enemies could not protect their homeland effectively everywhere. If we found the points of special importance, which were also vulnerable to attack by a small but determined force, skilful planning and the preparation of the necessary technical material could achieve substantial successes.

When I told Herr Schellenberg that I had decided to accept the job, he seemed very pleased. To my surprise he offered me not only a transfer to the SD, but the rank of a *sturmbannführer* in it. After a little reflection I declined the suggestion, stressing the fact that my main function was the command of fighting troops and I could perform it better as a Waffen SS officer. I had started the war as a ranker, been promoted to a commission and wished to remain an army officer while the war lasted.

A few days later my promotion to captain arrived. The Special Course which I now took over had previously been commanded by a Dutch captain, who had transferred to the Waffen SS. The company officers had all had long experience of the front.

But I was short of helpers for my part-time work for Section VI. Luck favoured me again. Some twenty young men, soldier lawyers, had just been transferred to the Political Intelligence Section. Among them I found Obersturmführer[1] Karl Radl, a countryman and old acquaintance of mine. I asked him whether he would like to join me in building up the new Section VI S. He not only agreed for himself, but brought with him two other experts. All three had done their military service. I could therefore use them for all purposes.

Nor was the then Director of the State Security Department, Dr. Ernst Kaltenbrunner, any stranger to me, as I had known him in my student days. He had been a member of a Students' Club in Graz, which was associated with mine, and we had seen a good deal of each other, though not after 1938. Now he was apparently one of the most important men in Germany. I had to present myself to him and was agreeably surprised to find that we were soon on the old footing. It struck me that even with all his glory, this man was not feeling quite at his ease.

He surprised me greatly by telling me about his worries during one conversation: "I took over this difficult department a year after the death of Obergruppenführer Heydrich," he said. "During

---

[1] For Waffen SS commissioned ranks and their army equivalents see Appendix.

the interregnum Reichsführer Himmler added it to all his other ministries and jobs and during that period my seven departmental chiefs achieved quite a degree of independence. They always went straight to Himmler himself and, even to-day, I am often side-tracked and there is much that I only find out afterwards. Your new chief, Schellenberg, and the Gestapo chief, Müller, are too fond of short circuits. Heydrich certainly knew his business, and built up his department in a cold, impersonal fashion, which we Ostmarkers don't like."

We had orders to expand the Oranienburg Special Course to battalion strength and the HQ of the Waffen SS instructed me to form the "Friedenthal" Special Formation, and gave me command of it. Thanks to my previous good relations with various front units, I was able to find enough officers, NCO's and men to form the first two companies within a very short time.

A suitable training area for the new unit was found at Frieden-thal, near Oranienburg. There was a modest old Frederickian hunting-lodge in a large, well-wooded park. The surrounding meadows were most favourable for our purpose. The planning was easy. What was not so easy was to get all our requirements from competent authorities. I fought ferociously with officialism and at length found my way through the labyrinth of red tape. But it was Karl Radl, now appointed my second-in-command, who became past-master in this art.

I had drawn up an extensive programme for my special unit. The men were to receive the most comprehensive training possible to enable them to be used at any point and for any purpose. Infantry and engineering training was a *sine qua non,* but each man must also be familiar with the handling of mortars, light field artillery and tank guns. It was elementary that he should be able to ride a motor-cycle and drive a car and lorry as well as specialized vehicles. The syllabus even included the driving of railway engines and the handling of motor-boats.

Riding and every kind of sport were to be a great feature, and a short course of parachute jumping was included. After this indi-vidual training, there would be group training for special operations, language and surveying courses and instruction on technical targets and tactics.

At that time I regarded the Soviet Union and the Near East as our main target by reason of the Anglo-American interests there. I am not certain that I quite appreciated that we were already in the fourth year of the war. Perhaps I deliberately put that thought behind me so that we could achieve at least as much as possible. I told myself that there is no " too late " for a soldier. It is never too late to start on something really important. It merely calls for speedier and more resolute action.

Preparations had already been made in Holland to establish and build up a school for agents. On my first tour of inspection I satisfied myself that in that country we could work on a bigger scale than at home. · This business was in the hands of Standartenführer Knolle. It was a difficult position for me. He was considerably higher in rank than I, though he was a soldier. But he solved the problem by offering to serve under me.

The school was quartered in what had been the modest country house of a titled Dutchman. Here, away from all prying eyes, training in wireless and sabotage activities was to be carried on.

What I learned in Holland about counter-espionage—the province of Section III of AA and the Security Police—was new to me. I learned for the first time of the intense activity of England in this field. Night after night, flights were carried out by fast aircraft which parachuted agents on a great variety of espionage and sabotage jobs or supplied previously parachuted agents with wireless sets, explosives, weapons and other suitable equipment.

The competent authorities calculated that half of these agents were caught soon after they landed, and almost three-quarters of the material dropped fell into German hands. We took an active part in securing this manna from heaven, so our difficult problem of procuring enough of the necessary equipment was solved almost entirely by our opponents themselves.

At my request I was given a large number of reports on the interrogation of English agents. From my study of them I realized what a lot of leeway we had to make up. I was particularly interested in the enemy's training and instruction methods. I asked our interrogators to devote special attention to that aspect. Before long we had a very good picture of the work of the " Secret Service " and its headquarters in England.

We knew most of what there was to be known about the carefully guarded restricted area in Scotland where most of the training schools were accommodated in lonely little houses. Agents who were willing to talk provided us with sketches of roads and other geographical features. The English method of instruction proved a valuable model.

It was in Holland too that I first made the acquaintance of the type known as the "double agent". Many men who had made espionage a profession were prepared to change sides when they were caught, and take service against their previous employers. But I soon realized that really dangerous enterprises could be entrusted only to soldiers who volunteered. Idealism and conviction are essential to a man who is prepared to give his life for his country. They alone could guarantee the cheerful resolution which meant success. If a man wants paying before he will risk his life, one cannot expect much force of character, though I admit that there were a few exceptions which proved the rule.

I also learned at this Dutch headquarters that we had excellent wireless communication with English stations. More than ten wireless sets, with all the code words and keys, had been captured. By using these, and with the help of agents, we were able to hoodwink the English with a regular wireless communication with that country. It enabled us to trace an organization in Holland consisting of several hundred persons. The "Underground" was quite inactive at the time, so we decided not to arrest them for the time being. We would get better results by biding our time and continuing the wireless correspondence.

I had read in the reports that the English training schools taught their agents to use revolvers with a silencer. The Germans had not yet invented such a weapon, nor had we found any specimen among the booty in occupied western countries. A bright idea occurred to me. What about using the surreptitious wireless to ask that one should be sent? Our post in Holland agreed to do so.

When I revisited Holland less than a fortnight later, I was handed one of these revolvers. It was a single-shot 7·65 weapon, somewhat primitive in construction and probably all the more accurate for that. In reply to our wireless call in the name of the agent "Treasure", the revolver had been promptly despatched by air from England and thankfully collected by us. I tried the weapon out from the window of the orderly-room on a number of ducks which were swimming on the lake. Practically nothing could be heard and the ducks took no notice of the shot falling quite close.

The weapons parachuted into Holland, Belgium and France also included the British Sten gun. When I was examining it I was impressed by the simplicity of its construction and the fact that it was obviously cheap to produce. There must be a silencer for this weapon also, but Britain was keeping this refinement a secret—which was a compelling reason why I should get hold of one. This time, however, the wireless request had no response. Either the British enemy smelt a rat, or the new weapon was being reserved for later use.

I learned quite casually that a Dutch sea captain was being despatched to Britain on another mission. He was proposing to make for a Scottish harbour, via Sweden, in his little cutter and collect some mail intended for British agents in Holland. At my request he was instructed to ask for a silencer for the Sten gun. In this way I became the first man in Germany to handle this device. I was most enthusiastic about the military possibilities of the weapon in its revised form. A reconnaissance party armed with it would avoid a lot of casualties! In the event of an unexpected meeting with the enemy, there would be no sound of firing to give it away. I felt sure that every soldier on an assault or reconnaissance mission would be enthusiastic about such a weapon.

But the ordnance department in Berlin thought otherwise. I demonstrated the silencer to some high-ranking officers in Frieden-thal one evening. It was dark and we were walking in a park. I arranged that a soldier just behind us should fire off a whole maga-zine into the air. My superiors were amazed when I subsequently showed them the empty cartridge cases on the ground. But objections were offered just the same. It was said that the force of impact was too small and accuracy was adversely affected by the silencer.

Others now joined with me in advocating the production of the simpler and pretty accurate Sten gun and its employment by the German Army. It could be rubbed in mud but would still fire—in contrast to our machine-pistols which even a little dust could upset. Moreover its manufacture required only a fraction of the material and man-hours involved in the production of the German weapon. But "Holy Bureaucracy" had its say again. Adolf Hitler's name was brought in. Had not the Führer himself said that only the best weapons must be issued to the German soldier? The accuracy of the Sten gun was certainly somewhat inferior to that of the German weapon, but it was forgotten that the Sten gun is a weapon for close quarters, and no one would think of firing it at a distant target.

This reminds me of the automatic repeater-rifle with which the Russian sharpshooters had been equipped since 1941. We were all very anxious to get hold of one of these rifles and before long every German company had one or more. A German automatic rifle was not introduced until 1944, although the manufacturers had designed them some years previously and offered to turn them out in quantity. But the idea was turned down. It was feared that its introduction would lead to an excessive consumption of ammunition and it was alleged that fire discipline would suffer. But at the same time the ·42 machine-gun, which fired more than a hundred rounds a minute, was brought out! These decisions of the higher authorities were not understood by the men in the ranks.

I had a visit one day from a lieutenant of the Brandenburg Division who was on leave. His name was Adrian von Foelkersam, and he had won the Ritterkreuz as early as 1941 for a smart piece of work in Russia. He told me that there was great dissatisfaction in the ranks of the old " Brandenburgers ". The division was no longer employed on special service, but used as a stop-gap at various points along the front—a rôle which any other division could have played equally well. Its losses had always been very high and it was almost impossible to make them good, having regard to the special training the men had received. The division consisted almost exclusively of men with a knowledge of languages and geography who had volunteered for special enterprises. He and ten other officers from his battalion would like to join my command, of the formation of which they had only just heard. Would I see what I could do to help them?

I immediately took a great fancy to von Foelkersam, both as a man and a soldier, and felt sure that in a tight corner I would certainly find him an experienced and valuable helper. I was only too pleased to assure him that I would do what I could.

It was in this connection that I came into contact, for the first and last time, with the well-known Admiral Canaris, Director of German Military Intelligence. I was told that Dr. Kaltenbrunner and Schellenberg were to have a conference with him about improved co-ordination between AAA and Section VI. I asked them if they would take me along and endorse my request to Admiral Canaris for the transfer to my unit of four officers and six ensigns of the Brandenburg Division.

We were ushered into a room which was half in darkness and sat down in low armchairs. Although I usually have a good memory for faces, I find it impossible, strange to say, to describe Admiral Canaris. All I can recollect is a heavily-built man of average height, with a bald head. He was wearing naval uniform. Of his features I remember only his colourless eyes, which wandered from one of us to the other when they were not fixed for a moment on a particular spot on the wall.

But I remember him very well as a negotiator. Unquestionably he was a man whom it was not easy to see through. One could never tell what he was really thinking or what he really wanted. He was a skilled conversationalist and a master of the art of interjecting a phrase designed to prevent one from pursuing a line of thought which he did not like. But I also know how to argue and bargain. For three hours we tried to persuade him to release the ten men we wanted, but he was always finding fresh excuses for refusing us. When we changed to some other topic and then produced an irrefutable answer to his last argument, he promptly produced another!

At length we got our way. His debating power seemed to give out and he approved of the release and transfer of the men. I glanced up in triumph and breathed a sigh of relief. The discussion had been terribly hard going. But when it came to instructing his Chief of Staff to issue the necessary orders, to everyone's surprise the Admiral revived all his previous objections and postponed consideration of the matter indefinitely.

I had had enough and thought it time to go. It was only a month later, in November, 1943, that after approaches from another quarter the ten volunteers from the Brandenburg Division were finally released. When I returned to my office from this meeting, a sadly disappointed man, I delivered myself thus to Radl:

"Admiral Canaris is certainly the most difficult opponent I have ever had to tackle. As a man, he seems to me quite impenetrable, and I cannot form any sort of opinion about him. He may be the ideal Intelligence officer. His eyes positively sparkle with intelligence, but you cannot get at him. He's like a jellyfish. You can push your finger right through it and see it come out the other side, but when you've withdrawn it the creature looks exactly the same as before. His debating technique never varies. He neither agrees nor disagrees. There is no black or white; always something in between, and at the end he hasn't admitted a thing—which is probably his object from the start. I don't mind such tactics against a stranger or an enemy—but against another German! "

At that time I also established contact with the intelligence service of the Luftwaffe, an institution disguised under the name of " Kurfürst ". It was one of the best-conducted departments with which I had to deal. In course of time the standard of co-operation became perfect. Most areas had been covered by photography from the air, and we had photographs of areas well beyond the Volga in the east, the Sea of Aral in the south-east, and including Mesopotamia and the Suez Canal in the south. It is true that most of the photographs dated from 1940 and 1941, when the Luftwaffe still ruled the skies. Their archives were also rich in material relating to the industrial potential of our enemies.

I had taken over a good deal of material about Soviet war industries in connection with " Operation Ulm ". When the Luftwaffe's store was also made available to me, I realized how much we still lacked and what a gigantic task lay ahead of me.

It was certain that Russia had removed the most important portions of her industry to regions east of the Urals, and also established new industries there. The area concerned was larger than the whole of Germany at that time. Aerial reconnaissance had seldom penetrated so far and we were thus dependent on other sources of information. The statements of prisoners were systematically collected and examined. Together with the information supplied by German, French and other concerns which had worked and exported there, they gave a good picture of the industrial structure of the Ural region. For the first time I was able to calculate how much systematic preliminary work was involved before we could devise any definite plan.

It was quite impossible for us to attack all the industrial establishments, whether from the air or by means of sabotage operations. We must find the nerve centres. In these days, every industry, particularly a centralized industry which has been built up by government planning in the course of a few years, has weak points. We soon found them out. In this case it was the electric power system, which had been planned on a central basis like the others and literally stamped out of the ground. The demand for power must be satisfied at once, and as the result of the frantic haste any considerable reserves of power are non-existent. A diminution of the power supply must in practice entail a corresponding diminution of industrial output. Even the grid covering such an area can become a soft spot when it is repeatedly and systematically disrupted.

With the help of some technical organs of the Luftwaffe—which was vitally concerned—we brought system into our planning and soon made rapid progress.

This systematic work was suddenly interrupted for months by an undoubtedly well-meant, but surely insufficiently considered, order from "high-up". One of the State Secretaries of Speer's Ministry of Munitions had given Himmler a memorandum on the importance of the vast blast furnaces at Magnitogorsk in the Urals. In his usual impulsive fashion, Himmler had issued the following order the very same day: "The Friedenthal Special Force will immediately prepare a sabotage operation against the blast furnaces at Magnitogorsk. These must be completely destroyed and put out of action permanently. Report to me monthly on the progress of the preparations and the prospective date of the operation."

I found this order in the form of a priority telephone message on my table.

After an immediate conference with all the experts we came to two conclusions: 1. No real information about Magnitogorsk and its industrial installations was available. It would take months of hard work to procure it. 2. Try as we might, we could not even imagine how the wretched saboteurs could get the vast quantities of explosives required anywhere near the target, which would be very well guarded at all times.

But how were such negative conclusions to be brought home to this superior of superiors? When I had committed these two objections to paper in plain language and proposed to send them for consideration "at top level", I was simply laughed at. Anyone could see I was a novice, I was told. I must learn the whole tricky business of handling those above me. The first thing was to display immense enthusiasm for any plan, however idiotic, which they put forward, and keep on reporting progress. Only later, and then in small doses, could one inject the truth. One became a master of the diplomatic art only when one managed to allow the plan to get completely forgotten—the royal road to enrolment in the ranks of the perfect subordinates.

Such was the teaching of Schellenberg, through whose department the order had come down to us. It took quite eighteen months before this wholly unrealizable scheme was definitely buried.

I gradually obtained a concrete and complete picture of what is understood by the terms "military commando operations" and "sabotage action by agents". As a soldier I was predisposed in favour of the former. But it was only fair to admit that Germany was not a good base for the activities of agents. It was true that we occupied almost the whole of Europe, but where were we to find Englishmen or Americans prepared to spy for us in their own countries? If money was the only attraction good results could not be expected.

How much easier it was for the Allies in the many occupied countries. There were plenty of patriots animated by the will to injure the "invader" in every possible way. I believed that more would be achieved by the voluntary devotion of German soldiers, assisted by one or two natives who knew the country. So, whenever possible, we proposed to carry out such enterprises as "commando operations" on a purely military basis.

CHAPTER IV

IN THE afternoon of the 26th July, 1943, I had a conversation in the Hotel Eden in Berlin with an old friend from Vienna, a university professor. I was wearing civilian clothes—which I preferred—and our prolonged lunch hour was all the more informal. After the meal we sat in the hall, drinking war-time coffee and chatting about Vienna, our homeland, and mutual friends. But gradually I found myself a prey to a vague and inexplicable feeling of apprehension. I had let the telephone operator know where I was to be found if a call came through. But who could know?

At length I rose and rang up my office. My secretary was in a state of wild excitement. They had been searching for me for two hours. "FHQ has sent for you, Chief. A plane will be waiting for you at five o'clock at the Tempelhofer airfield," she said. Now I understood what had been worrying me. I had never been summoned to FHQ before. I concealed my excitement and answered as calmly as possible: " Radl must go to my room at once, pack a uniform and linen and go straight to the airfield. He mustn't forget a thing! Is there no hint as to what it's all about?" "No," came the reply. "We know nothing at all. Radl will get busy at once; he won't forget anything."

To say good-bye to my friend was the matter of a moment. He was visibly impressed by the fact that I had been summoned to the Führer's headquarters and wished me luck.

I turned over all the possibilities in my mind as I drove through the streets of Berlin to the airport. Could it be connected with "Operation Franz"? It was not probable. Or "Operation Ulm"? This was possible, though I could not imagine why it should involve my going to FHQ. All I could do was wait and see. At the airport I found my Second with a parcel and a brief-case. In a matter of minutes I had changed. Karl Radl said that a radio message had just come in to the effect that there had been a change of government in Italy, but we did not associate that event with my sudden journey.

We walked on to the tarmac. A Junkers 52 drew up. A huge aircraft like that just for me! What a luxury! I was actually walking up the gangway when the most important point of all occurred to me: "You must be available at any moment. I'll ring up as soon as I know anything. Both our companies must be alerted. To be forewarned is to be forearmed!" I gave a signal and the aircraft turned into the runway.

After circling several times we gained height over Berlin and then my brain began to be plagued once more with useless queries. What was in store for me at FHQ? Whom should I meet? Everything was shrouded in mystery, a mystery impenetrable at the moment. I soon abandoned these hopeless speculations and took a look round. The twelve seats behind me were unoccupied. Just in front was a built-in cocktail cabinet. With my usual cheek I put my head through the pilot's door and asked whether I could help myself. Two glasses of good brandy soothed my nerves and I could sit back and contemplate the landscape below.

After crossing the Oder the lovely woods and meadows of the Neumark smiled up at us. I remembered that I had only a vague idea of the whereabouts of the Führer's headquarters, which was a secret carefully kept from ordinary mortals. Beyond its code name, "Wolfsschanze",[1] and the fact that it was somewhere in East

[1] Wolf's Den.

Prussia, I knew nothing. Radl had really thought of everything
and I found a map in the brief-case he had so carefully packed. We
had been flying for about an hour and a half when I recognized
Schneidemühl below us. The aircraft was flying at about one
thousand metres and the sun sparkled on the windows of the houses
and the canals. We continued on a straight north-easterly course.

I spent a short time in the pilots' cabin. They pointed out the
great stretch of water near Deutsch-Eylau which was beginning to
appear. The big intersection of the Warsaw-Danzig and Insterburg-
Posen lines lay just below us. I could not help thinking what a
magnificent target it would present for attack from the air. It was
too bad that such a splendid experience as this flight in glorious
weather could not banish thoughts of the war and I felt quite
angry with myself.

The sun was now low down on the horizon behind us. We had
lost height and were flying at about three hundred metres. The
landscape too had changed. It was flat and traversed in all directions by a number of water-courses. The foliage of the trees was
green and I wondered if they were birches.

When we had covered about five hundred kilometres a complex
of small lakes appeared, peering up at us like little blue eyes. By
now the sun was on the horizon and its light became paler every
moment. I glanced at the map. We were over the Masurian lake
region. It was here that old Hindenburg had dealt the Russians
a shattering blow. Thank God our eastern front was now at
Smolensk, a long, long way from our sacred East Prussia and
hundreds of kilometres from the German frontier!

At the edge of a lake near Lotzen I spied a small airfield. The
Junkers touched down and taxied in quietly and safely. The whole
flight had taken not quite three hours.

A big Mercedes was waiting for me near the barracks of the
airfield staff. "Are you Captain Skorzeny?" a sergeant asked.
"I'm to take you to Headquarters at once."

Driving along a road through lovely forests, we soon reached
an outer barrier. There was a pole across the road. The driver
had brought me a chit which I now showed, with my paybook, to
the officer at the guardhouse. My name was written in a book
which I signed. The barrier was then raised. The road narrowed
and led through a birch wood. We crossed some railway lines and
came to a second barrier, where I had to get out of the car again.

My papers were examined and noted in another book and then the duty officer spoke to someone on the telephone. He asked me who had sent for me. It was very disagreeable for me, but I had to admit that I did not know. "You are wanted at the office of the Führer's ADC at the Tea House," he said, obviously impressed by the answer he had received to his telephone enquiry. The information meant nothing to me. What would the Adjutant's office want with me?

The car proceeded a little further to a gate. The area we now entered was surrounded by a barbed-wire fence and resembled a park well laid out with birch plantations. Winding roads were bordered with low birch trees. Some buildings and barracks, apparently sited without any regard to symmetry, now came into view. Grass and small trees were growing on the flat roofs. Some of the buildings and roads were covered with camouflage nets, here and there surmounted by real tree-tops, to look like a group of trees in the bare places.

It was getting quite dark when we arrived at the Tea House. I saw a wooden building consisting of two wings connected by a passage roofed in. I learned subsequently that the left wing contained the dining-room where Field-Marshal Keitel, the Chief of the General Staff, his generals and a few other eminent personalities took their meals. The Tea House itself was on the right. When I entered I found myself in a large ante-room, furnished with comfortable chairs and several tables. The floor was covered with a plain Boucle carpet.

I was received by a Waffen SS captain and introduced to five officers who were standing round. One was an army colonel, another an army major and there were two Luftwaffe lieutenant-colonels and a Waffen SS major. I was annoyed that the captain pronounced my name wrong and corrected him: "My name's not all that difficult; if you pronounce it Skor-tsay-ny in ordinary German it's quite easy." My name is frequently mispronounced and I do not know why I attached so much importance to its being got right on this occasion.

Apparently my arrival was all that they were waiting for. The captain disappeared and I lit a cigarette. I was about to ask my Waffen SS colleague what his name was (as I had not caught any of the names during the introductions) when the officer came back. "I'll take you to the Führer, gentlemen. You'll be introduced and must tell him of your military careers, but keep it short. He may have some questions to ask you. Please come this way."

I thought I could not be hearing right and trembled in every limb. In a few minutes I should find myself face to face with Adolf Hitler, the Führer of the Reich and Supreme Commander of the Wehrmacht. What a colossal surprise! I should probably commit some frightful *gaffe,* or make a fool of myself! I hoped my men in Berlin were keeping their fingers crossed.

Meanwhile we had walked some hundred and fifty paces, but in what direction I have not the slightest idea. We entered another building and again found ourselves in a big ante-room, where we had to wait a moment. In the soft indirect lighting I glanced at the wall and saw a small picture in an unpretentious silver frame. It was Dürer's *The Violet*. It is curious that this detail remains in my memory, whereas I have almost forgotten far more important things.

Then we turned left through the door and entered a room about six metres by nine. The right wall had windows with plain, bright coloured curtains. In front of them was a massive table covered with maps. In the centre of the left wall was a fireplace and facing it a round table with four or five easy chairs. As the most junior in rank, I was on the left of the file. My eye fell on a writing table which was placed at an angle to the window. A number of coloured pencils, placed exactly parallel, were lying on it. So it is here that the great decisions of the age are taken! I reflected. Then a door on the left opened.

We clicked our heels and stood to attention. Now I was to meet the man who had played so great a part in German history. A soldier experiences a peculiar feeling when he suddenly finds himself facing his supreme commander.

It may be that I am mixing later impressions with my account of this occasion, for the situation at the time was so confusing and surprising that only incidents have stamped themselves clearly on my memory.

With slow steps Adolf Hitler entered the room. He greeted us with upraised arm—the gesture familiar to us from innumerable photographs. He was wearing a simple, open-necked field-grey uniform, which revealed the white shirt and black tie. On the left breast I saw the Iron Cross First Class, which he had won in the First World War, together with the black ribbon of the wounded.

When he asked the aide-de-camp to introduce him to the officer on the extreme right of the row, I could hardly see what he was doing. I had to hold myself back to avoid leaning forward to get a better view.

All I heard was the Führer's deep voice as he put his curt questions. The sound of that voice was well known to me through the wireless; there was no mistaking it. What struck me at the time was the unmistakable soft Austrian accent, even when he was emphatic. I thought that it was extraordinary that this man, who preached and embodied the old Prussian gospel, could not conceal his origin, despite long absence from his own homeland. I wondered whether he still retained something of the characteristic kindliness of the Austrian and whether he was a man of feeling. Heavens, what superfluous questions and ideas at such a moment!

All the officers who preceded me gave a short, soldierly account of their military careers. At length Adolf Hitler was standing before me and offering me his hand. I made a great effort not to bow too low and I think my bow was correct—smart and slight. In five sentences I gave my birthplace, education, military career and present assignment. While I was speaking he looked me straight in the face, not taking his eyes off me for a second.

Then he stepped back, took us in at a glance again and rapped out a question: "Which of you knows Italy?" I was the only one to reply. "I have twice been as far as Naples, my Führer." He addressed another question to the first man: "What do you think of Italy?" The enquiry came as a surprise, and we treated it as addressed to us all. The answers were hesitating: "Italy . . . Axis partner . . . Member of the Comintern alliance . . ." I broke in: "I am Austrian, my Führer!" It seemed unnecessary to say anything more as the loss of German South Tyrol, the loveliest region on earth, was the sorest possible subject with a real Austrian.

Adolf Hitler looked at me long and closely before he said: "The other gentlemen may go. I want you to stay, Captain Skorzeny."

I observed with satisfaction that he pronounced my name correctly. Then we were alone, face to face. When he began to talk to me he became quite animated. Although he was sparing in his gestures and the movements of his hands, there was, nevertheless, a compelling force about them.

"I have a very important commission for you. Mussolini, my friend and our loyal comrade in arms, was betrayed yesterday by his king and arrested by his own countrymen. I cannot and will not leave Italy's greatest son in the lurch. To me the Duce is the incarnation of the ancient grandeur of Rome. Italy under the new government will desert us! I will keep faith with my old ally and dear friend; he must be rescued promptly or he will be handed over to the Allies. I'm entrusting to you the execution of an undertaking which is of great importance to the future course of the war. You must do everything in your power to carry out this order; if you do, promotion will reward you!

"Now we come to the most important part," he continued. "It is absolutely essential that the affair should be kept a strict secret. Beside yourself only five people must know of it. You will be transferred to the Luftwaffe again and put under the orders of General Student. You must not talk to anyone else and you will get all the details from him. You must also devise with him all the military preparations to meet the situation if Badoglio Italy suddenly deserts us. Rome must not be lost! You'll have the task of finding out where the Duce is. The army commander in Italy and the German ambassador in Rome must know nothing about your assignment, as they have a completely mistaken view of the situation and would tackle the job in the wrong way. I repeat that I hold you responsible for the maintenance of absolute secrecy. I hope I shall hear from you soon and wish you the best of luck."

The longer Hitler spoke the more I could feel his influence upon me. His words seemed to me so convincing that at that moment I had not the slightest doubt about the success of the project. There was such a warm, human inflection in his voice when he spoke of his loyalty to his Italian friend that I was deeply moved. I could only reply: "I fully understand, my Führer, and will do my best."

We shook hands and the meeting ended. During those few minutes, which seemed to me an age, Adolf Hitler never took his eyes off me, and even when I turned away I felt he was still gazing after me. When I bowed myself out at the door my impression was confirmed; he was still watching me.

I was back in the Tea House. I soon felt more relaxed and lit a cigarette, though my head was still buzzing and it was some time before I could put my thoughts together. An orderly asked me whether there was anything I would like and then I realized that I was extremely hungry. I ordered coffee "and something with it". An excellent meal was on the table in no time. I discarded gloves, cap and belt and quietly sat down to do it justice, but I had hardly touched the cup before the orderly reappeared and called out: "Herr General Student wants you in the next room."

The door to a small adjacent room opened and I presented myself to General Student. He was a rotund individual of jovial appearance. A severe wound at Rotterdam in the year 1940 had left a deep scar. I told him that the broad outlines of the project had just been given me by the Führer.

There was a knock on the door and in stepped the Reichsführer, Himmler. I had only seen photographs of him until this meeting. He seemed to know the parachute general. The pair exchanged greetings while I waited to be introduced. A quick handshake, and then we were invited to sit down.

At first sight the most remarkable thing about Himmler's face was his old-fashioned eye-glasses. His far from impressive features betrayed nothing of the man's character. He gave us a friendly smile. He was wearing field-grey uniform, supplemented, I observed, only by the narrow shoulder-strap of the civil SS, riding breeches and boots. I was never to see him in these comfortable trousers again.

Himmler spoke first and gave us a picture of the political situation in Italy. He expressed the view that the new Badoglio government was unlikely to remain faithful to the Axis, and also mentioned the names of a large number of soldiers, Italian aristocrats and politicians, hardly any of whom were known to me. When he said that some were reliable and others traitors, I thought I had better write down some of the names. I had hardly produced my fountain-pen and some paper before he roared at me: "You must be mad to put anything on paper! This is dead secret. You must memorize the names!"

This is a good start, I thought. Of all these hundreds of names I'll be damned lucky if I retain one after all to-day's excitement.

General Student and I did not get a chance to speak, nor was there much to say while Himmler poured out his torrent of names and told us how to handle various individuals. I made a tremendous effort to take it all in, but it was too much at one go.

"Italy's defection is certain," he said, "the only question is when. It might be any day now. Italian representatives are already in Portugal negotiating with the Allies." He followed up this remark with another stream of names, places and secret reports which had come in.

Then he turned to discuss other matters with General Student. It was 11 o'clock by now and in Berlin my comrades must certainly have been on edge, waiting for a telephone call. I asked whether I could leave to ring them up, went out into the corridor, and while waiting to be put through, lit a cigarette and reflected on all I had learnt. I knew my assignment now, but the great question was how to tackle it. At that moment Himmler came out and stormed at me when he saw me smoking: "These eternal weeds! Can't you do anything without a cigarette in your mouth? I can see that you're not at all the sort of man we need for this job!" He glared at me and went on his way.

My second bloomer of the evening, I thought to myself. Herr Himmler does not like me and perhaps I've lost the job already! I extinguished my cigarette and felt quite bewildered. What was I to do now? At that moment the Führer's ADC reappeared. Apparently he had overheard the conversation. "Don't worry! The Reichsführer goes for everybody! He'll forget all about it. His nerves are probably on edge and it makes him jumpy. Go back to General Student and fix it all up with him."

Everything was soon arranged with the General. I was to fly with him to Rome as his orderly officer at 8 o'clock next morning, and at the same hour fifty men from my unit would leave by air from Berlin for the south of France. From there they would fly on to Rome to meet the 1st Division of the Parachute Corps, which was also to be sent by air direct to Italy. "We'll consider the next step when we get there," General Student said: "so here's to successful co-operation, and good-bye until to-morrow morning!"

The telephone rang outside. Radl was on the line in a state of great excitement. "What on earth has happened? We've been waiting ages for your call." "We have orders to move to-morrow morning," I replied. "I can't tell you any more now. I've got to think things out and I'll ring you later. All I can say is that sleep is off for everyone to-night. Get your transport ready, as we have to take equipment with us. Pick fifty men—only the best, and all with some knowledge of Italian. Let me know what officers you suggest and I'll give you my own ideas. Tropical kit required. We must have jumping and emergency rations also. Everything must be ready by 5 a.m."

I considered myself fortunate to find an officer still at the Tea House, for I did not then know that at FHQ no one knocked off until the early hours. I asked him to give me a room with a telephone and someone to teletype my instructions to my Special Force. A young woman in a plain green dress appeared. She asked me whether I had had any food and when I replied in the negative she went away and soon came back with an orderly carrying a tray of enticing snacks. As my nerves were in a pretty bad state, I could only manage a little bread and a lot of coffee. I made myself concentrate. What equipment, weapons and explosives should we require for fifty men? I went to work methodically and produced a long list. My little force must have the greatest possible fire-power, and yet be lightly armed. We might well have to drop by parachute, so we must have two machine-guns per group (9 men) and all the rest must be armed with machine-pistols. We must also have hand grenades, the egg variety being the best (they can be stuffed in one's pocket), and pioneer equipment for two parachute groups. Thirty kilograms of plastic explosive would be enough, preferably the English type which we had collected in Holland and which had proved better than our own. All sorts of fuses, not forgetting time fuses, went down on the list. Tropical helmets were important and also light underclothing for the men. Rations for six days and emergency rations for three I decided should be enough.

The first list went by teletype to Berlin. Then I started to consider which of my men were indispensable. There was Lieutenant Menzel, our one company commander, and Lieutenant Schwerdt, a particularly competent infantry and pioneer officer, who must certainly come with us. Lieutenant Warger knew Italian and was a good mountaineer. My list was soon made up and I realized that there would be great disappointment for the many I had had to omit.

When the names were completed, I put through a quick call to Berlin. Radl was at the other end: "We're sweating blood! How do you think we can get through all this by the morning? Your teletype's frightfully long." "You've damn well got to, and there's still more to come!" I rapped out. "I'm sweating too. I've been talking to the Führer and the Reichsführer!" (I could hear my second-in-command gasp). "It's a direct order from the Führer himself." Then we compared lists of those we proposed to take with us. Both contained practically the same names. Great minds think alike!

"There's a fearful rumpus in the company," Radl continued. "Everybody wants to go and refuses to be left out."

"Give them the names of the certainties at once," I advised. "It will keep them quiet."

Had I forgotten anything? Yes, there was wireless gear. We must fix up a wireless correspondence in Berlin and arrange a cypher for a month and the times for putting calls through (as many as possible), both by day and night. A further telegram was called for. Everything went as "top secret" over the wires. We had to be extremely careful. If the Italians or their Intelligence got wind of the business we should be wasting our time.

I put through four or five further calls to Berlin. Fresh points which might be important continually came to mind: tracer for the machine-guns in case of fighting at night, Verey pistols, medical orderlies and stores for tropical regions. Civilian clothes for the officers would probably be necessary. It was nearly three-thirty when I put through my last call. Everything was still upside down there. Lorries were racing all over the place collecting what I had asked for. But I knew that we would be on time.

Finally I was told that we should need to take Intelligence officers with us and hoped we should have occasion to use them!

Before I slept that night I had time to think quietly and for the first time I realized what a formidable task I had been set. Our first problem was to find out where Mussolini was. But if we managed to find him, what next? The Duce would certainly be in some very safe place and extremely well guarded! Should we have to storm a fortress or a prison? I conjured up all sorts of fantastic situations.

Turning over and over in bed, I tried to banish thought, but five minutes later was wrestling with my problems again. The longer I cogitated the poorer seemed the prospect of success. The chances were that I should never get back alive, but I could show what I was made of, do my best and, if necessary, make a respectable exit from this pleasant world.

I remember thinking that I was a family man. I had been through the war so far without making a will, and it occurred to me that it was high time that I did so. I switched on the light and hastily made one.

Another thought that came to me while the stuffy air and noise of the ventilators kept me awake, was that this day had certainly brought one chapter of my life to a close. Skorzeny the soldier had been given an order which, whatever the outcome, would have a decisive influence on his future. A great event had occurred which would single me out from the great mass of German soldiers—if I survived. Curiously enough, I did not find this thought at all disturbing.

By 6 o'clock I knew I should never sleep, so I crept along the corridor in my pyjamas and found an orderly who told me where I could get a shower. The water did me good, and half an hour later I was able to put all idle and superfluous speculations behind me.

At 6.45 I was back in the Tea House. I had ordered a car for 7.30 to take me to the aerodrome. I had an enormous appetite and kept the orderly busy.

Outside the grass was steaming in the early sunshine.

I caught sight of a sergeant with a sheep dog and went out to get a closer look at it, as it was my favourite breed. The dog fetched, crouched to command and jumped smartly through a circle, quite five feet above ground, made by the man's arms. He told me that the dog was Hitler's "Blondi", doing its morning exercises.

At length I was ready, my briefcase my only luggage. I had just received a telegram that my men had left Berlin.

I was taken to a different aerodrome which was laid out almost on the top of a hill. What a target for enemy bombing, I thought. It seemed a miracle that it had not been attacked already.

A few minutes later General Student arrived. He had slept at the Luftwaffe headquarters. A two-engined He 111, which would make better time than our good old Junkers, was waiting for us. I was introduced to the General's pilot, Captain Gerlach. I quite looked forward to the flight, which promised to be pleasant if the splendid weather held.

We climbed into the plane and found the pilot, rear-gunner and wireless operator already in their places. After taking off we quickly gained height and set a course southwards. We passed over the same lake and forest area as before. Our speed was something like 270 kilometres an hour and our altitude 3,000 metres. The noise was too great to allow sustained conversation between General Student and myself, but I managed to let him know that my men had left Berlin. In due course he went to sleep and I had a look round. It was the first time I had been in an He 111, and there was plenty to see. I was allowed to sit for a considerable time in the second pilot's seat, from which I had a wonderful all-round view.

On arrival at Rome, I wanted to get rid of my fur-lined flying suit, but suddenly remembered that I had no Luftwaffe uniform underneath. A Waffen SS officer as orderly to Student, the parachute general, would strike everyone as very odd, so I had to go on stewing.

Frascati, a typically Italian and idyllic little town, was the headquarters of the German forces in Italy, under the command of Field-Marshal Kesselring. We drove to the headquarters of General von Richthofen, commanding the Air Fleet, and were invited to lunch. I did not know how I should explain my peculiar appearance, but Captain Melzer, commanding the advance party of parachutists, came to my rescue and found me a parachutist's tropical kit, as well as a pass for a staff officer of the Parachute Corps.

I had a room next to that of General Student in the villa Tusculum II, from which we had a splendid view of Rome. He had been asked over for the evening by Field-Marshal Kesselring and told to bring me with him. Who would have thought twenty-four hours earlier that Captain Skorzeny would be spending this evening with the German Commander-in-Chief in Italy?

We drove to the Field-Marshal's house just before 9 o'clock. I was presented to him in the hall. To me he was one of the most attractive characters among the top-ranking generals, both for his fine soldierly qualities and his personal charm. Major-General Westfal, his Chief-of-Staff, was the typical outstanding young staff officer, all intelligence and reserve.

Following dinner, coffee was served in the hall. I was joined by some junior officers and the conversation was almost exclusively concerned with the fall of the Duce. One of the officers said that he had asked a high Italian officer if he knew where the Duce was. (Of course I pricked up my ears at once.) The Italian had given him his word of honour that even the chiefs of the Italian Army were quite in the dark. In my impulsive way I burst out: "I should doubt whether that can be true!" Field-Marshal Kesselring, who had come in unnoticed, apparently heard my remark. He seemed annoyed and spoke up for our ally: "I believe it absolutely," he said. "I have no reason to doubt the word of honour of an Italian officer and it would be as well for you to feel the same, Captain." I made up my mind not to volunteer opinions in future.

Next day news began to come in of the arrival of the Parachute Division. The first aircraft landed about midday at Pratica di Mare, an airfield on the coast south-west of Rome. General Student drove down with me to give some orders on the spot. We watched a number of very large, but slow, planes of the *Gigant* type come down on the tarmac.

My own unit had not yet arrived.

The wait next day proved less pleasant as news came through that the echelons had been attacked by enemy fighters, and there had been losses of men and aircraft. Every commander is an egotist and I could only hope that my own men were not involved. On the following morning the good news arrived that my unit would be with the next echelon. I went down to the airfield and found the men in high spirits.

We were allotted three groups of wooden huts close to the airfield and the men took up their quarters, installed their gear and were then drawn up for my inspection by Lieutenant Menzel. I told them that we should probably have an important assignment: "You must keep in perfect physical condition, so be at your best when the moment arrives—Dismiss!" I gave Menzel orders to get them acclimatized. Military training must be confined to morning and evening. They could fill in the rest of the time with swimming and sport.

I took Karl Radl along to Frascati and it was only in my room, which he was to share with me, that I let him into the secret. He was as surprised and excited as I had been, but we were in no doubt whatever about the difficulties facing us in trying to find out the whereabouts of the Duce. We did not get as far as thinking out how we were to liberate him. The chance seemed too remote at the moment.

We also gave some thought to the other side of the operation, which to us meant the rescue of Mussolini and nothing else. General Student had taken over the defence of Rome with the one available Parachute division—the other was fighting in Sicily. Hitler considered that we should be prepared for the defection of the new Badoglio government. In that eventuality drastic steps must be taken to keep Rome and its vicinity, railway stations and airfields in German hands. If the city were lost as a supply centre for any appreciable time, the consequences might be disastrous.

Of the vast number of names mentioned by Himmler I had been lucky enough to retain the two most important—Kappler and Dollmann. Himmler had said that both must be contacted and cooperate in the task of finding the captive. Apparently Himmler had a particularly high opinion of Dollmann, who had lived many years in Italy and was said to have excellent connections with the most influential circles. Kappler was the German Police Attaché in Rome, and must also be in a good position to help.

I had presented Radl to General Student and told him of my intention to get in touch with these two men the next day so that we could make a start with our enquiries at the earliest possible moment. I said we could not yet decide how we would tackle our problem. I was told at this meeting that Field-Marshal Kesselring, in his capacity as Commander-in-Chief, had paid a visit to the Crown Prince Umberto and enquired officially as to the whereabouts of Mussolini. The Crown Prince had replied that he did not know. I had my own views as to his truthfulness, but cautiously said nothing, though there was no doubt that General Student's opinion was the same as mine.

The offices of the Police Attaché were in an ordinary commercial building. Kappler was a young *regierungsrat* and he gave us a great welcome and proved a wonderful help and support in our work.

We learned that all sorts of rumours were flying round as to where Mussolini could be found. Many professed to know that he had committed suicide, while some said he was very ill and had been sent to a sanatorium. Such speculations turned out to be rubbish and we found no real clue. All we established for certain was that the Duce, against the advice of his wife, had sought an audience with the King in the afternoon of the 25th July, and had not been seen since. Presumably he had been arrested at the palace.

The sagacious foreign policy of the Allies had borne fruit, and it was impossible to doubt that the secret flight of certain Italian politicians to Portugal was connected with it. The only surprising feature was the arrest and imprisonment of the Duce, which presented us with our problem. I could not understand why this *coup* had had no reaction among Italian circles which were still Fascist. Why no protest, or demonstration? It seemed to me that there could only be one explanation; the few genuine Fascists were in the Black Shirt brigade at the front and the Italian Army must be backing the royal house. The Crown Prince had been the focus of opposition to the régime for many years.

The German Police Attaché had been in close touch with an officer of the Carabinieri, who was probably still a loyal Fascist at heart. In the course of conversation this officer dropped a hint which was to be the first clue in our search; the Duce had been bundled off in an ambulance from the royal palace to one of the Carabinieri barracks in Rome.

Subsequent investigation showed that this news was true. We found out the exact part of the building in which he was detained. Unfortunately, ten days had passed since the 25th July and it was highly probable that he had been transferred elsewhere meanwhile. But we must assume the contrary and consider how we could spirit him away from this building. To Radl and myself, the only solution seemed to be a swift commando operation.

CHAPTER V

THE SCOPE of this book does not permit me to give a detailed description of our labours in the next few weeks and I will confine myself to a few incidents and the result of our enquiries.

For many days we made no progress at all, but then the queerest chance came to our rescue. In a restaurant in Rome we made the acquaintance of a grocer who often visited his customers at Terracino, a little town on the Gulf of Gaeta. His best customer had a servant who was being courted by a soldier of the Carabinieri stationed on the island of Ponza, a penal settlement. As he got very little leave, he used to write to his beloved and in one of his letters there was a hint that a very high-ranking prisoner had arrived on the island.

This news was confirmed, though much later, by an incautious remark dropped by a young Italian naval officer to the effect that on the 7th August, the Duce had been taken from Ponza on a cruiser to the port of Spezia and from there to an unknown destination.

This information was sent on to FHQ by General Student, whom I was seeing almost daily. An order came back by return that I was to set about rescuing the Duce from the cruiser. For twenty-four hours I was given my worst headache. As if it was quite simple to spirit a man away under the noses of a warship's company! Fortunately, by next morning we had received confirmation that the Duce had been moved somewhere else.

I might mention as a curiosity that we subsequently learned that in Berlin clairvoyants and astrologers were consulted in the hope of discovering Mussolini's place of detention. It was Himmler who was alleged to attach importance to their somewhat dubious lore. Radl and I did not place our trust in such things and managed to reach our goal without supernatural intervention.

Then Captain Hunäus, an old and somewhat gouty sea-dog, who was the liaison officer with the Italian commander of the naval station of Santa Maddalena in Sardinia, reported that a particularly important prisoner was being held on the island. The information seemed to me serious enough to call for a personal visit and investigation. I took with me Lieutenant Warger, who spoke Italian perfectly, as it would be easier for him to make the necessary enquiries. The good captain took me on a German R-boat (minesweeper) for a comprehensive and instructive tour of the harbour. Concealed under an awning, I took a number of photographs. On the outskirts of the little town lay the Villa Weber—the house indicated—and I took photographs of that too, though from several hundred metres distance. The next step, the important one, was to ascertain for certain who the " high-ranking prisoner " was. Lieutenant Warger, with his fluent Italian, could be very useful.

He was rigged up as an ordinary German sailor and was attached to Captain Hunäus as interpreter. I was gambling on the Italian passion for betting. Warger was to haunt the dockside pot-houses, mix with the crowd and keep his ears open. If the Duce's name was mentioned, he was to assert that he had reliable information that Mussolini had died of a serious disease. When he was contradicted he was to bet that he was right. To make the scheme more plausible he would get slightly drunk. But here I came up against an unexpected obstacle. Warger was a teetotaller! After much argument and an appeal to his duty as a soldier, I persuaded him to sacrifice his principles for this one occasion.

Our plan succeeded. A fruiterer, who took his wares to the Villa Weber daily, was the unconscious victim of his own love of a gamble. He easily won his bet and thereby rendered us a very valuable service. He took Warger to a house adjoining the villa and pointed out the Duce sitting on the terrace. The vanished dictator was found at last!

Warger paid several further visits to this observation post to get a better idea of how, and how well, he was guarded. Now it was time for us to plan his rescue from the naval fortress, but I felt I must first get a better picture of the area, the anti-aircraft defences, and so forth. The available maps were inadequate and I decided to fly over the harbour—which was out of bounds to aircraft—at a considerable height with a view to getting some good photographs.

By Wednesday, the 18th August, I was ready. The He 111 assigned to me by General Student left from Pratica airfield and first set course to the north. Enemy air activity over the sea was already very considerable and for security reasons flights to Sardinia were routed by Elba and Corsica. We came down on the airfield at Pausania in Sardinia to refuel and then I soon covered the fifty kilometres north to meet Hunäus and Warger at Palau.

I learned that the position had not changed, though the security measures were being strengthened every day.

With a sense of relief I returned to the airfield to start my reconnaissance flight. I proposed to include Corsica in it and contact the Waffen SS brigade stationed there, as I felt certain that we should have to employ a considerable body of troops in the enterprise.

The crew had refuelled and we started soon after 3 p.m. I had given orders that we should go straight up to 5,000 metres and cross the harbour at that altitude. I lay in the forward turret behind the port gun, with the camera and a marine chart—which I wanted to fill in—beside me. I was engaged in admiring the wonderful colours of the water when the voice of the rear-gunner came through the microphone: "Look out! Two aircraft behind us. British pursuit planes!" Our pilot swerved and I kept my finger on the button of the gun, ready to fire if they came within range. The pilot recovered control and I was beginning to think that we were out of trouble when I noticed that the nose of the plane was pointing practically straight down. I turned round and saw the anguished face of the pilot, who was trying to pull out. A glance outside showed me that the port engine had stopped. We were racing headlong downwards and there was no hope of recovery. Through the microphone came a yell: "Hold tight."

I instinctively clutched the two handles of the gun as we hit the water with a resounding smack. I must have knocked my head somewhere as I was " out " for a moment, conscious only of things smashing and clattering all round me. Then I felt myself being pulled up by the back of my coat. The plane was submerged for a moment or two and when it came up the water was up to our knees, everything in front was wrecked and the sea continued to pour in.

We shouted down the passage to the rear cockpit, but there was no reply. Were our two comrades dead? We had to act quickly. We joined forces and shoved open the hatch at the top of the cockpit. More water poured in. We quickly got the second pilot out and then I took a deep breath, forced myself upwards and found that I had got free of the wreck. My predecessor was swimming about and the pilot also emerged.

Then something quite remarkable happened. Relieved of our weight, the plane came to the surface. The pilot and his comrade forced open the rear cockpit and we saw the two " dead " men squatting in a corner. They were somewhat frightened, but quite undamaged. They crawled along the wings. It appeared that neither could swim, though they both hailed from the water-front at Hamburg. The pilot managed to release the rubber dinghy and inflate it.

I had to go back to fetch my brief-case and camera and shortly afterwards the plane reared up and vanished for ever. We clung to our dinghy and looked round to find that there were some steep cliffs not very far away. We reached them and climbed to the top. The pilot had retrieved a signal pistol and proposed to fire it, but I thought we should wait to see whether a ship came in sight. Half an hour later, one slowly approached. We fired the red emergency signal. The ship hove to and put out a boat. When we were safely on board, we discovered that we had been rescued by an Italian anti-aircraft ship. When I was examined by a doctor a few days later, it turned out that I had three broken ribs.

Meanwhile, Radl had had a very anxious time. When he returned, as arranged, on the evening of the 18th August, he enquired what had happened to my plane and received the laconic reply: " Missing, probably in the drink ! " My wireless message had not come through.

I returned to the mainland on the 20th, went straight to the men's quarters and met Radl on the way. Everyone was very pleased. We were convinced that prompt action must be taken. Our captive had been located; of that we felt no doubt. General Student fully shared our opinion.

Then, out of a clear blue sky, came a shattering order from FHQ: "FHQ is informed by Security (Admiral Canaris) that Mussolini is held prisoner on a small island near Elba. Captain Skorzeny must immediately organize a parachute attack on this island and notify the earliest possible moment when he can be ready. FHQ will fix the time."

Whatever has happened? thought Radl and I. The Security people seemed to have particularly good sources of information in Italy. Only a few days before we had been reading a "secret" Security report for the information of all local commanders from which I will quote an extract: "The new Badoglio government guarantees that Italy will continue the struggle at our side under all circumstances. It will act even more vigorously than its predecessor."

We had different views. To-day it is difficult to understand how Admiral Canaris came to give this totally inaccurate information to FHQ. We thought that quite another construction could be placed on the obvious concentration of several divisions in the vicinity of Rome.

General Student now endeavoured to get permission for us to report in person at FHQ. After a certain amount of coming and going an order arrived for us to go to East Prussia. When we presented ourselves we were told that the Führer would see us in half an hour. We were taken to the same room in which I had seen Hitler on the first occasion.

Now, however, all the chairs at the round table by the fireplace were occupied. I had the rare privilege of meeting some of the men at the head of affairs in Germany. On Adolf Hitler's right sat the Foreign Minister, von Ribbentrop, and on his left Field-Marshal Keitel, and then Colonel-General Jodl, next to whom I was placed. To Ribbentrop's right came Himmler, and then General Student and Grand-Admiral Dönitz, between whom and myself sat the massive figure of Reichsmarschall Göring.

After a few introductory words from General Student I was asked to speak. I will admit that at first I was a bit overcome at the thought of speaking out quite frankly in front of such an audience. Eight pairs of eyes were concentrated on me. I had taken the precaution of making some notes, but soon forgot all about them. I gave a detailed account of our investigations. The weight of argument in favour of our view that the Duce was held prisoner at Santa

Maddalena obviously impressed my hearers and some of them, Dönitz and Göring in particular, smiled at the story of Warger's bet.

When I had concluded I was astonished to find from a glance at my watch that I had been talking for nearly half an hour. Hitler promptly got up, put his hand out and said: "I believe you, Captain Skorzeny! You're right. I withdraw my order for the parachute attack on the island. Have you a plan for a similar operation at Santa Maddalena? If you have, tell us all about it."

I drew out a pencil sketch and explained the plan I had worked out a few days before. I said that in addition to a flotilla of E-boats, I should need several R and M-boats, and that my own unit should be supplemented by a selected company of volunteers from the SS Corsica Brigade. The anti-aircraft batteries of the Corsica Brigade and the batteries posted in Sardinia should be available to cover the withdrawal. Our plan of a surprise attack at daybreak seemed to meet with approval. At this point I was interrupted by a number of questions from Hitler, Göring and Jodl. When I had answered them all Hitler said: "I approve your plan. Carried out with the utmost resolution and faith in the cause, it is feasible. Grand-Admiral Dönitz, please issue the necessary orders to the navy. The formations required will be put under Captain Skorzeny's command for the duration of the operation. Colonel-General Jodl will take care of everything else. One word more for you, Captain Skorzeny. My friend Mussolini must be freed at the earliest possible moment. There must be no delay whatever over the operation. It is possible that you will receive starting orders while Italy is officially still our ally. If the enterprise fails for any reason, it may be that I shall have publicly to disavow your action. I should then say that you had concocted an insane plan with the commanders on the spot and acted without authority. You must be prepared to be thrown over in the interest of our cause and for Germany's sake!"

I was not given much time to consider my decision, but of course there was no room for hesitation where the welfare of Germany was concerned. A few minutes' conversation followed and I answered additional questions. When Göring asked for details about the plane crash there was no holding me: "The He III is certainly a grand all-purpose aircraft. It can even be used as a submarine," a remark which he rewarded with a smile. So it was true that the Reichsmarschall had a sense of humour!

Hitler shook hands warmly when we parted. "You'll bring it off, Skorzeny!" There was such a confident ring in his voice that his conviction communicated itself to me. Having already heard a great deal about his almost hypnotic powers, I had a sample of them on this occasion.

I spent some time in the aide-de-camp's dining-room with Field-Marshal Keitel and other individuals, of whom I remember Prince Philip of Hesse, Flight-Captain Bauer, Standartenführer Rattenhuber, Major John von Freyand and Herr Sundermann. They assumed from my tropical uniform that I had just come from Italy, so it was natural that the conversation should turn to the situation there. I gave them my impression that the country was obviously very tired of the war and that we must be prepared for surprises.

I was just about to mention the so-called "Crown Prince Umberto Party", when I felt someone treading on my toe—Flight-Captain Bauer. I took the hint and switched to another topic. Bauer told me later that Prince Philip was the brother-in-law of Crown Prince Umberto. Once again it was brought home to me how dangerous backstairs influence was at FHQ. It rather alarmed me to think that one could not speak freely there.

This time I slept much better in the "Wolf's Den" than I had on the first occasion. To begin with, I asked for a bed outside the bunker, to be away from the din of the ventilators, to which I preferred the risk of being woken up by an air-raid warning.

Early next morning we flew back to Italy. On arrival I told my trusty Radl that if things went wrong I should be held personally responsible, but the only answer I got was: "In that case I'll go to gaol with you; or perhaps we'll be packed off to an asylum and share a padded cell."

Captain Schulz, the commodore of the E-boat flotilla allotted to me, threw himself heart and soul into the business. He had always been longing for such a job. The whole plan, phase by phase, was thrashed out again with him. All the possibilities were considered.

On the day before D-day, the E-boats would enter Santa Maddalena Bay on an official visit and lie up against a breakwater of the town of the same name. On the previous day the R and M-boats under Radl's command would collect the assault force from Corsica and anchor at the mole of Palau, opposite Santa Maddalena. The men must keep below decks out of sight.

At dawn on D-day both flotillas would leave the harbour as if for an exercise. The R and M-boats would then land their men at top-speed. Some of them would be required to guard our flank on the town side. The E-boats would provide covering fire if required.

With the bulk of my force in close order we would make for the villa. I calculated that the close order would intensify the effect of surprise. As far as possible I wanted to avoid shooting or the use of force during the approach. Further decisions would be dictated by the situation as it arose. I could disregard the possibility of a premature alarm as all the telephone wires from the villa and other buildings to the town would have been cut.

Once the Duce was in our hands and we had disposed of the 150-odd guards, I meant to take him immediately on board one of the E-boats. Simultaneously one of the booms would be secured by a special commando and we should thus be able to make our exit unhindered. If the need arose, the Italian anti-aircraft batteries on the hills round the harbour should be kept in check by German anti-aircraft batteries from the opposite side.

Only one feature caused me anxiety. Below the Villa Weber there were some military barracks in the port. They were occupied by about 200 Italian naval cadets undergoing training. We must be secured on this dangerous flank. Just off the coast, two somewhat antiquated Italian seaplanes and a rescue plane, painted white and with the red cross, lay at anchor. To prevent immediate pursuit the two former must be put out of action.

On the 26th August, the day before D-day, I embarked with Radl on the E-boat flotilla in the harbour of Anzio and reached Santa Maddalena after a rough crossing. Radl immediately went off to Corsica on a mine-sweeper to supervise the embarkation of the other troops. He was to have them in the harbour of Santa Maddalena by dusk.

I have often been overcome by an invincible feeling of doubt when an important assignment has had to be carried out by someone else and I have not checked the data personally. That feeling assailed me just as violently now.

Warger had been to see me and we had again scrutinized his accurate plans, with the latest emendations showing the enemy positions. Nothing could have exceeded the care he had taken, but I felt that I must make assurance doubly sure and decided on a final personal reconnaissance, which I had to make of course in a normal sailor's uniform.

Even before I reached the villa I was in a bad temper, as I discovered a telephone line leading into the garden which Warger had not indicated. I blasted him properly, remarking that an operation such as that in which we were engaged could easily be frustrated by such an oversight. Otherwise everything was exactly as he had described. Two parties of Carabinieri were marching up and down the road and there was a machine-gun post at the gate. Unfortunately a high wall prevented us from seeing inside the garden.

No one took any notice of us. I had donned a sailor's blouse and we carried a basket full of dirty clothes. We made for a house adjoining, but rather higher than the villa and therefore giving us a view into what interested us—the ground floor. Warger took his linen to this house to be washed.

To get a better view into the Villa Weber I climbed the hill behind. The absence of certain intimate rooms in the more humble Italian houses gave me an excuse for seeking cover behind a rock.

I certainly got a very good view and could slip back to the laundress's house with an excellent picture of the villa, its surroundings and the garden paths in my mind. There I found a carabiniere of the guard, who was paying a call. I entered into conversation with him while little Warger translated. I resorted again to the well-tried trick and began to talk cautiously about Mussolini. The soldier did not seem particularly interested in the subject; he only woke up when I asserted that, to my knowledge, the Duce was dead. His southern temperament manifested itself when he vehemently retorted that it was not true. I egged him on still further by saying that I was in possession of detailed information through a doctor friend of mine.

That really set him going: "No, no, Signor, it's impossible. I saw the Duce with my own eyes this morning. I was a member of his escort. We conducted him to the white aeroplane with the red cross and I saw it take him away."

I got a tremendous shock. What the man said rang true and seemed to fit in. I recollected that the white red-cross aircraft was not there that morning! I had registered the fact, but regarded it as unimportant. And now it struck me as also significant that— as I had observed myself—the guards were strolling about unconcernedly on the broad terrace of the villa. Another indication that the bird had flown! The man had spoken the truth and we were very lucky to find out in time. What a rumpus there would have been if we had staged our show in vain!

Now the preparations had to be called off as quick as possible. I got Karl Radl on the telephone just as he was leaving Corsica. The men were already on board! Right-about-turn was now the order of the day, though we did not actually call off the operation for a few days in case the Duce was brought back. It was observed that the full guard routine inside and outside the villa was carefully kept up. I suspected that the Italian secret police did this to cover up the tracks and preserve the illusion. The prisoner was so important that they did not mind the trouble and worry of frequent moves. The dogs had been shaken off once more.

So there we were, back at the beginning and all our efforts had been in vain. All sorts of rumours were flying round, but none proved trustworthy.

It was only on a tour of·inspection with General Student on the Lago di Bracciano that, quite casually, we were given another clue. The arrival of the white sea-rescue plane had been observed! There were indications that the Duce's place of detention was somewhere in the Apennines. A rumour that it was on Lake Trasimene turned out to be false, but thanks to a motor accident to two high-ranking Italian officers we learned that the Abruzzi mountains were the object of our search. Even now we were first led on a false trail to the eastern Abruzzi.

We became gradually convinced that many of the unfounded rumours were spread intentionally. The Italian secret service was not to be despised as an opponent! Other German authorities, such as Field-Marshal Kesselring's staff, were interested on their own account in finding the whereabouts of the missing Dictator. Mussolini's sixtieth birthday, the 29th July, was used by Field-Marshal Kesselring as an excuse for a further attempt to draw Marshal Badoglio on the subject. By way of a birthday present, Adolf Hitler had sent Italy a unique edition de luxe of the works of the philosopher Nietzsche. Kesselring told Badoglio that he was to present this gift from the head of the German state to the Duce in person. But the attempt failed, Badoglio offering some transparent excuse as to why this was impossible.

Meanwhile the situation in Rome was becoming more uncomfortable every week. One Italian division after another was transferred to the vicinity, as security, we were told, against an allied landing. We had different ideas. The one German parachute division and the few Staff and Communications units of GHQ and the Luftwaffe saw themselves facing the appalling superiority of seven divisions. Intelligence had its hands full to trace and record the daily arrival of fresh Italian units.

My own handful of Intelligence people now brought me the news —amounting to practical certainty—that Benito Mussolini was held in a mountain hotel in the Campo Imperatore (Gran Sasso *massif*) and was guarded by a Carabiniere unit. For days on end we made great efforts to acquire accurate maps of that region, but in vain. The hotel had been built only a few years before the war and was not shown on any military maps, or even on the latest mountaineering maps. The only information we obtained was the description given by a German living in Italy who in 1938 had spent a winter holiday in this ski hotel, then quite new. Another, but very vague source of information, was the advertisement of a travel agency extolling the beauties of this skiing paradise in the Abruzzi.

These data were far too scanty for the planning of so important a military operation. We must get air photographs of the locality as soon as possible.

On the 8th September, we emplaned in a German He 111 which had an automatic air photography camera built into it. On this vitally important expedition I had with me Radl and the Corps Intelligence officer (Ic), for whom we should have a special job on the great day.

As it was important that the Italians should not recognize the aircraft for what it was, we ascended to a high altitude in order to pass over the Abruzzi-*massif* at 5,000 metres. Even the pilot did not know what our real mission was, and assumed that we were going to take photographs of some of the harbours on the Adriatic.

When we were still 30 kilometres short of our objective we tried to take some photographs with the special camera and then dis-covered that some of the working parts would not function, either because they were frozen up, or for some other reason. Fortunately, we also had a hand camera.

We were wearing our "African" uniforms and consequently suffered severely from the cold. As we could not open the entrance hatch during the flight, we had to make a big hole in the perspex through which the photographer could force his head, shoulders and arms, not to mention the camera.

I had not expected the outside air and slip-stream to be so cold. With Radl holding my legs I managed to get my thinly-clad upper torso through the opening. We were just passing over our target, the hotel, and I saw beneath me the rugged Camp Imperatore, a plateau lying at an altitude of about 2,000 metres, with the lofty crest of the Gran Sasso rising to 2,900 metres on its north-eastern rim. We had a vision of grey-brown rocks, deep hollows and here and there patches of snow and grass. When we were immediately over the building it looked to be of considerable size.

I took the first photograph and, when turning the spindle of the rather heavy camera to bring up the next film, made the discovery that my fingers had become quite stiff. I took another photograph and immediately afterwards noticed a little meadow, virtually triangular in shape, just behind the hotel. In a flash came the thought —this is our landing ground!

A small path winding up the cliff indicated that this was probably a nursery slope for ski beginners. I quickly took another photo and then gave a kick as a signal to be pulled up.

As Radl made some sarcastic remark about the cold I decided that he should have his turn on the way back.

I crawled into the pilot's cockpit, and seeing in the distance a blue strip, which could only be the Adriatic, I ordered the pilot to descend to 2,500 metres and follow the coast northwards. We pretended to be absorbed in maps and, to keep the pilot guessing, made preparations to photograph the port of Ancona.

The view of the Adriatic coast from above is quite unique. The little harbours lay bathed in the afternoon sunshine and we soon reached the well-known resorts of Rimini and Riccione. Somewhat further north I told the pilot to turn west and we pretended to take some more pictures, after which fresh orders were given to ascend to 5,500 metres and pass over the summit of the Gran Sasso at that altitude.

Now it was Radl's turn. We crawled into the stern of the aircraft, which had now become extremely cold—certainly below zero, so that we heartily cursed the tropical uniforms which we usually thought so smart. I thrust the camera into Radl's hand and explained its workings, a very necessary preliminary as he was a poet by temperament and took very little interest in technical matters.

Perhaps that is why we made such a good pair. When he was pushed through the opening I hung on to his legs.

We passed over the crest and when I knew that we should be above the target in about a minute gave him a signal to be ready. Though the noise of the engine prevented me from hearing anything myself, I gave him a yell: "Now! Get as many as you can!"

I noticed that he was making some sort of signal with his arm. Perhaps we were not directly over the hotel so that his photographs would be at an angle. It did not matter. Pictures from an angle are often more revealing; they show up undulations in the ground better.

He soon signalled that I was to pull him in. A face, blue with cold, appeared: "To hell with sunny Italy," was his comment this time.

When I gave orders for the descent we lay on the floor and covered ourselves with lifebelts and oiled paper that was lying about. A little later I called out to the pilot: "Don't make direct for the airfield. Keep north so as to strike the Mediterranean coast above Rome. Then come right down and fly in."

A quarter of an hour later we were to discover that this sudden decision had probably saved our lives. We reached the coast and by then the interior of the plane was getting pleasantly warm. I sat next to the pilot for a bit and was casually looking in the direction of the Sabine Hills when I saw something which made me think I must be dreaming. Dense formations of aircraft were coming from the south and concentrating on Frascati. They could only be the enemy's. I used my glasses and could actually see the bomb-doors opening and discharging their deadly load on our headquarters. Two further waves followed. Now we realized that it was only by luck that we were not in their path. It was only because we were flying practically at ground level that we were not discovered and shot down by the escorting fighters.

We found the house occupied by General Student quite un-damaged, but our own house, villa Tusculum II, was in a bad way, having been hit by two bombs, fortunately not of heavy calibre. We were stopped by an officer who said that there were two time bombs in the cellar, a remark which did not prevent us from going to our room to collect our belongings and files. We scrambled over and through masses of rubble and found the safe upside down but intact.

The casualties among the civil population must have been very
high, but few German-occupied buildings had been hit. The troops
worked tirelessly to restore the telephone network, emergency lines
were laid and it was soon known that the essential repairs would
be effected in a few hours.

Radl and I had to go to Rome for an important meeting with
some Italian officers who I had been told were planning to rescue
Mussolini. I was concerned to know what they had in mind, as I
could not let their plans prejudice and perhaps ruin mine. I soon
ascertained that though their intentions were excellent, their preparations had not nearly reached the same stage as ours.

Meanwhile the daylight had gone. I was driving through the
streets of Rome to fetch Radl from another German office when
I noticed crowds gathered round the public loudspeakers. When
I turned into the Via Veneto the throng was so great that I could
hardly make any progress. An announcement over the loudspeakers
was greeted with loud cheers: Cries of "Viva il Re" could be
heard. Women kissed each other and excited groups engaged in
fierce argument. I stopped and heard the shattering news: "The
Italian government has capitulated."

I knew that this meant an extreme crisis for our troops in the
peninsula. Not that the Italian government's action was unexpected. It was only the timing that came as a surprise. The new
situation would hold up, if not entirely frustrate, the whole object
of my presence in Italy!

I met Lieutenant Radl at the German Embassy.

I learned later that the news of the Italian capitulation had
already been given by General Dwight D. Eisenhower over the
Algiers radio. The fact that General Badoglio broadcast the same
news afterwards through loudspeakers, indicated that the Allies
meant to force their new partner's hand, at any rate as regards the
time of the announcement.

The Allies had fixed on the night of the 8th September for their
landing at Salerno, and had to keep to this time-table. This operation and the air attack on Frascati were planned to give a breathing
space to the Italian government. Our Intelligence Service had given
us information from which we deducted that General Eisenhower's
HQ was considering a parachute landing near Rome. With our
meagre forces, such a landing could be very unpleasant.

I cudgelled my brains for days as to the best means of clearing up doubts whether the Duce was actually to be found at the mountain hotel on the Gran Sasso. So far my source of information was two Italians, who had talked to me without knowing the object of my questions. I was most anxious to have their statements confirmed by a German. It seemed obvious that no one would be allowed to go to the hotel itself, which was isolated from the valley below apart from a cable railway. But I thought I could find some German who could get as near as possible on some innocent pretext.

An opportunity presented itself of which I immediately availed myself. I knew a German staff surgeon in Rome who was supposed to have ambitions to win a decoration. I met him and explained how he could render a very valuable service to his general.

All malaria cases among the troops had hitherto been sent for treatment to the mountains in the Tyrol. I suggested off my own bat that he might like to inspect a sports hotel in the Gran Sasso of which I had heard, as it had occurred to me that such a resort at an altitude of 2000 metres would be highly suitable. I said that he must move heaven and earth to see the manager personally, find out the number of beds and make all the necessary arrangements. The doctor agreed to set out next morning and I confess that I had certain misgivings about the chances of his return.

The personnel of the German Embassy were taken to Frascati in a convoy so that they could have the protection of German troops. I and Radl went on ahead and I went straight to General Student to discuss the situation. We agreed that we must postpone the attempt to rescue Mussolini for a short time as the position in Rome must first be cleared up, which meant that the city must remain in German hands as the most important supply base for the troops fighting in the south.

Now we knew the reason for that concentrated air attack on Frascati which I have already described. The Allied GHQ and the Italian government were clearly working together to paralyse the nerve centre of German military operations in Italy. The attempt had not suceeded, as we still were in touch with all our formations and they were in a position to carry out all orders at a moment's notice. The night passed quietly, apart from a few clashes between German and Italian troops in the south of Rome.

In the early hours of the 9th September began the first serious fighting round Frascati. During that day our troops established themselves firmly in the whole area of the Sabine mountains. The German front was slowly withdrawn nearer to Rome, which was occupied solely by Italian troops.

The staff surgeon reappeared that morning. He was very unhappy to hear that the new turn of affairs meant the abandonment of the plan for a convalescence home. He told me how he had got to Aquila and from there into the valley and to the lower station of the cable railway. But there his journey had ended, despite all his efforts. The road was closed by a barrier and a detachment of Carabinieri. He had had a long discussion with the soldiers and eventually persuaded them to let him telephone the hotel. On speaking to an officer, he had been informed that the Campo Imperatore was now a military training area and closed for all other purposes. He thought that the training must be on a pretty big scale, as he had seen a wireless truck in the valley and the cable railway was kept very busy. He had also heard some remarkable stories from the local inhabitants. They said that only a short time before all the civilians had been evacuated from the hotel and preparations made for the reception of about 200 soldiers. Many high-ranking officers had arrived in the valley.

The good doctor added that he had met some who said that they thought that no less a person than Mussolini was held prisoner there. Of course that was only a rumour, and most unlikely to be true. I said nothing to make him change his mind.

CHAPTER VI

SEPTEMBER 10TH, 1943. We had not been out of our uniforms for two nights and days, and though our general was in the same case it was essential that I should see him with a view to making the great decision.

But first I discussed all the possibilities with Radl. We both fully realized that speed was absolutely vital. Every day, every hour that we delayed increased the danger that the Duce might be removed elsewhere, nay even worse, delivered over to the Allies.

This supposition subsequently turned out to be most realistic. One of the terms of the armistice agreed by General Eisenhower was that the Duce should be handed over.

A ground operation seemed hopeless from the start. An attack up the steep, rocky slopes would have cost us very heavy losses, apart from giving good notice to the enemy and leaving them time to conceal their prisoner. To forestall that eventuality the whole *massif* would have to be surrounded by good mountain troops. A division at least would be required. So a ground operation was ruled out.

The factor of surprise could be our only trump as it was to be feared that the prisoner's guards had orders to kill him if there was any danger of rescue. This supposition later also proved well founded. Such an order could only be frustrated by a lightning intervention.

There remained only two alternatives—parachute landings or gliders.

We pondered long over both and then decided in favour of the second. At such altitudes, and in the thin air, a parachute drop would involve too rapid a rate of descent for anyone equipped with the normal parachute only. We also feared that in this rocky region the parachutists would get scattered too widely, so that an immediate attack by a compact detachment would not be possible.

So a glider landing remained the only solution. The final decision was in the hands of the Parachute Corps experts and General Student.

What were the prospects of success with glider landings? When we took our air photographs to the big laboratory at Frascati on the afternoon of the 8th, we had found it completely destroyed. I asked one of my officers to look for somewhere else and he eventually found an emergency laboratory at an airstrip. Unfortunately, we could not have the usual big stereos which would have shown up all the details of the mountain zone. We had to be content with ordinary prints approximately 14 by 14 cm.

These proved good enough to enable me to recognize the triangular meadow which I had noticed as we flew over. On the suitability of this meadow as a landing-ground we based our whole plan and I accordingly drew up detailed orders for the individual parties.

General Student suggested that a parachute battalion infiltrate by

night into the valley and seize the lower station of the funicular at
the hour appointed for the landing. In that way we should have
cover on that side and also a line of retreat if withdrawal became
necessary after the operation was complete.

The talk with General Student had the desired result. Of course
he realized that there were many most serious objections, but he
agreed that there was only one possible way short of abandoning
the enterprise altogether. Then the experts in air landings—the
Chief-of-Staff and the Ia Air of the Parachute Corps—were called
in to give their reactions.

These two officers were at first wholly adverse to the plan. They
objected that an air landing of this kind at such an altitude and
without a prepared landing-ground had never been attempted
before. In their view the projected operation would result in the
loss of at least 80 per cent of the troops employed. The survivors
would be too few to have any chance of success.

My answer was that I was fully aware of this danger, but every
novel venture must have a beginning. We knew the meadow
was flat and a careful landing should enable us to avoid serious
casualties. "Of course, gentlemen, I am ready to carry out any
alternative scheme you may suggest."

After careful consideration, General Student gave his final
approval and issued his orders: "The twelve gliders required are
to be flown from the south of France to Rome at once. I fix 6 a.m.
on the 12th September as zero-hour. At that moment the machines
must land on the plateau and the funicular station be seized by our
battalion. We can assume that at that early hour the dangerous air
currents so common in Italian mountain regions will be relatively
weak. I will instruct the pilots personally and impress upon them
the importance of the utmost care in landing. I am sure you are
right, Captain Skorzeny. The operation cannot be carried out in
any other way!"

After this decision had been given Radl and I worked out the
details of our plan. We had to make careful calculations of the
distances, make up our minds as to what arms and equipment the
men should carry and, above all, prepare a large-scale plan showing
the exact landing-place for each of the twelve gliders. Each glider
could take ten men, i.e., a group, in addition to the pilot. Each
group must know exactly what it had to do. I decided that I would
go myself in the third glider so that the immediate assault by my

own and the fourth group could be covered by the two groups already landed.

At the conclusion of these labours we spent a little time discussing our chances. We did not bluff ourselves that they were other than very slim. No one could really say whether Mussolini was still on the mountain and would not be spirited away elsewhere before we arrived. There was the further question whether we could overpower the guards quickly enough to prevent anyone killing him first, and we had not forgotten the warning given by the staff officers.

We must, in any event, allow for casualties in the landings. Even without any casualties we should only be 108 men and they could not all be available at the same moment. They would have to tackle 150 Italians, who knew the ground perfectly and could use the hotel as a fortress. In weapons the two opponents could be regarded as approximately equals, as our parachutists' tommy-guns gave us an advantage, compensating to some extent for the enemy's superiority in numbers, particularly if we had not suffered too badly at the outset.

While we were immersed in these calculations Radl interrupted: " May I suggest, sir, that we forget all about figures and trying to compute our chances; we both know that they are very small, but we also know that, however small, we shall stake our lives on success! "

One more thought occurred to me: how could we increase the effect of surprise, obviously our most potent weapon? We racked our brains for a long time and then Radl suddenly had a bright idea: " Why not take with us an Italian officer, someone who must be reasonably well known to the Carabinieri up there? His very presence will bluff the guards for a short time and restrain them from immediately reacting to our arrival by violence against the Duce. We must make the best possible use of the interval."

This was an excellent idea, which I promptly approved and considered how best to exploit. General Student must confer with the officer in question during the evening before the operation and somehow persuade him to come with us. To prevent leakage or betrayal, he must remain with us until the following morning.

We discussed the choice of the most suitable person with someone who knew the situation in Rome and decided upon some high-ranking officer of the former Italian headquarters in that city who had adopted a substantially neutral attitude during the recent disturbances. He must be invited to a conference at Frascati after General Student had approved the idea.

Fresh troubles now descended upon us. The reports we received during the 11th September about the movement of the gliders was very unsatisfactory. Owing to enemy air activity they had had to make various detours and bad weather had not helped. Despite these misfortunes, we hoped to the last that they would arrive in time, but we hoped in vain.

The selected Italian officer, a general, appeared punctually, but had to be politely put off till the next day and invited to a conference with General Student for 8 p.m. at the Practica de Mare airfield. Zero-hour had to be postponed, as we received news that the gliders could not arrive in Rome before the early hours of the 12th. General Student fixed it for 2 o'clock on the Sunday (12th September) as we certainly could not wait another twenty-four hours. This postponement involved awkward changes in our plans and further prejudiced our chances. Owing to the air currents and local winds to be anticipated in the middle of the day the landing would be more dangerous, and the fact that the assault was to be made at 2 p.m. (i.e., in broad daylight) set a difficult task for the detachment operating in the valley. Various changes were necessary and had to be made with the utmost speed.

In the afternoon of the Saturday I visited the garden of a monastery in Frascati where my own men and the Mors battalion had pitched their tents. For this enterprise I meant to take volunteers only, and I had no intention of keeping them in the dark as to the dangers involved. I had them paraded and made a short speech: "The long waiting-time is over. We have an important job to do to-morrow. Adolf Hitler has ordered it personally. Serious losses must be anticipated and, unfortunately, cannot be avoided. I shall of course lead you and can promise you that I will do my utmost. If we all stick together the assault will and must succeed. Anyone prepared to volunteer take one step forward! "

It gave me the greatest pleasure to see that not one of my men wanted to be left behind. To my officers and von Berlepsch, commanding the one parachute company, I left the disagreeable task of refusing some of them, as the party must not exceed 108 in all. I myself selected 18 of my Waffen SS men. A small special commando was chosen for the valley detachment and another for an operation to rescue the Duce's family. I remained at the camp a little longer and was delighted with the spirit and enthusiasm everywhere displayed.

At that moment we got a terrible shock from an allied wireless message which came through. It was to the effect that the Duce had arrived as a prisoner in Africa on board an Italian man-of-war, which had come from Spezia. When I recovered from the first fright I took a map and compasses. As we knew the exact moment when part of the Italian fleet left Spezia I could easily calculate that even the fastest ship could not possibly have reached Africa so soon. The wireless message must, therefore, be a hoax. Was I not justified in regarding all news from enemy sources with the greatest suspicion ever after?

Sunday, the 12th September, 1943. At 5 a.m. we marched in close order to the airfield. There we learned that the gliders were expected at 10 a.m.

I again inspected the equipment of my men, who were all wearing parachute uniform. Parachute rations for five days had been issued. I had arranged that several boxes of fruit should be sent up and we sat about, pleasantly idle, in the shade of the buildings and trees. There was an atmosphere of tension, of course, but we took care to prevent any manifestation of apprehension or nerves.

By 8 o'clock, the Italian officer had not showed up so I had to send Radl off to Rome, telling him that the man had to be produced, alive, in double quick time. The trusty Radl duly produced him, though he had the greatest difficulty in finding him in the city.

General Student had a short talk with him in my presence, Lieutenant Warger acting as interpreter. We told him of Adolf Hitler's request for his participation in the operation, with a view to minimizing the chance of bloodshed. The officer was greatly flattered by this personal request from the head of the German state and found it impossible to refuse. He agreed, thereby placing an important trump in our hands.

About eleven the first gliders came in. The towing planes were quickly refuelled and the coupled aircraft drawn up in the order in which they were to start. General Student dismissed the men of Berlepsch's company and then my men.

The pilots and the twelve group commanders were summoned to an inner room, where General Student made a short speech in which he again laid great stress on the absolute necessity for a smooth landing. He categorically forbade crash landings, in view of the danger involved.

I then gave the glider commanders detailed instructions and drew a sketch on a blackboard showing the exact landing-place of each craft, after which I cleared up all outstanding points with the commanders of each group and explained the tasks allotted to them. The men had decided on their password, something guaranteed to shift all obstacles. It was "Take it easy", and that battle-cry remained the watchword of the SS commandos right up to the end of the war.

Flying times, altitudes and distances were then discussed with the Ic (Intelligence officer) of the Parachute Corps, who had been on the photographic expedition with us. He was to take his place in the first towing plane as, apart from Radl and myself, he alone knew the appearance of the ground from the air. The flying time for the 100 kilometres to be covered would be approximately one hour, so it was essential that we should start at 1 o'clock prompt.

At 12.30, there was a sudden air-raid warning. Enemy bombers were reported and before long we were hearing bomb bursts quite near. We all took cover and I cursed at the prospect of the whole enterprise being knocked on the head at the last moment. Just when I was in the depths of despair, I heard Radl's voice beside me: "Take it easy!" and confidence returned in a flash. The raid ended just before 1 o'clock. We rushed out on to the tarmac and noticed several craters, though our gliders were unharmed. The men raced out to their aircraft and I gave the order to emplane, inviting the Italian General to sit in front of me on the narrow board, which was all that was available in the cramped space into which we were packed like herrings. There was in fact hardly any room for our weapons. The General looked as if he were already regretting his decision and had already shown some hesitation in following me into the glider. But I felt it was too late to bother about his feelings. There was no time for that sort of thing!

I glanced at my watch. 1 o'clock! I gave the signal to start. The engines began to roar and we were soon gliding along the tarmac and then rising into the air. We were off.

We slowly gained altitude in wide circles and the procession of gliders set course towards the north-east. The weather seemed almost ideal for our purpose. Vast banks of white cloud hung lazily at about 3,000 metres. If they did not disperse we should reach our target practically unobserved and drop out of the sky before anyone realized we were there.

The interior of the glider was most unpleasantly hot and stuffy. I suddenly noticed that the corporal sitting behind me was being sick and that the general in front had turned as green as his uniform. Flying obviously did not suit him; he certainly was not enjoying himself. The pilot reported our position as best he could and I carefully followed his indications on my map, noting when we passed over Tivoli. From the inside of the glider we could see little of the country. The cellophane side-windows were too thick and the gaps in the fabric (of which there were many) too narrow to give us any view. The German glider, type DFS 230, comprised a few steel members covered with canvas. We were somewhat backward in this field, I reflected, thinking enviously of an elegant aluminium frame.

We thrust through a thick bank of clouds to reach the altitude of 3,500 metres which had been specified. For a short time we were in a dense grey world, seeing nothing of our surroundings, and then we emerged into bright sunshine, leaving the clouds below us. At that moment the pilot of our towing machine, a Hentschel, came through on the telephone to the commander of my glider: "Flights 1 and 2 no longer ahead of us! Who's to take over the lead now?"

This was bad news. What had happened to them? At that time I did not know that I also had only seven machines instead of nine behind me. Two had fallen foul of a couple of bomb craters at the very start. I had a message put through: "We'll take over the lead ourselves!"

I got out my knife and slashed right and left in the fabric to make a hole big enough to give us something of a view. I changed my mind about our old-fashioned glider. At least it was made of something we could cut!

My peephole was enough to let us get our bearings when the cloud permitted. We had to be very smart in picking up bridges, roads, river bends and other geographical features on our maps. Even so, we had to correct our course from time to time. Our excursion should not fail through going astray. I did not dwell on the thought that we should be without covering fire when we landed.

It was just short of zero-hour when I recognized the valley of Aquila below us and also the leading vehicles of our own formation hastening along it. It would clearly be at the right place at the right time, though it must certainly have had its troubles, too. We must not fail it!

"Helmets on!" I shouted as the hotel, our destination, came in sight, and then: "Slip the tow-ropes!" My words were followed by a sudden silence, broken only by the sound of the wind rushing past. The pilot turned in a wide circle, searching the ground—as I was doing—for the flat meadow appointed as our landing-ground. But a further, and ghastly, surprise was in store for us. It was triangular all right, but so far from being flat it was a steep, a very steep hillside! It could even have been a ski-jump.

We were now much nearer the rocky plateau than when we were photographing it and the conformation of the ground was more fully revealed. It was easy to see that a landing on this "meadow" was out of the question. My pilot, Lieutenant Meyer, must also have realized that the situation was critical, as I caught him looking all round. I was faced with a ticklish decision. If I obeyed the express orders of my General I should abandon the operation and try to glide down to the valley. If I was not prepared to do so, the forbidden crash-landing was the only alternative.

It did not take me long to decide. I called out: "Crash landing! As near to the hotel as you can get!" The pilot, not hesitating for a second, tilted the starboard wing and down we came with a rush. I wondered for a moment whether the glider could take the strain in the thin air, but there was little time for speculation. With the wind shrieking in our ears we approached our target. I saw Lieutenant Meyer release the parachute brake, and then followed a crash and the noise of shattering wood. I closed my eyes and stopped thinking. One last mighty heave, and we came to rest.

The bolt of the exit hatch had been wrenched away, the first man was out like a shot and I let myself fall sideways out of the glider, clutching my weapons. We were within 15 metres of the hotel! We were surrounded by jagged rocks of all sizes, which may have nearly smashed us up but had also acted as a brake so that we had taxied barely 20 metres. The parachute brake now folded up immediately behind the glider.

The first Italian sentry was standing on the edge of a slight rise at one corner of the hotel. He seemed lost in amazement. I had no time to bother about our Italian passenger, though I had noticed him falling out of the glider at my side, but rushed straight into the hotel. I was glad that I had given the order that no one must fire a shot before I did. It was essential that the surprise should be complete. I could hear my men panting behind me. I knew that they were the pick of the bunch and would stick to me like glue and ask no explanations.

We reached the hotel. All the surprised and shocked sentry required was a shout of "*mani in alto*" (hands up). Passing through an open door, we spotted an Italian soldier engaged in using a wireless set. A hasty kick sent his chair flying from under him and a few hearty blows from my machine-pistol wrecked his apparatus. On finding that the room had no exit into the interior of the hotel we hastily retraced our steps and went outside again.

We raced along the façade of the building and round the corner, to find ourselves faced with a terrace 2·50 to 3 metres high. Corporal Himmel offered me his back and I was up and over in a trice. The others followed in a bunch.

My eyes swept the façade and lit on a well-known face at one of the windows of the first storey. It was the Duce! Now I knew that our effort had not been in vain! I yelled at him: "Away from the window!" and we rushed into the entrance hall, colliding with a lot of Italian soldiers pouring out. Two machine-guns were set up on the floor of the terrace. We jumped over them and put them out of action. The Carabinieri continued to stream out and it took a few far from gentle blows from my weapon to force a way through them. My men yelled out "*mani in alto*". So far no one had fired a shot.

I was now well inside the hall. I could not look round or bother about what was happening behind me. On the right was a staircase. I leaped up it, three steps at a time, turned left along a corridor and flung open a door on the right. It was a happy choice. Mussolini and two Italian officers were standing in the middle of the room. I thrust them aside and made them stand with their backs to the door. In a moment my Untersturmführer Schwerdt appeared. He took the situation in at a glance and jostled the mightily surprised Italian officers out of the room and into the corridor. The door closed behind us.

We had succeeded in the first part of our venture. The Duce was safely in our hands. Not more than three or four minutes had passed since we arrived!

. At that moment the heads of Holzer and Benz, two of my subordinates, appeared at the window. They had not been able to force their way through the crowd in the hall and so had been compelled to join me via the lightning-conductor. There was no question of my men leaving me in the lurch. I sent them to guard the corridor.

I went to the window and saw Radl and his SS men running towards the hotel. Behind them crawled Obersturmführer Menzel, the company commander of our Friedenthal special unit and in charge of glider No. 4 behind me. His glider had grounded about 100 metres from the hotel and he had broken his ankle on landing. The third group in glider No. 5 also arrived while I was watching.

I shouted out: "Everything's all right! Mount guard everywhere!"

I stayed a little while longer to watch gliders 6 and 7 crash-land with Lieutenant Berlepsch and his parachute company. Then before my very eyes followed a tragedy. Glider 8 must have been caught in a gust; it wobbled and then fell like a stone, landed on a rocky slope and was smashed to smithereens.

Sounds of firing could now be heard in the distance and I put my head into the corridor and shouted for the officer-in-command at the hotel. A colonel appeared from nearby and I summoned him to surrender forthwith, assuring him that any further resistance was useless. He asked me for time to consider the matter. I gave him one minute, during which Radl turned up. He had had to fight his way through and I assumed that the Italians were still holding the entrance, as no one had joined us.

The Italian colonel returned, carrying a goblet of red wine which he proffered to me with a slight bow and the words: "To the victor!"

A white bedspread, hung from the window, performed the functions of a white flag.

After giving a few orders to my men outside the hotel I was able to devote attention to Mussolini, who was standing in a corner with Untersturmführer Schwerdt in front of him. I introduced myself: "Duce, the Führer has sent me! You are free!"

Mussolini embraced me: "I knew my friend Adolf Hitler would not leave me in the lurch," he said.

The surrender was speedily carried out. The Italian other ranks had to deposit their arms in the dining-room of the hotel, but I allowed the officers to keep their revolvers. I learned that we had captured a general in addition to the colonel.

I was informed by telephone that the station of the funicular had also fallen undamaged into our hands. There had been a little fighting, but the troops had arrived to the second and the surprise had been complete.

Lieutenant von Berlepsch had already replaced his monocle when I called to him from the window and gave orders that reinforcements must be sent up by the funicular. I wanted to make assurance doubly sure and also show the Italian colonel that we had troops in the valley also. I then had our wireless truck in the valley called up on the telephone with instructions to send out a message to General Student that the operation had succeeded.

The first to arrive by the funicular was Major Mors, commanding the parachute formation in the valley. Of course the inevitable journalist put in an appearance. He immediately made a film to immortalize the hotel, the damaged gliders and the actors in the drama. He made a mess of it and later on I was very annoyed that the pictures in the magazine suggested that he had himself taken part in the operation. We certainly had too much to do in the first moments to find time to pose for reporters.

Major Mors then asked me to present him to the Duce, a request I was very pleased to comply with.

I was now responsible for Mussolini and my first anxiety was how we were to get him to Rome. Our plan had provided for three possibilities.

Both he and I considered that it would be too dangerous to travel 150 kilometres by road through an area which had not been occupied by German troops since the defection of Italy. I had therefore agreed with General Student that Plan A should be the sudden *coup de main* against the Italian airfield of Aquila de Abruzzi, at the entrance to the valley. We should hold it only a short time. I would give the zero-hour for this attack by wireless and a few minutes later three German He 111s would land. One of them would pick up the Duce and myself and leave at once, while the two others gave us cover and drew off any aircraft pursuing.

Plan B provided that a Fieseler-Storch should land in one of the meadows adjoining the valley station. Plan C was for Captain Gerlach to attempt a landing with the Fieseler-Storch on the plateau itself.

Our wireless truck got through to Rome with the report of our success, but when I had fixed up a new time-table with Lieutenant Berlepsch and tried to give the parachutists the zero-hour, 4 o'clock, for the attack on the airfield we found we could not make contact. That was the end of Plan A.

I had watched the landing of one of the Fieseler-Storchs in the valley through my glasses. I at once used the telephone of the funicular to have the pilot instructed to prepare to take off again at once. The answer came back that the aircraft had suffered some damage on landing and could not be ready straight away. So only the last and most dangerous alternative, Plan C, remained.

After they had been disarmed, the Italian other ranks showed themselves extremely helpful and some of them had joined with the men we had sent out to rescue the victims of the glider crash. Through our glasses we had seen some of them moving, so that we could hope that it had not been fatal to all its occupants. Other Carabinieri now helped in clearing a small strip. The biggest boulders were hastily removed, while Captain Gerlach circled overhead and waited for the agreed signal to land. He proved himself a master in the art of emergency landing, but when I told him how we proposed to make a getaway with his help he was anything but pleased with the prospect, and when I added that there would be three of us he said bluntly that the idea was impracticable.

I had to take him aside for a short but tense discussion. The strength of my arguments convinced him at last. I had indeed considered every aspect of the matter most carefully and fully realized my heavy responsibility in joining the other two. But could I possibly justify letting the Duce go alone with Gerlach? If there was a disaster, all that was left for me was a bullet from my own revolver: Adolf Hitler would never forgive such an end to our venture. As there was no other way of getting the Duce safely to Rome it was better to share the danger with him, even though my presence added to it. If we failed, the same fate would overtake us all.

In this critical hour I did not fail to consult my trusty friend, Radl.

I then discussed with him and Major Mors the question of how we were to get back. The only men we wanted to take with us were the general and the colonel, and we must get them to Rome as soon as possible. The Carabinieri and their officers could be left at the hotel. The Duce had told me that he had been properly treated, so that there was no reason not to be generous. My pleasure at our success was so great that I wanted to spare my opponents.

To guard against sabotage to the cable railway I ordered that two Italian officers should ride in each cage and that after we had got away the machinery should be damaged sufficiently to prevent its being put in working order again for some time. All other details I left to Major Mors.

Now at last, I had time to pay a little attention to the Duce. I had seen him once before, in 1943, when he was addressing the crowd from the balcony of the Palazzo Venezia. I must admit that the familiar photographs of him in full uniform bore little resemblance to the man in the ill-fitting and far from smart civilian suit who now stood before me. But there was no mistaking his striking features, though he struck me as having aged a lot. Actually he looked very ill, an impression intensified by the fact that he was unshaved and his usually smooth, powerful head was covered with short, stubbly hair. But the big, black, burning eyes were unmistakably those of the Italian dictator. They seemed to bore right into me as he talked on in his lively, southern fashion.

He gave me some intensely interesting details about his fall and imprisonment. In return I managed to give him some pleasant news: "We have also concerned ourselves with the fate of your family, Duce. Your wife and the two youngest children were interned by the new government in your country place at Rocca della Caminata. We got in touch with Donna Rachele some weeks ago. While we were landing here another of my commandos, under Hauptsturmführer Mandel, was sent to fetch your family. I'm sure they are free by now!"

The Duce shook my hand warmly. "So everything's all right. I'm very grateful to you!"

Donning a loose winter overcoat and a dark, soft hat, the Duce came out of the door. I went ahead to the waiting Storch. Mussolini took the rear seat and I stowed myself in behind. I noticed his slight hesitation before he climbed in and recollected that he was a pilot himself and could well appreciate the risks he was running.

The engine worked up to full speed and we nodded to the comrades we were leaving behind. I seized a stay in each hand and by
moving my body up and down, tried to give the aircraft more
thrust or lessen the weight. Gerlach signalled the men holding the
wings and tail to let go and the airscrew drew us forward. I
thought I heard a mixture of "Eviva's" and "Heil's" through the
cellophane windows.

But, although our speed increased and we were rapidly approaching the end of the strip, we failed to rise. I swayed about madly and
we had hopped over many a boulder when a yawning gully
appeared right in our path. I was just thinking that this really
was the end when our bird suddenly rose into the air. I breathed
a silent prayer of thanksgiving!

Then the left landing-wheel hit the ground again, the machine
tipped downwards and we made straight for the gully. Veering
left, we shot over the edge. I closed my eyes, held my breath and
again awaited the inevitable end. The wind roared in our
ears.

It must have been all over in a matter of seconds, for when I
looked round again Gerlach had got the machine out of its dive
and almost on a level keel. Now we had sufficient air speed, even
in this thin air. Flying barely 30 metres above the ground, we
emerged in the Arezzano valley.

All three of us were decidedly paler than we had been a few
minutes earlier, but no words were wasted. In most unsoldierly
fashion I laid my hand on the shoulder of Benito Mussolini, whose
rescue was now beyond doubt.

Having recovered his composure, he was soon telling me stories
about the region through which we were flying at an altitude of
100 metres, carefully avoiding the hilltops. "Just here I addressed
a huge crowd twenty years ago." . . . "Here's where we buried
an old friend." . . . the Duce reminisced.

At length Rome lay below us, on our way to Practica di Mare.
"Hold tight! Two-point landing," Gerlach shouted, reminding
me of the damage to our landing gear. Balancing on the right
front and tail landing-wheels, we carefully touched down. Our
trip was over.

Captain Melzer welcomed us in the name of General Student
and congratulated us warmly on our success. Three He 111s were
waiting for us, and after the conventions had been observed by my

formally presenting their crews to the Duce, I gratefully shook
Gerlach's hand on parting. There was no time to lose if we were
to reach Vienna before dark.

CHAPTER VII

THE HEINKEL was a far more comfortable form of transport,
but the noise of the engines made conversation impossible and the
Duce sat back with closed eyes, while I took refuge in thought. We
had brought our undertaking to a successful conclusion. Healthy
optimism and unflinching resolution had triumphed over all our
trials and tribulations.

It was clear to me that soldier's luck had been on our side and
made no small contribution—particularly to-day. How easily things
could have gone quite differently! When I thought of all our
fortunate escapes I could only feel intensely grateful to all my
comrades who had volunteered to join me. But without their
iron discipline and reckless courage nothing could have been
achieved.

We passed over the Karavanken Alps and the Austrian frontier,
and then flew into bad weather. We could now break wireless
silence, which had been imposed on us until we reached our own
country. We wanted to contact the airfield and the wireless
operator was soon at work, but he soon reported that there was no
answer to his call to Aspern (Vienna).

There was little to be seen from the pilot's cockpit as rain-clouds
hid the landscape and we had to maintain an altitude of over 2,000
metres in order to keep above the mountain tops. Direction was
by compass.

The Duce seemed to have gone to sleep. "No contact" was
repeated and the light began to fade, slowly and almost impercep-
tibly, in the dark storm clouds. It was nearing 7.30. We must
soon arrive at our destination, and still no wireless contact! I was
getting very worried. It was no picnic to be hanging about with
so exalted a passenger in such a plane, particularly as petrol was

getting low. The pilot muttered something about a belly landing. Not on your life! I thought. We checked our course again and decided that we must certainly be in the vicinity of Vienna.

When it was quite dark I lay in the nose of the cockpit and half-closed my eyes. We had reduced speed and I suddenly saw a sheet of water glimmering through a gap in the clouds. It could only be Lake Neusiedler. It meant a happy end to our journey, as I knew this country like the palm of my hand. We dropped cautiously through the clouds. I was right; the lake spread its broad sheet barely fifty metres below us. I told the pilot to steer north (we could safely fly to the Danube at that height) then turn left and follow the river into Vienna. We landed at Aspern in total darkness.

Leaving the Heinkel in one corner of the airfield, with the Duce in charge of its crew, I went to the control tower to find out if we were expected. I was informed that some cars had arrived from the city but had been sent off to Schwechat, a suburb of Vienna, when the news had come through that an aircraft had made an emergency landing there. My Heinkel had been expected an hour before.

After a certain amount of fuss the Commandant got hold of a car to take us to Vienna. I was not in a position to tell him who was with me. I was told why we had not been able to establish wireless contact with the airfield. It was Sunday duty only at Aspern. And this was total war!

I returned in the car to our Heinkel and asked the Duce to step in. On our way to the city we met the returning cars conveying a group of high-ranking officers and Gruppenführer Querner, the SS and Police Chief of Vienna. They were all very delighted to find my protégé safe and sound. Having assumed that the plane which had made the emergency landing was mine, they were glad to find that it was our escort to which the mishap had occurred. I ascertained later that the second plane, which had left Rome with us, had also made a belly-landing at Wiener-Neustadt. Fortunately, both crews got off comparatively unscathed.

When we had changed cars and were sitting in the Gruppen-führer's car, I breathed freely again. Responsibility had passed to someone else and I had survived this critical day. We soon reached the Hotel Imperial, where a suite had been prepared for the Duce. Here I had a short but very cheerful talk with him. We had no luggage so that Querner had to set about producing pyjamas and toilet articles for him. When I took them into his bedroom, he made an enlightening remark: "It's unhealthy to sleep in night clothes. I never wear anything at night and should advise you to do the same, Captain Skorzeny." A merry twinkle in his eyes betrayed that he had a wide experience of life. I could not restrain a sly smile. Thereupon I left him until next morning.

The telephone suddenly rang and I heard Himmler at the other end. He congratulated me on my success and asked me a few questions before adopting a particularly friendly tone and remarking: "You're Viennese, aren't you, Skorzeny? Have you let your wife know? Get her to come up to the hotel for the night. You mustn't leave Mussolini; you have to bring him to FHQ in a few days."

I needed no second invitation to send for my wife, and to give her an even greater surprise I had her fetched by Querner's ADC in his car.

A few minutes before midnight a colonel, the Chief-of-Staff of the Vienna garrison, was solemnly announced. He strode ceremoniously into the room and introduced himself. My eyes almost left my head when I heard his solemn words: "I am here on the orders of the Führer, Captain, to bestow on you the Knight's Cross of the Iron Cross!" He removed an order from his neck and placed it round mine. The ceremony was concluded with a glass of champagne, which helped me to recover from my surprise, and I was busy for quite a time in shaking hands and acknowledging congratulations. My poor wife still had not the slightest idea what all the fuss was about and could only gape in astonishment at what, to her, were mysterious and unintelligible proceedings.

Just as midnight struck the telephone rang again. General Querner answered it. "Skorzeny, the Führer himself wishes to speak to you!"

Adolf Hitler's gratitude was most moving.

"You have performed a military feat which will become part of history. You have given me back my friend Mussolini. I have awarded you the Knight's Cross and promoted you to Sturmbannführer. Heartiest congratulations!" He also made my wife come to the telephone to be congratulated, after which I had a few kind words from Göring and Keitel.

A little later the news came in from Munich that my commando had successfully performed its task at Rocca della Caminata and arrived in Munich with the Duce's family, so I felt that I could regard this eventful day as really ended and bid my visitors good-night. I recalled my father's words at the beginning of the war: " You mustn't win the Knight's Cross straight off! "

The programme for the next day had been fixed up. Ambassador Dörnberg, who was half a head taller than I, came to say that he would travel with us. I also met Baldur von Schirach, the gauleiter of Vienna, when he paid a visit to Mussolini. There was a constant stream of callers.

The Duce seemed years younger, thanks partly to the barber, and had recovered his old vitality. Apparently he had been using the night hours to work out a great new plan. Then, and during our subsequent flight together, he developed his scheme for a reconstruction of the Party, which was to take the name of the Fascist-Republican Party.

" I made one great and critical mistake," he said, " and have had to pay the price. I never realized that the Italian royal house was, and would remain, my enemy. I ought to have made Italy a republic after the end of the Abyssinian campaign."

Just before twelve we returned to Aspern airfield, where a comfortable civilian Junkers was waiting for us. I sat opposite the Duce and this time conversation was possible. The Duce gave me all the details of his scheme for the reorganization of the party and the formation of a new government.

At Riem airport, outside Munich, we were met by his family. On this occasion Dr. Kaltenbrunner was present and now became personally responsible for the Duce's safety.

For the next twenty-four hours we were the guests of the government at the guest-house in Munich. I had all my meals with Mussolini's family and passed several hours in conversation with him. Among other things, he told me how he had been arrested. About 5 o'clock in the evening of the 25th July, in the teeth of many warnings, including his wife's, he had been to the palace to take his leave of the Italian king. The latter had thanked him in the most exaggerated terms for all he had done for Italy. " You will always be deemed Italy's greatest son," he had said, " and I shall always call you my cousin! " (This was a reference to the award to Mussolini some years before of a high order of the House of Savoy.) The words were uttered as the Duce embraced his royal master, who then accompanied him to the door where some officers were waiting to arrest him and take him in an ambulance to the Carabinieri barracks in Rome.

I made the acquaintance of two other members of Mussolini's family at this juncture. One was Count Ciano, who had secretly moved to Germany with his wife in August and was living at a country estate in the vicinity of Munich. Edda Ciano arrived on the Monday to arrange a meeting between her husband and the Duce. The Countess looked very ill and appeared to be in great trouble. At first the Duce and Donna Rachele flatly refused to see their son-in-law, who had supported the opposition to Mussolini. Then the latter agreed to grant Ciano a short interview, though nothing would make Donna Rachele relent. "I hate him; I'd like to kill him," she said, with her southern vehemence. The Duce himself told me of this sudden outburst on the part of his wife, but he did not let it influence the final decision he had long taken.

At Mussolini's request I was present at the meeting. Count Ciano, wearing a smart dark civilian suit, began by offering congratulations. Then he seemed to be trying to explain away his actions at the meeting of the Fascist Grand Council, but the atmosphere became so chilly that it was positively embarrassing for a mere bystander like me. It was over in a few minutes and I accompanied the Count to the door, where we parted.

Mussolini then asked me to join him by the fireplace. He began to tell me that, in a very short time, he would bring the leaders of the revolt of the 25th July to justice. Having regard to the interview just ended, I asked a most undiplomatic question: "Won't you have to charge Count Ciano, too?" "Yes," replied the Duce. "I realize that my son-in-law will be one of the first to face the tribunal, and I have no illusions about the result!" The tragedy of the situation was not lost on me. Here was the head of the Italian state being compelled to bring a member of his own family to justice for treason. To outward appearances the Duce was hard enough to act, without hesitation, against the husband of his favourite daughter. What he really felt he never betrayed, even to his intimates. But, remembering the strong sense of family which animates all Italians, and which I had seen that he shared, I can imagine what it cost him later to sign Count Ciano's death warrant.

Early in the morning of the 15th September, we started on our flight to FHQ in East Prussia. We were accompanied by Ambassador Dörnberg and Dr. Kaltenbrunner, who had taken up his quarters in Berlin as the head of the German Security Police. It was a great relief to me, as I still felt responsible for our august guest, and one never knew what might happen.

Brilliant sunshine greeted us at FHQ airfield. When the Ju 52 touched down and we climbed out the Duce was warmly welcomed by the Führer in person, and the two men stood together for a considerable time hand in hand. Then Adolf Hitler greeted me, too, and in the afternoon I gave him a full description of our exploit. Our conference lasted nearly two hours. There seemed no limit to his gratitude. "I will not forget what I owe you," he said.

He invited me to midnight tea with him, which I knew to be a great and rare honour. It was nearly one o'clock when I was fetched. He always took tea at the big round table in his work-room. When he said midnight "tea", he meant it. He drank it out of a glass on a silver saucer. The guests could have coffee if they preferred.

The company included two secretaries, Fräulein Wolf and Frau Traudl Jung, who sat left and right of him. Ambassador Hewel and Dr. Kaltenbrunner were also of the party. I was surprised at Hitler's courtesy towards his secretaries. There was nothing of the boss and employee attitude about it and when they left he kissed their hands. Ambassador Hewel was a talkative and much-travelled man, but Dr. Kaltenbrunner spoke little except when the subject of rebuilding his home town, Linz, came up, when he intervened actively in the conversation, half of which was carried on by Adolf Hitler that evening.

Everything under the sun was discussed, though little was said about the topic ever present to our minds—the war. One of the Führer's hobby horses was his plans for rebuilding cities. On this subject he was inexhaustible and tossed one idea after another, including the incorporation of a university city in the plans for Linz, into the discussion. When the conversation turned to the projected picture-gallery he took not merely a general interest, but went into great detail about the pictures he wished to be collected in advance. I had an idea that his love of his home country played quite a large part in his life. History and philosophy also came into the discussion.

That he was aware even during the war that the state of affairs in the NSDAP sometimes gave cause for concern, and had made up his mind to intervene at the right moment, appears from the following remarks: "Germany must be cleaned up after the war. We will draw our coming men from the fighting soldiers, but traitors must be rooted out *now*. Don't forget how Clemenceau dealt with the enemy within, in 1914. He ruthlessly rounded them up and had them shot, thereby saving France. We must get rid of deserters and mutineers behind the front. Traitors always work on the same lines—to let the enemy in by the back door."

Next day Marshal Göring arrived by special train. During a walk with him I had to give him a detailed description of our exploit and he gave me the gold flying badge, though he also cooled my ardour with some caustic remarks about my "criminal" folly in risking the Duce in the Storch. I asked him, and he agreed, to give Captain Gerlach and Lieutenant Meyer the Knight's Cross. The Führer had previously acceded to my request that my men should also receive a decoration.

The officer in charge of security at FHQ asked me to call on him. I had unwittingly worried him greatly. He feared that the idea of a commando raid on the enemy's headquarters might now occur to the Allies also, and he wanted me to advise him what counter-measures he should take. I did not deny that there was a distinct possibility of a successful attack on FHQ. No headquarters could be immune from such attack and I have always wondered why it had not been attempted already. Before long we were so absorbed in our discussion that I nearly forgot that I had been invited to lunch by Reichsleiter Martin Bormann, who had hitherto been only a name to me. The result was that I arrived late and this time deserved the snub I received from Himmler, who was also present.

Strange to say, Bormann's personality made so little impression upon me that I cannot say what he looked like. My only recollection is that he was of medium height and powerfully built. It was only at and after the end of the war that I learned of the fateful part this second *eminence grise* played behind the scenes. Even at a first meeting he struck one as a rigid doctrinaire. He regarded himself as Hitler's personal bodyguard and, unfortunately, was only too successful in his efforts to keep him isolated from the outer world. Whatever the reason, the atmosphere at table was rather chilly. I put it down to my being late, and never felt at my ease.

It was just the same when I went to tea with the Foreign Minister, von Ribbentrop, that afternoon. Conversation remained on conventional levels, without a trace of human warmth. Even the good manners in vogue throughout FHQ were absent here. The minister sat on a kind of throne while visitors took lower and less comfortable chairs. The aide-de-camp on duty stood behind him throughout. The only thing I liked was that smoking was not forbidden.

After three days, I had had enough and returned to my comrades in Italy. During my absence enough German troops had arrived to disarm all hostile Badoglio forces throughout the part of the country we occupied and there was no immediate danger of a repetition of the crisis we had passed through when Italy went over to the Allies on the 8th September. Apart from the Allied bridgeheads, Italy was once more firmly in German hands, to quote the official announcement.

When I was back at Frascati, there was news both pleasant and unpleasant. It was not nice to hear that a Propaganda concern was on its way to Gran Sasso to make a belated film of the "actual attack". Unfortunately, I was not able to prevent these photographs appearing later in periodicals.

But it was with a certain amount of satisfaction that I learned that on the 12th September, at the very time we were in the air on our way to the Abruzzi, GHQ in Italy had ordered that Sardinia should be evacuated without a fight, though Mussolini, held prisoner on the island of Santa Maddalena, must be rescued and brought away at all costs. Obviously our own little private Intelligence service had worked faster, and the insistence of General Student and myself on complete silence had had its effect everywhere.

When I returned to Friedenthal I proposed to send my men away for a short leave, but the first day, the 26th September, brought my first and last public appearance. I, and all the participants in the Mussolini affair, were invited to the Harvest Thanksgiving in the Sportpalast in Berlin. I was asked to present three Knight's Crosses of the War Service Cross to civilian recipients. It was usual for this civil order to be handed over by a military Knight's Cross holder, thereby symbolizing the intimate connection between the fighting forces and the men behind the front.

Dr. Joseph Goebbels, whom I met for the first time on this occasion, made the chief speech. Without saying anything to me in advance, he suddenly presented me to the audience. It gave me a curious sensation to hear cheering provoked by a speech by someone else, and which was meant for everyone who had taken any part in the Duce affair.

After the meeting I was invited to lunch by Dr. Goebbels. His villa was in the Hermann-Göring Strasse, near the Brandenburg Gate, and was included in the same group of edifices as the Reichs Chancellery. I was introduced to Frau Goebbels and the State Secretary Dr. Naumann. I took Frau Goebbels in to lunch while our host gave his arm to his eldest daughter. The big table in the dining-room was decorated simply but tastefully. A butler in livery handed round the food. I was surprised that the latter was quite ordinary, comprising soup and a goulash, washed down with the usual light beer.

Coffee—real bean coffee, I was glad to see—was always taken in the hostess's boudoir. The conversation, in which she took an active part, became very animated.

I met Dr. Goebbels on three or four subsequent occasions. It was known that he could be very caustic when commenting on conditions or personalities at home, but I was very surprised at his candour when talking to me. He criticized his colleague Göring in very severe terms. Admittedly, few of us had any good words for the head of the German Luftwaffe, who had promised so much and performed so little. But I had never heard such scathing remarks about the Reichmarschall's love of luxury and show.

Dr. Goebbels could best be appreciated when very few people were present, for only then could it be seen how quickly his keen intellect could grasp the facts of any situation. I can see now that he made one great mistake—he always thought that the enemy must draw the same conclusions as himself from any set of facts.

To give an instance, in 1945 the loss of the industrial region of Silesia was a terrible, if not fatal, blow to Germany. Goebbels believed that even England would not tolerate this slap in the face of Europe, as the British Empire could not stand by and see the Silesian arsenal exploited from the east. He was convinced that the disaster presented a fresh opportunity for negotiations with England.

A Wehrmacht lieutenant, Dr. Goebbels' aide-de-camp, told me

the following trivial, but significant story in a train in 1944. At a conference of political and military leaders, a high-ranking general ironically asked Goebbels: "How do you think you are going to win *your* war, Herr Minister?" The Propaganda Minister, who is generally credited with a fiery tongue, flashed back: "Why put that question to *me*, General? Isn't it more appropriate for me to ask you when you are going to win *your* war with the help of your soldiers? I don't know how we are going to win a war at all if we have generals who are under the delusion that it is not *theirs*!"

CHAPTER VIII

I HAD BARELY had five weeks in which to devote myself to building up my special force before I received an order from FHQ that I was to go to Paris immediately with one company and wait there for further orders, after reporting to General Oberg, commanding the SS and the police in France.

In Paris I was informed that there was another crisis in the Vichy government and that it was possible that Marshal Pétain, then residing in unoccupied southern France, was in touch with General de Gaulle and, voluntarily or otherwise, might leave Vichy and go to North Africa, which was then in allied hands. Such an eventuality must be prevented at all costs, if necessary by removing him and his colleagues to the neighbourhood of Paris. I was to be prepared to deal with both situations and the code phrase, "the wolf howls", would be the signal from FHQ for immediate action.

After various comings and goings in the offices of the Military Governor of Paris I was allotted the troops I needed for my plans. There were two rifle battalions of a new SS division, the Hohenstaufen, and two police battalions, the use of which could only be decided by a police general. These units alone were to appear "on show", but I had also had three companies of infantry as a reserve, which I stationed at an airfield north of Vichy.

The police battalions were distributed all round the town and given the specific job of traffic control, which we thought would disguise our intentions. If and when our intervention was ordered, they would tighten the ring so that no one, or at any rate no vehicle, could get out. The three companies in reserve would also close the roads leading out of the town and, if necessary, surround the government buildings. In that case a few hundred men of the armed French Garde Nationale would have to be dealt with.

Lieutenant von Foelkersam, who was later to become my chief staff officer, and I chose quarters in the centre of the town for the critical period, so as to familiarize ourselves with local conditions and be close·at hand if required.

One thing we certainly learned at this time, the importance of patience! Paris gave the alarm signal time and time again, and as often withdrew it. I was also made aware in those few days that conflicting views of the situation prevailed among the German authorities everywhere. Everyone I consulted to clear my mind seemed to have a different idea. The Counsellor of the Foreign Office did not agree with the head of the Security Service and the Intelligence Chief was much better informed than the military Chief-of-Staff, or the Chief-of-Staff of the Police.

Before long I had had quite enough of all this dissension. How could a successful *coup* be brought off if based on unreliable inform-ation? This time I had no chance of probing the facts myself or organizing my own intelligence service, so I was more than delighted when, on the 2nd December, I received a clear order from FHQ to call off my preparations and withdraw my troops. The wolf did not howl after all!

I had fourteen days' leave at Christmas, 1943. I had only had one previous leave! With my wife and baby girl I forgot the troubles and anxieties of the times, especially as the navy had invited us to a leave-centre for submarine personnel at Zurs on the Arlberg. We had a week's excellent skiing.

Meanwhile, at Friedenthal my people had been making prepara-tions for a great paper war, which I found myself obliged to wage on my return, against the headquarters of the Waffen SS. Every military unit in Germany has to have its KStN and KAN. Readers who dislike abbreviations should be told that these letters stand for the German equivalents of " strengths ", in personnel and *matériel*. Each company had a hefty file. Captain von Foelkersam (he had just been promoted) and I took it into our heads that it would be a good idea if we prepared the corresponding KStN and KAN lists for our special formation and got them approved. In our simple fashion we assumed that if they were sanctioned a steady flow of personnel and equipment would be forthcoming.

After weeks of waiting and much haggling over every man, revolver and motor vehicle, we got as far as being told that our lists were to be approved and we should get what we needed. But when the great day came, it brought nothing but disillusionment to Foelkersam, myself and our colleagues. The KStN and KAN lists were certainly approved and the formation of Commando battalion 502 was ordered, with Sturmbannführer Otto Skorzeny as its commander, but the last sentence, which I remember well, shook us to the core and seemed a very bad joke: "SS Headquarters must, however, make it quite clear that the allotment of personnel or material is not to be counted on."

So we were left with a handsome piece of paper, but nothing else! We had to swallow our rage and remember our slogan, and then we made two decisions: that we would resort to any subterfuge to get round that last sentence and broaden the basis of our recruitment by drawing men from every branch of the armed forces. To this latter decision I owe the fact that the army, the navy, the Luftwaffe and the Waffen SS were all represented in my formations, fought side by side and acquitted themselves brilliantly.

The appointment of Lieutenant Hunke to be my subsequent Ia came about in a very odd fashion. The Far Eastern department of Section VI wanted someone who knew Chinese. By some means which I have never been able to fathom they ascertained that there was a person with the requisite qualifications in a Finnish division. After long negotiations and much waste of paper, this Chinese expert, Werner Hunke, was transferred to Section VI and told to occupy himself with political "Intelligence". Two surprises were in store for all concerned. Firstly, though he had been born in China, he had left the country at the tender age of eighteen months. In the second place, he had not the slightest desire to spend his military career in "Intelligence"!

I came across him, and taking a great liking to him, got him transferred to Commando Battalion 502 as a company commander. Thereafter he was known to us as "Ping-Fu".

In February, 1944, I took on another sphere of work, additional

The author when a witness in the Nüremberg war crime trials in 1945

The Albergo Campo Imperatore Hotel where Mussolini was kept
prisoner

Otto Skorzeny with some of his men in Italy after the rescue of Mussolini. Radl (in peaked cap) is sitting in the front row

Mussolini greeting Hitler on his arrival at the Führer's headquarters in East Prussia, 16th September, 1943

Hitler congratulating Otto Skorzeny on the rescue of Mussolini, September, 1943

A portrait of the author, then a Major in the Waffen-SS, taken about the same time

In paratroop uniform in Italy at a presentation of decorations to his men

A similar event at Friedenthal, Germany, in November 1944

An American picture of Otto Skorzeny at the time of his arrest by the
United States Army

As a prisoner of war, 1946

In the Denazification Camp at Darmstadt, May 1948. Radl is on the
extreme right

Otto Skorzeny with
Wing Commander Yeo
Thomas in Madrid
1952

to my previous activities, which can compendiously be called
"Special Weapons"! After the northern part of Italy had resumed
fighting at our side under the leadership of Mussolini, the liaison
between the armed forces of the two countries became much closer
and we were initiated into the mysteries of one of the best of the
Italian organizations, the X-MAS Flotilla, then under the command of Colonel Prince Borghese, a member of one of the oldest
noble families of Italy.

This unit had developed a number of so-called auxiliary methods
of waging war at sea. They had produced among other weapons
a boat filled with explosives and manned by a steersman who was
ejected when the target was nearly reached, and also a torpedo on
which two men sat astride and which could approach an enemy
ship under water. With the latter contrivance, two resounding
successes had been obtained by Italian special commandos against
ships in the harbours of Alexandria and Gibraltar. X-MAS Flotilla
had also established a school of swimmers (frogmen), who
approached an enemy ship underwater and fastened explosive
charges to the hull. This technique was improved by the invention
of two Austrian NCO's, Hass and N., whose names were known,
though they were then students, even before the war. Rubber flap-
pers attached to their feet made them far nimbler underwater and
increased their capacity for all sorts of acrobatics. Captain H., a
German in Section II of the Secret Service, had, single-handed, sunk
more than 50,000 tons of enemy shipping with the help of this
device.

One day I received an order to report to Vice-Admiral Heye.
An active man of about fifty years of age rose to receive me. He
was the commodore of the newly-established "Naval Auxiliary
Units" (KdK). On Himmler's orders some of the suitable soldiers
in my commando battalion were to assist with their training.

The fundamental ideas explained by the Admiral, with whom I
was soon working on the best of terms, were most convincing and
impressed me deeply. Apart from the U-boat, E-boat and mine-
laying services, it was no longer possible for the navy to operate in
large formations on the high seas or damage the enemy fleets in
action, though there was much important activity against their
supply lines. The result was that large numbers of sailors, both men
and officers, were looking for other outlets for their energy and
fighting spirit.

Following the example of the Italians, Admiral Heye and his colleague developed various new and effective special weapons. The basic principle was that whenever possible we should use and transform existing material. Speed was absolutely essential as we all knew that there was no time to be lost. There were plenty of men in Germany only too anxious to take on assignments which would certainly be dangerous and in most cases a one-man job. All wanted to contribute to a German victory, and what could be more attractive to such men than the chance of attacking enemy ships single-handed or with only a few comrades.

So the naval designers converted ordinary torpedoes into a " one-man torpedo " (which was given the code name " nigger ") by removing the explosive charge, furnishing it with a glass cupola and a steering apparatus and affixing a second, live torpedo underneath. It had a range of about ten sea miles and, though we knew that the first specimens were a highly primitive and imperfect weapon, we were justified in banking on the effect of surprise on the enemy. Many improvements were made and in the course of a few weeks Admiral Heye's outfits had developed one-man torpedoes capable of diving and already not unlike the smallest U-boats.

The first occasion on which this new weapon was employed was a great success. In the grey morning light of a summer day in 1944, twenty commandos shoved their little contraptions into the water north of the allied bridgehead at Anzio. They reached their targets, the warships and transports lying at anchor, unnoticed.· The lower torpedo was released and a few seconds later a number of explosions announced that the peace of the convoy had been rudely disturbed. More than 6,000 tons of shipping was sunk or damaged. Seven men returned and six others landed on the enemy bridgehead and, a few nights later, returned through our lines.

We had similar successes, though on a smaller scale, in the Mediterranean and on the Channel coast. The enemy soon learned to spot the glass cupolas and then fired at them with everything they had. Sometimes we defeated them by adopting a ruse. On nights when the wind and current was favourable we released empty cupolas which had been made buoyant. The enemy concentrated their fire on them while the deadly steered torpedoes approached from quite another direction.

It is not my purpose here to describe all the special weapons and commando exploits of the navy, but I should like to touch on a few points because, with my technical training, I was an enthusiast for the new ideas and saw a possibility of occasionally enlivening a defensive war and thought that the very fact that we carried out unexpected *coups* on all fronts would help to shake the enemy's confidence.

The boat filled with explosives, an Italian invention, bore the code name "Linse". Remote control, the essence of the "Goliath" tanks, was adopted and enabled two unmanned explosive boats to be steered by one manned torpedo. *Linses* were used on several occasions in the Mediterranean, and on the invasion coast, though the public did not hear of them.

Another special weapon was the midget submarine, which had previously been employed by the Japanese and also the English in Norway. There were several varieties, which were used on a small scale, and with a high casualty rate, up to the end of the war. They were being continuously improved.

By the spring of 1944, all our thoughts were turning to the question of where we must expect the inevitable great and decisive landing on the continent. I myself saw the air photographs taken in May, 1944, of the south-eastern harbours of England and helped in solving the puzzle presented by the first appearance of long strings of little rectangles. It was only after a considerable time that we were satisfied that they represented part of an artificial portable harbour.

It was only logical that my staff should concern themselves with the question, how best we could contribute to the disruption of the enemy's supply lines during the coming invasion. I first asked Admiral Heye for the professional opinion of the navy chiefs as to where the landing would take place. He gave me a list of ten sectors, No. 1 of which was the Cherbourg Peninsula, with all the possible landing-places marked. This information was of course conveyed to all military quarters concerned.

I set Captain von Foelkersam to work on a programme which we could carry out at once. We suggested that we should establish small units at the points of greatest danger with a commission to attack prospective enemy headquarters and communication centres. Our pet scheme was to bury explosives at suitable places with a view to their being detonated from our own aircraft by a newly invented apparatus. In accordance with instructions received, we submitted this plan to GHQ, West, for approval. After many enquiries this organization, which was "overwhelmed with work", informed us that our idea was sound and practicable, but . . . And the "buts" culminated in rejection!

I have never suggested that our plans would have foiled the invasion, but I cannot help considering the probability that many other suggestions were turned down for similar reasons. We were all fully aware that the coming invasion would mean the final decision of the war, and thereby settle Germany's fate.

We also discussed these special developments with the Luftwaffe. Squadron 200 was selected to carry out the experiments. Captain Lange and his immediate associates took a very active part in the work and, in fact, carried the project a step further. They were quite prepared to sacrifice their own lives in steering a flying bomb to its target, a ship for instance.

Such men are not to be regarded as mental, or the victims of heated imaginations. The general opinion (which I shared when I first heard of the idea) was that a normal man should not seek death voluntarily and that suicide was going too far and incompatible with the outlook of a German or any European. I heard about this time that Adolf Hitler had not committed himself definitely on the subject. His view was that such self-sacrifice was not in character for the white races and opposed to German mentality. We should not imitate the Japanese *kamikaze*.

I was one day given the hint to discuss the matter with the well-known German airwoman, Hanna Reitsch, and I was only too glad to follow it up, as I was keen to make the acquaintance of the woman who for years had proved as brave as a man in flying new types of aircraft. I was particularly impressed by the fact that she had taken part in tests of the most modern rocket planes and was none the worse for a serious crash two years before.

One afternoon I found myself face to face with a small, slight woman in a modest, but tastefully furnished room in her home. Traces of the accident still showed themselves in her face. She surveyed me critically with her big, flashing blue eyes.

She gave me her views quite frankly and told me that, not only had she been strenuously supporting Lange's efforts, but she herself was prepared to be available for such suicide attacks. "We're no lunatics, throwing away our lives for fun," she said, and added in her emotional way: "We're Germans with a passionate love of our country, and our own safety is nothing to us when its welfare and happiness are at stake. So, of course, we are ready to sacrifice our lives if it is necessary!"

One day an idea came to me when I was on a casual visit to Peenemünde. I had flown with a Luftwaffe colonel in a Bucker-Jungmann courier aircraft to the Baltic island of Usedom, because I wanted to see the testing grounds of the V1 and other secret weapons. I do not think that I was shown everything, but what I did see was sufficient for my purpose. While I was inspecting the V1 and watching it start on its journey, an idea occurred to me. Why could not such a rocket weapon be manned in the same way as the one-man torpedo? I asked for, and obtained, figures of the total weight and the weights of fuel and explosive respectively, and also the data about velocity, range and the steering apparatus.

Unfortunately, I was not an aircraft engineer, and was thus dependent on the advice of others, though I meant to make up the deficiency as soon as possible.

I reflected on the possibilities on our return flight. We landed on the works' airfield of the Heinkel concern in Berlin. Radl met me and, even before the aircraft came to rest I greeted him with: "Hot night, to-night! No sleep for us!"

We managed to collect the people we needed for a meeting that night at the Wannsee. My guests included Herr L., the designer of the V1, Dipl.-Ing. F., another engineer of the Fieseler concern, the commander of Squadron 200, Staff-Engineer K., and some other aeronautic experts. I managed to get these gentlemen quite enthusiastic about my idea and soon we were making an effective picture, with uniformed officers sprawling over drawing-paper spread out over the floor, and occupied in drawing and filling sheets of paper with all sorts of calculations. No one looked at the clock and we all forgot the time.

By 5 o'clock, the experts assured me that the idea of a manned V1 was practicable and could be realized with a very modest outlay of material and man-hours. But when we were sitting over our wine and congratulating ourselves on the success of our labours, faces grew long again and I was informed that we should have to beat down resistance of bureaucracy entrenched in the Reich's Air Ministry. It was there that our troubles would begin.

The first and, as I then thought, decisive obstacle we surmounted by resorting to a little ruse. We had to obtain the consent of Field-Marshal Milch, whom I did not know personally. I asked his

adjutant for a meeting at short notice " on a most urgent matter ",
and an appointment was made for the next day. Hopefully I
entered his beautifully furnished room and was given a very kind
reception.

Now is the moment, I thought, feeling that first impressions would
be vital. Holding out the plans and diagrams which were the fruits
of our night's labours, I began:

" Herr Feldmarschall, I have come to you with a project of
which the Führer knows and in the fate of which he is extremely
interested. I have to report to him on the matter as soon as
possible." I am afraid that it was not true and I had to pull myself
together not to give the show away. All I had got was a promise
that within a few days the committee of experts, appointed for the
purpose, would look into the proposal, and if they passed it a final
decision would be given almost immediately at the conference of
the chiefs of the Air Ministry.

I had succeeded in convincing Engineer-General Hermann of the
practicability of the project after close and careful investigation
by him and I found him of the greatest help. We went together
to the meeting of the Committee. I was rather surprised to see that
the chairman was an admiral. He had a peaked naval beard, which
he was continually stroking while he delivered a long harangue,
which began with Noah's ark and was not concluded two hours
later, when he was telling us interesting stories about naval battles
in the First World War. At that point our united efforts managed
to bring him back to the real object of the meeting.

Eventually there were a number in favour and a much larger
number against. Then the exposition of Staff Engineer K., who did
wonders with plans and figures, which General Hermann confirmed,
combined with an intimation from me that I had to report to the
Führer on the matter " at once ", did the trick.

I was promised that the main committee, with Field-Marshal
Milch presiding, should meet the following day and give a final
decision.

The conference room at RLM was most imposing. When we
started, we again had the same array of pros and cons, but before
long we reached a critical stage when the question of personnel
came up. I needed engineers, foremen and so forth. Fortunately,
I had made previous enquiries. I found that the position was
favourable for our little enterprise, though I was shocked by what

I learned, viz., that at this critical moment in the summer of 1944, marked by the ever-growing intensity of the allied air attacks, a great part of our aircraft industry was not only not overworked, but almost unemployed, as the result of frequent changes in our aircraft programme. I mentioned this fact quite casually—because I did not wish to appear to be criticizing—and explained that all I was asking for was the release of three engineers and fifteen qualified foremen and workmen from the Hentschel concern. We had been promised the use of an erection shed at its works. This disposed of the last argument and our proposal was approved in principle.

In the technical discussion which followed I was asked how long would it be before we could have our first test of a manned V1? Basing my reply on the data furnished to me by the experts, I promptly answered: "I'm hoping for the first test-flight in about four weeks." This remark met with a sympathetic smile from the majority of those present. A general made himself their spokesman. "My dear Skorzeny, your optimism does you honour, but with our expert experience we can only tell you to think again! It will certainly be three to four months before you've got to that stage!"

This cold douche in no way discouraged me and simply stimulated my professional ambition. All the greater need for speed!

I had discussed with the engineers how we should set about our task. We had to form a closed community to obtain maximum results, and to ensure complete secrecy and no waste of time everyone engaged on the project agreed to isolate ourselves completely. Our world became the big workroom, the two construction offices and a small hall, which served as common sleeping quarters for both engineers and workmen. We were soon going ahead at top speed.

There was one person who was overjoyed at my victory over the bureaucracy—Hanna Reitsch.

Working fifteen hours a day, the engineers and technicians achieved the "impossible". In ten days—not four months—the first three machines were all set to start on the testing-ground near Rechlin, where the new rocket fighters were carrying out their final tests.

It was a fine summer day when I joined Hanna Reitsch, to fly in her own Bücker-Jungmann to witness the start. As the skies over Germany were now a happy hunting-ground for enemy aircraft, we had to keep low and "hedge-hop".

In a plane Hanna Reitsch was another being. I could hardly believe my ears when she began to sing at the top of her voice the folksongs of her native Silesia. When we reached Rechlin everything was ready for the start. The Vi nestled like a young bird under one wing of the He 111. After a final inspection of the jets, the combination flew off and the spectators followed its progress with bated breath. In a moment the Vi detached itself from the He 111, and then we noticed how much faster it was—600 kilometres an hour against 300. At about a thousand metres the pilot of the Vi was travelling in wide circles and everything looked all right to us from below, but then he patently throttled back the jets and started to come down to land. He passed over the airfield up-wind at about 50 metres, and we fervently hoped he was not travelling too fast and could make his landing.

He passed over the airfield again, but this time was only two or three metres above ground, and seemed to be in trouble. He pulled out, however, and started to climb instead of landing. We wondered whether he was worrying about his landing and the tension increased, particularly when we saw him skim a low hill, touch the top of some trees and disappear behind a rise. A moment later, two clouds of dust showed us that something had happened!

We found the pilot alive, but unconscious, and sent him to hospital. The tracks showed that he had tried to land in a ploughed field. But why?

The technicians submitted the debris to the most exhaustive examination, but could find nothing wrong, so we decided to try again next day. The second pilot was quite willing. But the same thing happened. The Vi got away in fine style, the pilot was longer in the air, but could not touch down and there was another crash almost on the same spot. Again the pilot was seriously hurt and unconscious.

The Ministry instructed me that there must be no further experiments and a fresh committee would consider the matter and give its decision later. I had a horror of committees, as I knew they meant weeks of delay. When our two casualties recovered, they mentioned vibrations in the steering, but otherwise knew of no reason for the accidents.

About a week later, I had a visit from Hanna Reitsch, the engineer in charge of the constructional work, and Staff Engineer K., from the Ministry. I was expecting bad news, but to my sur-

prise, Hanna told me that all three were convinced that they knew
the real explanation of the accidents. They had seen the service
records of the two pilots and ascertained that neither had ever flown
a really fast aircraft. No one without great experience could control
such a very small machine at very high speeds. They felt certain
that there was no fundamental constructional fault and backed
their opinion with an offer to make fresh test flights with the new
prototype themselves. But what about the ban, on which the
Ministry insisted? They calmly said that they would ignore it if
I agreed.

"Nothing doing, Hanna," I said. "If anything happened to you
the Führer would tear me in pieces himself!" But they gave me
no peace, attacked me from all sides and boldly appealed to the
principle enshrined in the words: "In an emergency a soldier must
even be prepared to act against orders." With a heavy heart I
gave way. The airfield commandant must simply be disregarded.
We would tell him we had received permission to carry out fresh
tests.

I do not think I was ever in such a fluster as next day when
Hanna was closing the cockpit and the airscrews began to turn.
The start and the release of the V1 were perfect and the handling
of the machine and its beautiful circles soon showed what an amazing pilot this girl was. Before long she came hurtling down
towards us. I sweated inside and out. There was a cloud of dust
on the tarmac and when we rushed up a smiling Hanna greeted
us from the cockpit. "Nothing wrong with it at all!" was her
verdict.

The two men followed her example, and between the three of
them twenty starts were made without any sort of mishap. Both
the idea and the machine had been vindicated.

Field-Marshal Milch turned pale when I subsequently told him
that Hanna Reitsch had flown the V1. "That could have cost
you your head," he remarked. But we got our permission to carry
on with the work of production and training. Before long our little
workshop was busily turning out machines—prototypes, then dual-
control training models, and finally the service type in series.

We already had all the volunteers we needed. Thirty men of
my special force had previously taken a pilot's course, and sixty
Luftwaffe pilots had volunteered and arrived at Friedenthal. We
were all set!

Now came the climax. I had asked the Ministry for an allocation of five cubic metres of aircraft fuel for each trainee. It may seem incredible, but the fact is that this proved an obstacle which we never surmounted. Week after week went by and all we got was ten on one occasion and fifteen the next. The promised bulk quantity never materialized. I badgered all the relevant authorities unmercifully, but, beyond promises and regrets, nothing was forthcoming. In the autumn, I abandoned the scheme as hopeless, particularly as the general situation had taken a further turn for the worse.

Most of the volunteers remained with me. I could offer them no prospect of flying against the enemy, but they were gradually incorporated in my battalions, where they did their duty manfully.

CHAPTER IX

MEANWHILE THE invasion had begun. For some weeks the outcome was in doubt, and it was only the irruption from Avranches that brought a decision in favour of the Allies. I had to accept it as a brilliant military feat on the part of the enemy, which had been crowned by a resounding triumph. No clear-sighted man could doubt that from a purely military point of view, we had lost the war. I myself shared that view and it was discussed dispassionately in conversation with intimates like von Foelkersam and Radl.

It was natural that we officers should conceal from the men our knowledge that the situation was desperately serious. We were now fighting on our own soil with an enemy who demanded unconditional surrender. Our determination to resist him with our last breath could be the only answer. No honourable man who loved his country could have done anything else. The desperate efforts of Tito and the Russian partisans and the struggles of the French and Norwegian *maquis* were called heroic. Was our resistance less heroic?

Sometime later, I was pleasantly but unexpectedly reminded of the Mussolini rescue in the summer of 1944, when the Italian ambassador sent me a gold wrist-watch for each man who had taken part. The pocket-watch for myself had the letter "M" in rubies, and it was accompanied by an invitation to spend a few days at Lake Garda.

My first audience with Mussolini took place at the headquarters of the Fascist-Republican Government at Gargano, and I was particularly astonished to note that the guard was furnished by an SS battalion and not by Italian troops. The whole quarter was sealed off by road blocks and all visitors were subjected to the closest scrutiny. I could not help wondering how well-intentioned Italians must be affected by the fact that security was in the hands of the Germans. Could not the Duce rely on his own troops? Did not it look as if he ruled solely by the favour of Hitler?

The Duce gave me the warmest of welcomes and asked me to draw chairs up to the table. It was only natural that we should discuss the war. "I'm doing my best to help the Axis to win the war," he said, but it seemed to me that his optimism, which had struck me so forcibly nine months before, had departed, despite all the quiet assurance in his voice. I realized that he must be in a moral dilemma. I wondered whether he was simply a fatalist. It looked like it when he added: "My dear Skorzeny, do you remember the journey from Vienna to Munich and our talk about my historic mistake? Now the cowardly flight of the royal house has robbed me of the possibility of an honourable internal revolution. The Italian Republic has, unfortunately, been established without a fight."

The next day was oppressively hot. In the morning I had a meeting with Prince Borghese, the commander of the X-MAS Flotilla. I found him the model of what an officer should be and have never heard the European vision put in better words: "In this war, Europe, the real Europe, is fighting against Asia. If Germany fails, the true core of Europe will disappear and so I and my men are prepared to stand at your side to the bitter end and fight on at the gates of Berlin, if need be. The Western Allies, who are now helping to overthrow Germany, will bitterly regret their action."

It was a shrewd glance into the future.

On my second visit to the Duce, he talked about German history and drew various parallels between the past and the present. He certainly had a better knowledge of German history and philosophy than the average German professor.   Then he turned to various forms of government and said that his ideal was a particular form of corporative state, based on purely democratic principles.   The Senate was to be organized in estates, but its members should be appointed by the government.   Two-thirds of the lower house should be elective and the remainder deputed for life.   He added that these were just his preliminary ideas, on which he had reflected deeply, and that he must await the successful outcome of the war before they could be translated into action.

It struck me that the Duce spent a good deal of his time in quiet reflection and was not very interested in the actual business of government.   When I got back, I summarized my impressions in a phrase: in the summer of 1944, the Duce was no longer the active head of a state, but had become a political philosopher.   It never occurred to me that I had seen him for the last time.

In Sesto Calente, which I visited on my return journey, I found a number of Italian volunteers from the X-MAS Flotilla and a company of the KdK undergoing training.   They were all amazed that I was driving in an open car, with only two officers as escort, as the autostrada from Milan to Lake Maggiore was the happy hunting-ground of the Italian partisans, who were particularly active at the time.   Cars travelled only in convoy.   My own view was that these convoys, having regard to the excellent intelligence of the partisans, were easier to catch than a solitary vehicle, as well as being more attractive bait by reason of their presumably more valuable freight.

At Valdagno I participated in the exercises of the frogmen, and was surprised to find that a little mountain town had such a fine swimming-bath.   The Italian volunteers, men of splendid physique, were under the command of a *capitano*, who was a White Russian emigrant.   They enjoyed seeing my first struggles with the breathing apparatus, but as I had long been a water-rat, I was able to put up quite a fair show.

We went on to Venice the same day as our time was very limited. Here the frogmen had their real element, the sea, at their disposal, and spent up to ten hours a day in the water.   The curriculum included walking as much as twelve kilometres underwater.

Much though I enjoyed such a tour of inspection, short though it was, I seldom repeated it, unwisely as I think.   The trouble was that we were kept far too busy in Friedenthal, even though half our time was spent on the paper war and the acquisition of personnel and supplies. Still, we saved some of our energy for wide-ranging plans and projects. I had given my staff officers orders to study most carefully all the reports of allied commando operations which we could get hold of, and the result was that we soon knew all about the activities of Lord Mountbatten and his special formations.

We had to admit—enviously—that the allied commando operations were always aimed at our nerve centres—an oil depot on a Norwegian island, a radar station on the Channel coast at Dieppe, or Rommel's headquarters in Africa, the attack on which probably failed only as a result of imperfect information.

As so few Ju 290's were given us, and the experts said that the He 117 was a failure, we had to think about substitutes. It occurred to us that there must be quite a number of American four-engined bombers which had come down in Germany or the occupied countries, and could be made airworthy again. The Luftwaffe welcomed the suggestion, and after a conference with General Koller I was given a promise that a special workshop should be established to recover and repair such aircraft.

Another problem was how to secure safe landing at the destination. The heavy aircraft would hardly ever be able to land, and we must, therefore, resort to gliders. Unfortunately, our DFS 230 type was only built for a maximum speed of 250 kilometres and we must plan for speeds of 350 to 400. Here we had the right man in Professor Georgi, an old glider specialist and a friend of Hanna Reitsch. He designed a glider to carry about twelve men and capable of the towing speed required.

There was another serious worry. What chance was there of getting the men back after a raid? As things stood at that time only two courses were open to them, to give themselves up or find their way back, perhaps through hundreds of kilometres of enemy-held territory. Their chance of return would be almost nil.

I believed that a soldier with a real chance of getting back would fight all the better for it, and soon came to the conclusion that, some-how or other, we must retrieve the glider itself.

I ascertained after enquiry that this problem was being worked out at the Ainring airfield, where the engineers had designed an apparatus by which the towing aircraft could retrieve the glider without itself landing. With this we had great success with our light gliders, but its application with the necessarily heavy and faster machines called for much trial and error and above all plenty of oil and time. These two last requirements were met in decreasing measure and finally not at all.

I often wondered why allied divisions were not dropped in the vicinity of Berlin in the winter of 1944, when FHQ and the ministries were concentrated there. A well-prepared surprise assault could have thrown them all out of gear and I must admit that I had my moments of apprehension about what was a real possibility. It may well be that there were strategic and political objections to such a *coup*, but it would have been a wonderful feather in the cap of the British commandos, or the American "Office of Strategic Service", under its chief, Major-General William O'Donovan. "Wild Bill" and his merry men were quite capable of making a job of it.

As a faithful chronicler, I must not omit to mention some of our plans, even though they did not materialize. Particularly attractive to us was the idea of some enterprise in the Near East, which was then practically under the complete control of England and France. Here the great pipeline from Irak reached the Mediterranean in two separate branches.

We knew that friendly Arabs were always trying to interrupt the flow of oil to the two refineries at Haifa and Tripoli, by blowing up this line at various points. In this war nothing was more coveted and bitterly fought for than oil.

To form Arab demolition parties and set them to work was one of our most promising and yet dubious ambitions. Success was most problematical and the effect would not be permanent. The Achilles heel of the pipeline was the pumping-stations and if these were destroyed the whole system might be put out of action for two or three months.

German engineers devised small floating mines with the same specific weight as that of oil. These mines were to be introduced into the pipes through a little oval hole produced by an explosive charge and immediately closed by a lid of the same shape. I thought that the destructive effect of these mines would be confined to the inlet valves of the pumping station and so rejected the suggestion.

Other technicians put forward a proposal to use the extreme heat of thermite bombs to fuse lengths of pipe at the bottom of valleys, but nothing effective eventuated. Finally the Luftwaffe proposed to destroy considerable sections of the pipelines by air bombing or the use of small magnetic mines, but here again we never got beyond the experimental stage.

So our last resource was commando raids on the pumping-stations, with their diesel-pump units. Air photographs showed that each pumping-station had its landing-ground, used by the aircraft which carried out a regular patrol of the installations, and a small fort for the reception of the personnel if they were attacked by rebellious Arabs. The actual pumping building was a few hundred metres away. However, we were never given the necessary long-range aircraft to put our plans into active operation.

Another weak point in the Allies' armour was certain sections of the Suez Canal. If this waterway could be blocked they would be forced to send their supplies for the Far East round by the Cape, involving a delay of two months. We had frogmen all ready to start, but the enemy's complete air control of the Mediterranean in 1944 made the enterprise impracticable.

The Baku oilfields and various points on the English coast were also promising targets, but plans to attack them had to be abandoned in view of the difficulty of carrying the agencies of destruction to the places where they would be required.

Another operation of the same kind had a certain measure of success and might have had more. The activities of the partisans in what had been Jugoslavia had been a source of anxiety to our High Command since 1943. The country, created by nature for a resistance movement on a large scale, tied down very considerable German forces which suffered serious losses almost every day. The discovery and elimination of Tito's headquarters would bring considerable relief to the army. At the beginning of the year I was asked to occupy myself with this problem.

By early summer our Intelligence network had done its job and all the reports received had been tested and found accurate. Tito's travelling HQ had been definitely located in a valley near Dvar, in western Bosnia. It was time to get our attack under way and concentrate the men and supplies. I said I would lead the party myself. I sent my chief staff officer, Captain von Foelkersam, to the officer commanding in the Bania Luka area to arrange about liaison and fix up certain details. On his return von Foelkersam told me that he had met with a somewhat chilly reception, but that did not worry us. We had a job to do and personal antipathies were irrelevant.

One day we received a remarkable report from our representative at headquarters in Agram: " The 10th Corps is preparing an operation against Tito's headquarters. It is called ' Rosselsprung ', and the 2nd June has been fixed as the date."

Now we could understand why von Foelkersam was not welcome. We had been regarded as rivals to be kept in the dark about what was brewing! It was an unworthy attitude to adopt, as I would gladly have co-operated and served with the Corps if necessary.

But I felt that the situation called for action rather than irritation, so I put a call through to Corps HQ and advised them against the projected operation, as I was certain that, if my people knew about it already, it could be no secret to Tito's Intelligence staff.

In the next few days I received a steady flow of information at Friedenthal which decided me to give a fresh warning and press for at least the postponement of the date fixed. But in vain! The Corps operation started on the appointed day. A parachute battalion of the Waffen SS, incorporated in the Corps, was dropped in a valley. Reinforcements followed in gliders. After a bloody fight, the valley and a village were in German hands, but the nest was empty—as could have been anticipated. Tito's HQ was represented by two English liaison officers, whom he was probably quite glad to leave behind. The only trace of Tito himself was a brand new marshal's uniform. He had left the village in time and removed his HQ elsewhere. Petty jealousy was responsible for the failure of a great plan.

This failure practically reduced to nil the chances of another raid. All we could do was to follow Tito's tracks to the coast, and then an island in the Adriatic. No opportunity presented itself for another attempt, though we toyed with the idea for a considerable time.

CHAPTER X

J ULY, 1944, in Berlin. The military situation was continually deteriorating, as a tremendous Russian offensive in June had rolled up almost the whole of our central eastern front and more than thirty German divisions had been taken prisoners. How such a thing could have happened was a mystery to all of us. No one could say whether the disaster was due to the High Command or the troops themselves.

In the west, the invasion had succeeded and the enemy, backed by all his enormous superiority in material, was thrusting towards the German frontier.

The wireless announcement of an unsuccessful attempt on the life of Adolf Hitler came like a thunderbolt. How was such a thing possible, and at FHQ, too? Had our enemies found a means of getting there? Were the previous anxieties of the troops guarding it shown to be justified? It never entered our heads that the bomb should have been placed by one of our own people, so I saw no reason to postpone an urgent journey to Vienna to attend some frogmen exercises in the Diana baths.

At 6 o'clock, Radl and I arrived at the Anhalt station. We made ourselves comfortable in the sleeping coach, produced some real coffee, which I had brought from Italy, and lit a spirit lamp. When we stopped at Lichterfelde West, the last station in Greater Berlin, we saw an officer running along the platform and could just hear him shouting: "Sturmbannführer Skorzeny! Sturmbannführer Skorzeny!" He flung himself into our compartment, quite out of breath. "You must return to Berlin at once, Sturmbannführer! Orders from Headquarters. There's a military revolt behind the attempt on the Führer's life!"

"You'll have to go on alone, Radl, and handle the conference yourself. I'll follow to-morrow morning if I can." I had my suit-case on the platform in a second and followed it as the train was moving out.

At Section VI, Brigadier Schellenberg told me that the source of the conspiracy was supposed to be the Bendlerstrasse, the head-quarters of the C.-in-C., Home Forces. "The situation is obscure and dangerous," said Schellenberg, who looked pale as death and had a revolver on the table in front of him. "I'll defend myself here if they come this way," he continued. "I've armed all the employees with machine-pistols. Couldn't you get a detachment of your men here to protect the house?"

I rang up Friedenthal and von Foelkersam answered. "Alert the whole battalion at once," I said. "Await further orders, which I alone will give. No. 1 Company is to come here at once. I appoint Ostafel my adjutant and you and he must jump into a car and come along without waiting for the others." I went on to give him a short résumé of the situation. The company could be with us within an hour.

"Brigadeführer," I said, turning to Schellenberg, "have most of your staff disarmed at once. You've no idea how dangerous such men can be with firearms! I've just had to send a chap down to the cellar to prevent damage from his machine-pistol. If 'they' arrive before my company, you'd do far better to slip away next door. You wouldn't do any good fighting it out here."

I waited impatiently in the street for the arrival of Foelkersam and Ostafel. They must have driven like mad, as their car soon appeared round the corner.

As I had no immediate orders, I thought I would go on a tour of inspection in Berlin. I told Foelkersam to remain in Berka Street and I would keep in touch with him. It was maddening to think that the German army was not equipped with a portable wireless. The American "walky-talky" would have been just the thing.

First I drove to the government buildings area. Everything was quiet, so I continued to Fehrbellinerplatz for a visit to General B., commanding the armoured formations. Here something was afoot. There were two tanks across the road. I stood up and was allowed to pass. "The revolt can't be that bad," I remarked to Ostafel.

General B. received me at once. He seemed rather undecided, saying that all the armoured forces from Wunsdorf were marching on Berlin and that he was concentrating them in the vicinity of Fehrbellinerplatz, so that he could keep them under his eye. "I'm going to take my orders from General Guderian alone," he added, "as he's the Inspector of Armoured Forces. God knows what's going on! I had an order to keep the Berlin barracks of the Waffen SS under armed observation. What do you think of *that*, Major Skorzeny?"

"Surely it hasn't got to civil war?" I countered. "I should have thought it quite wrong to pay any attention to such an order, General. If you like I'll have a look round Lichterfelde Waffen SS barracks and see what's happening. I'll ring you up from there. I'm sure our first duty is to prevent incidents." The General agreed and I drove on.

Everything was quiet at Lichterfelde, my old barracks, though the depot battalion and other units were alerted. I talked to the commander, Lieutenant-Colonel Mohnke, and advised him to be sensible and keep his men in barracks whatever happened.

I reported to General B., and he seemed satisfied. Incomprehensible orders from Home Forces and the Bendlerstrasse had ceased to come in. Von Foelkersam told me that the company from Friedenthal had arrived and I instructed him to keep it concentrated in the courtyard of the SS Headquarters on the Berka Strasse.

I do not know to this day what was really happening. Some sort of general alert must have been issued, probably about midday. Nothing seemed to have any method or precise object and before long the affair could hardly be taken seriously. The armoured formations stood to attention, so to speak, but adopted a neutral attitude. No orders were issued to the Waffen SS. Who were the rebels, and against whom?

I suddenly remembered that General Student would be in Berlin, so I drove at top speed to Parachute headquarters at the Wannsee. The officers there had heard nothing and had not received any orders. The General himself was at his house in Lichterfelde. His ADC came with me to pick up any orders he might issue.

Meanwhile night had fallen and it was getting on for nine o'clock.

A pleasant, domestic scene met our eyes at the nice little villa at Lichterfelde. Under a shaded lamp on the terrace the General was poring over a mass of papers. He was wearing a long, light-coloured dressing-gown and our visit was the last thing he expected at that time of night. His wife was sitting beside him, sewing. I could not help thinking that the situation had its comic side. Here was one of our most important generals quietly working away at papers while a revolt was supposed to be in full swing in the city. I had to cough quite loudly to attract his attention.

Though he was surprised by our visit at such an hour, we were given a very kind welcome. Mutual trust, dating from the Italian days, was still a strong bond. When I told him what I knew he burst out: "No, no, my dear Skorzeny, it can't be true! A plot! It's impossible!" I had the greatest difficulty in convincing him that the situation was really serious. "No more than obscure, you mean," he replied and started to draft a short order to his parachute troops: "Alert! No orders are to be obeyed unless issued by General Student personally."

At that moment the telephone bell rang. Reichsmarschall Göring was on the other end. He confirmed my report and gave us some further information to the effect that the attempt on Hitler's life had been made, probably by an officer in Home Forces and that orders had been issued from the Bendlerstrasse under the code phrase "Hitler is dead". Göring went on to say that no one was to pay any attention to any orders except those issued from Wehrmacht headquarters.

General Student got on the telephone and repeated these orders, adding: "Keep calm and do nothing likely to lead to civil war." By now he also was convinced that something extraordinary was afoot and he quickly issued his orders accordingly. He said that General B. and I must keep in close touch with him.

I drove back to the Berka Strasse at top speed. Nothing much had happened. Oberführer Schellenberg asked me for the loan of an officer and ten men as he had been ordered to arrest Admiral Canaris and did not wish to go alone. I could only spare him the officer. He was back an hour later.

There was nothing new from the Fehrbellin Platz or General Student, and I was thinking of returning to Friedenthal, when a call, probably prompted by Hermann Göring, came through for me: "You must take your troops straight to the Bendlerstrasse to support Major Remer, commander of the 'Grossdeutschland' battalion, which is keeping the block isolated." I replied that I had only one company in Berlin and was informed that I must make do with that.

It was midnight when I entered the Bendlerstrasse from the Tiergarten. Two cars barred our way, and when I got out I recognized

SS-Obergruppenführer Dr. Kaltenbrunner and Colonel-General Fromm, C.-in-C. Home Forces. I heard the latter say: " I'm going home; you can get me there if you want me," and saw the two men shake hands. We continued up the street and Dr. Kaltenbrunner called out that he would come with us. I thought it very odd that the C.-in-C. should go home at such a time, but of course it was none of my business.

At the door of the building I met Major Remer and introduced myself. He said his job was to isolate the whole block and we agreed that my company should be posted inside. I left the company in the courtyard and went upstairs with Foelkersam and Ostafel, as I knew my way about the building, having frequently been there on service business. In the corridor we passed several officers, all armed with machine-pistols, and there was an atmosphere of hostile suspense.

In General Olbricht's ante-room I found several staff officers whom I knew, and they gave me a brief account of what had happened during the day. It appeared that early in the afternoon they had noticed there was something odd about some " alert " orders which had been issued. There had been a number of conferences in Colonel-General Fromm's room, to which only a few officers were summoned. Most of the other officers in the building had become alarmed, armed themselves with machine-pistols, and demanded an explanation of what was going on from the C.-in-C. He had replied that a revolt had broken out which he was investigating. Then Colonel-General Beck had shot himself and three officers, including the Chief-of-Staff, Colonel von Stauffenberg (who was suspected of having carried out the attempt on Hitler's life), had been court-martialled, Fromm presiding. The death sentence had been carried out only half an hour before by a squad of NCO's. There had also been a little shooting in the corridors on the first floor.

This all sounded very wild, though it confirmed what I had learned previously.

None the less, I was very much in the dark and left wondering what to do. I should like to have rung up FHQ, but I could not get through. It was soon made plain that no one was allowed to leave the building. I considered how best to restore peace and order to this disturbed hive and, reflecting that the resumption of work was the best cure, gathered round me the officers I knew personally and suggested they should get on with their jobs, reminding them that the fronts were still holding and calling for reinforcements and supplies. They all agreed and a sensible colonel pointed out that something must be done about some of the orders relating to the revolt which Colonel von Stauffenberg had given. I said I would make myself responsible for any decisions necessary and in particular for the cancellation of the alert all over Europe, which had been issued under the code word "Walkure". It soon appeared that action along those lines had been taken already.

In a few hours the machinery was functioning perfectly once more, though I often shudder at the thought of all the decisions I had to take in the absence of the three top men at the Bendlerstrasse, Fromm, Olbricht and von Stauffenberg.

I got FHQ on the telephone at last and pressed hard for the appointment of a general to be put in charge of headquarters staff, and for my release. Though I repeated this request every few hours until the early hours of the 22nd July, all the answer I got was that nothing had been decided and I must carry on.

That morning Himmler arrived with the SS Chief-of-Staff, Obergruppenführer Jüttner. To everyone's surprise he had been appointed C.-in-C. Home Forces. Now, at last, I could return in peace to Friedenthal, and though I tumbled into bed tired, I was profoundly relieved to think that my active intervention was at an end.

I should, perhaps, be creating a false impression if I spoke of the "defeat" of the plot and the plotters, because everyone with direct knowledge of the affair will agree that after their first blow had failed, all of them, with the exception of Colonel von Stauffenberg himself, became hopelessly irresolute and resigned to the worst, so that a slight push from a handful of opponents brought the whole house of cards tumbling to the ground.

I may say that I have the greatest respect for any man who is prepared to give his life for his convictions. In that respect there is no difference between the battlefield and the concentration camp. No normal human being wants to lose his life, but a moment may come for all of us in which we have to choose between our existence and what we believe in.

After more than ten hours sleep I was a different man, but it was only natural that I was constantly reviewing the events of the last two days. My first feeling was one of fury against men who had apparently tried to stab the German nation in the back when it was fighting for its life. Yet they must have had honourable motives as well. I suddenly recalled details of very frank conversations I had had at various times with all sorts of officers in the Bendlerstrasse. Many of them had made it quite plain that they were anything but followers of Hitler or advocates of national socialism. They were simply Germans who always, and in all circumstances, put Germany's interests first.

The "rebels" had agreed only on one thing—that Hitler must not remain head of the state—but were at sixes and sevens as to what was to happen afterwards and, in particular, how they were to achieve their main object, a tolerable peace after a hopeless war. One section, to which Stauffenberg belonged, advocated a separate peace with Russia, while the others favoured the Western Allies. Yet according to an announcement on the English radio as early as the 20th July (Hitler's death must have been assumed), neither approach would have had any chance of success, as any new German government would have to make peace with west and east simultaneously, and only on the Casablanca "unconditional surrender" basis. In that case, what could either section have achieved?

One direct result of these fateful days was an extension of my activities. Section 2 of the former Counter-espionage department, which had been converted into Military Section D in March, was put under my command. As I knew my limitations, I established good personal relations with Colonel Neumann, the previous chief of Section 2. He became my deputy, and I retained only the most important decision for myself.

The work of the Intelligence Units at the front had become routine and I made no change in it.

What interested me even more was that large numbers of men from the "Brandenburg" Division now volunteered for service with me, men who were tired of the ordinary duties of a unit in the line and keen on service with commando units. After various negotiations with the divisional staff in Berlin and the Wehrmacht chiefs, two orders were issued which promised well for our chances of future employment. On Jodl's orders my commando battalion was expanded to a formation of six battalions, and 1,800 officers and men from the Brandenburg Division who had volunteered were transferred to it.

Before I go on to my next chapter I should like to refer briefly to a few of the exploits of my formation in the summer and autumn of 1944.

After the invasion succeeded, our High Command feared that the Allies would violate the neutrality of Switzerland, and I was ordered to have my frogmen ready to blow up the Rhine bridges at Basle. A few weeks later these orders were countermanded, as it became clear that our enemies had no such intention.

In the autumn of 1944, my commando battalion 502 carried out an extremely interesting exercise under the command of von Foelkersam and Hunke. We arranged with the manager of a munition factory near Berlin that on a certain day some of my men should try to enter it disguised as foreign saboteurs and put it out of action.

The experiment was amazingly successful. Furnished with forged identity cards, twenty of our commandos got into the works without being detected by workmen or the special anti-sabotage personnel, and placed "explosives" in the most delicate and important parts of the machinery.

The personnel in question had to make a long and detailed report to the relevant authorities and I suspect that the instructions and orders to factory managers were subsequently very much tightened up.

This affair taught me that the success of enemy agents in Germany could not have been very great, because otherwise we should have had more, and more serious, reports of sabotage damage in our war industries. It also taught me that enemy saboteurs had little to fear from "anti-sabotage squads" and similar organizations.

Work had also been found for us in the east. In August, 1944, I received an urgent summons to FHQ, where Colonel-General Jodl referred me to two staff officers, who gave me the following information:

After the collapse of the Centre Army Group in June, a reconnaissance commando (a formation from the Intelligence Units detailed to serve with each army) had received a wireless message from a Russian agent, who had been in German service since the beginning of the war, to the effect that in the forest region north of Minsk there was a body of German troops which had not surrendered. This information was confirmed by some German soldiers who managed to get back, and supplemented by the agent himself when he got through to our lines. He said that the isolated force was a battle group of about two thousand men under the command of a Lieutenant-Colonel Scherhorn, and he was able to give a fairly close description of exactly where it was.

The staff officers added that various attempts had been made by the reconnaissance commando to get in touch with the missing battle group, but without success. GHQ now wanted every effort to be made to find the Scherhorn group, and get it back to our lines. Could I do it?

I replied that we could certainly do what was at all possible, as I knew that our most suitable officers and men for the job—Balts— would jump at the chance of rescuing their countrymen.

A plan was quickly worked out at Friedenthal and given the code name of " Freischütz ". Its execution was entrusted to Battalion " East ", which I had just formed. The essential features of the scheme was that there should be four groups, each of five men, of whom two would be drawn from Commando East, and the other three would be Russians. Each group would have a wireless trans- mitting set, parachute rations for four weeks, tents, etc., and Russian machine-pistols. It goes without saying that all the men had to be disguised as Russian soldiers. All the necessary papers and passes were prepared and, as far as we could tell, no detail was forgotten. The men even had to get used to the Russian " machorka " cigar- ettes, had their heads shaved and forgot about washing and shaving in the days immediately preceding the raid. They were given a supply of Russian black bread and tinned stuff, which they could produce even if they did not eat it.

Two of the groups were to be put down near Borisov and Cervenj, east of Minsk, and search the area to the west. If they did not find the Scherhorn group, they were to try and fight their way back through the Russian lines. The third and fourth groups were to be dropped near Djerzinsk and Viteika respectively, and make a con- centric approach to Minsk. If they did not contact Scherhorn they too were to get back as best they could.

We appreciated that our plan could only be a basis for the opera- tion and that once on Russian soil the groups might have to be left to their own devices and to act as the situation required, though we hoped we should be able to keep in wireless contact with them and issue further instructions in any emergency. Our idea was that if the Scherhorn group was found, a temporary landing strip could be constructed and we could gradually get the men out by air.

At the end of August the first group, commanded by Sergeant P., was dropped by a He 111 of Squadron 200. Waiting for news of the return of the aircraft was an anxious business, for at that time the Vistula was the front line, the dropping zone was five hundred kilometres away to the east, fighter escort was impossible and the flight could only be made at night in the prevailing weather.

That night we heard that it had passed without incident and the group had been duly dropped at the appointed spot. Early next morning the reconnaissance commando got a wireless message from P.'s group: "We made a bad landing. Trying to regroup under machine-gun fire." . . . At that point the message broke off. It looked as if the group had had to bolt and leave the transmitter behind. Night after night, our wireless man remained glued to his receiver, but nothing more came through from the group. Not a very encouraging start!

At the beginning of September, the second group set out under the command of Ensign Sch. On their return, the air-crew reported a smooth and successful drop. For four days we heard nothing at all from the group and began to fear the worst and wonder what had happened. On the sixth night, an answer was received to the call signal. The correct password was given and also the secret codeword indicating that the speaker was not being held by the Russians. Then came the splendid news that Scherhorn's group had been found!

Next evening, Lieutenant-Colonel Scherhorn spoke to us himself. His few simple, soldierly words of thanks were ample reward for what we had done.

The third group was dropped on the night after the second. We never heard from it at all. It was swallowed up in the vast distances of Russia.

The fourth and last group, under the command of Sergeant R., was dropped a day later. For the first few days it reported fairly regularly. The men had all landed together, but they had lost direction a bit, as they had to keep out of the way of Russian police troops. They had met some Russian deserters, who took them for deserters also. The people of White Russia were friendly.

On the fourth day the wireless messages suddenly stopped, so we were no longer able to let R. know the approximate position of Scherhorn's group. The nerve-racking waiting for news began again. I asked for a daily report from Adrian von Foelkersam, who was specially concerned in the affair, both as Chief-of-Staff of the commando formations, and as a countryman of the Balts employed in it. Always the same answer came back: "No news from groups R., M. and F."

But three weeks later a telephone call came from a corps, which was somewhere on the Lithuanian frontier: "Group R. has turned up, and without loss."

What Sergeant R. had to say was of the greatest military interest, as he was one of the few Germans who had actually seen what was going on behind the Russian front. He told us what the Russian leaders really meant by "total war"! Every woman and child was roped in to work for the army, if occasion required. Where transport was lacking, the civil population was employed in carrying petrol containers right up to the front line and shells were passed from hand to hand to the artillery positions. We had a lot to learn from the Russians!

Sergeant R. had even had the audacity to enter an officers' mess disguised as a Russian lieutenant. Lest my readers be surprised at my use of the words "officers' mess", I should remind them that, in the course of the war, the Russian army revived many of the old traditions—the broad Czarist shoulder-strap, for instance. The guest spoke such perfect Russian that his hosts had not the slightest suspicion who he was. A few days later he returned to our lines and naturally played a most active part in our further efforts to help the Scherhorn group.

The most urgent requirements of this group were medical supplies and a doctor. The dropping ground indicated was lit so badly that the first doctor we put down broke both legs and a later message reported that he had subsequently died. The arrival of the second was more than welcome. Next on the list came food, and then small arms and ammunition. As a result of their privations, the health of the men was so bad that there could be no question at the moment of an attempt to find their way back.

Squadron 200 flew a supply plane every second or third night, but we received complaints that the dropping was inaccurate and much was being lost. Each lost consignment had to be replaced.

Then we worked out with the squadron's technical experts a plan for bringing out Scherhorn's group. A landing-strip must be laid down from which the casualties first, and then as many men as possible, could be evacuated. We fixed the dark nights of October as the most suitable time.

An aerodrome technician was put down by parachute. Unfortunately, we learned by wireless that the construction of the landing-strip and take-off was soon discovered by the Russians and made impossible by gunfire, so we had to think up a new idea, which met with Scherhorn's approval. The group was to find its way to a lake region 250 kilometres to the north, on the former Russian-Lithuanian frontier near Dvinsk. These lakes usually froze over towards the beginning of December and could then be used as aerodromes.

To facilitate the march of so large a formation behind the Russian lines, Scherhorn divided it into two sections. He was to take over the command of the southern party himself, while the advance party of the northern would be led by our Ensign Sch.

For this march the men needed warm clothes and a mass of other things. Formidable quantities were involved. In addition, we had to supply nine more wireless sets—and Russians to work them—to maintain wireless communication between the two sections if they got widely separated.

It was a great day for me when I sent Ensign Sch. the notification of his promotion to lieutenant and of the award to him of the Knight's Cross of the Iron Cross. The receipt of my congratulations was very warmly acknowledged.

In November, 1944, the two columns started off. The wounded were taken in Russian *panje* carts. Progress was slower than we had hoped—not more than 8 to 10 kilometres a day. As occasional stops for a day or so proved necessary, it was found that 30 to 40 kilometres a week was the usual rule. Then the wireless messages spoke increasingly of clashes with Russian police troops and all of us who knew the country began to shed our illusions. There was very little chance of the Scherhorn force getting back.

It was true that our supply aircraft had not so far to go, but the dropping zones, which were constantly changing, were becoming more difficult to find, even though they were indicated and plotted on our squared maps, and Verey lights were fired at the moment appointed. I have no idea how much of the stuff we dropped was picked up by the very efficient Russian Security Police.

But that was not our only worry. Every week fuel supplies were getting shorter. From time to time, I managed to extract a special

ration of four or five tons for "Operation Freischutz", but it became more and more difficult. I can well believe that, in their
desperation, Scherhorn and his men were quite at a loss to account
for our behaviour, though I did my best in personal messages to
convince him that we were doing all we could.

In February, 1945, I was commanding a division on the eastern
front. Although we were engaged in fierce action every day, I was
still in charge of all the commando operations. News of "Freischutz" arrived almost every night and it got more and more
depressing. The only cheering feature was that the Scherhorn
group had joined up with P.'s commando, which had been missing
for months. The trouble was that the distance was now nearly
800 kilometres and we could not send a plane more than once a
week. I racked my brains to devise some other method, but all in
vain.

At the end of February we were refused any more petrol—a
development which made me furious when I remembered what vast
stores of oil were falling into the hands of the advancing enemy
every day. There were hundreds of tons of it on the airfields in the
Warthegau, now in Russian occupation.

About this time Lieutenant Sch. wirelessed: "My advance guard
has reached the lake region. We shall starve if we don't get some
food at once." The despairing cry was heard time and again, but
we were helpless. At the very end he was asking merely for enough
juice to charge the batteries of his wireless accumulators. "All I
want is to remain in touch with you and hear your voices," he said.
But the war was rushing to its close and the relevant authorities far
too bewildered to pay any attention to us. It was the end. We
must abandon thoughts of bringing the Scherhorn group back, or
even reaching it.

Yet the retreat and constant changes of position did not prevent
our wireless men from listening patiently every night. They still
got occasional contact. Then came the 8th of May and "Operation
Freischütz" was over.

When I became a prisoner, I spent many a sleepless night thinking about it. None of Scherhorn's or my own men ever got back.
I wondered whether the Russians were having a game with us all
the time. Of course we had taken precautions against the possibility. Every wireless operator was given a special keyword, which he
must use to show that he could speak freely. But, during my cap-

tivity, I learned so much about methods of detection that I have my doubts. I had a wholesome respect for the skill of the Russians and their allies. Perhaps the puzzle will be solved some day.

CHAPTER XI

FOELKERSAM AND I had vainly hoped that we should be able to get on with the business of making the Special Force what we intended it to be—a self-contained, effective force capable of carrying out an offensive operation, at any rate on a small scale. But about 10th September, 1944, I got a sudden call to come to FHQ at the "Wolf's Den".

This was no longer far behind the front, which was now only 100 kilometres away. General Jodl informed me that I was to attend conferences at FHQ because an important assignment for me and my formation in the south-eastern area was under consideration. This was the first time I was called on to be present at the Führer's Staff Conference, though, of course, I attended only the discussions about that front, which were usually conducted by Colonel-General Jodl himself. Yet during those conferences I learned quite a lot about the confusing conditions prevailing at the summit of the military hierarchy. The Supreme Command of the Army (OKH) was in charge of the eastern front only. All the other fronts, including the Balkan, took their orders from the High Command of the Wehrmacht. The navy and the Luftwaffe sent their own officers to the conferences. The only co-ordinating factor in the whole set-up was Adolf Hitler, who had made himself head of all the fighting forces in 1941.

At the heart of the "Wolf's Den" was the central building, fifty metres from the new "Führer Bunker", which had just been built and provided a good bomb shelter with its seven metres of steel and concrete. It had no windows, but a complicated system of ventilation. Yet the atmosphere inside was unhealthy. I was told that the concrete had never properly dried out; it steamed most unpleasantly.

The main building, provided with big windows and containing

the main conference room hall, and several smaller conference and telephone rooms, was also far more inviting. The conferences, or "appreciations of the situation", were held daily at 2 and 11 p.m., and it was at these that the great decisions were taken.

The conference room was about 7 by 21 metres. On the window side was a long table, on which the war maps were laid out. The door was in the centre of the wall opposite the windows and near it was a round table and a number of armchairs.

When I entered for my first conference, most of the generals, staff officers and civil officials had already arrived. I knew very few of them and had to be introduced. A brisk command announced the entrance of Adolf Hitler. He was accompanied by Keitel and Jodl.

I was deeply shocked at the appearance of the Supreme Commander, remembering how he looked when I last saw him only the previous autumn. He stooped and seemed years older, and there was a weary tone in his deep base voice. I wondered whether he had been smitten by some insidious disease. His left hand trembled so violently that he had to steady himself with his right when he got up. His condition could have been the result of the bomb explosion on the 20th July, or he might be just giving way under the enormous burden of responsibility he had been carrying for so long. I could not help speculating whether this tired old man could still have sufficient energy to carry on.

Adolf Hitler shook hands with some of the officers present and then addressed a few kind words to me and ordered me to attend every conference on the situation in the Balkans. Then he asked for the reports. Two stenographers took their places at the table. There was a stool for the Führer, which he rarely used, but everyone else remained standing. His glasses and array of coloured pencils were within easy reach.

Field-Marshal Keitel stood on his left, Jodl on his right. The latter opened the proceedings by describing the general situation. His report could be followed on the big General Staff map. Various corps, divisions and armoured regiments were referred to by their numbers. Here the Russians had attacked but been beaten off. There the enemy had effected a deep penetration, but countermeasures were being taken. The Führer's memory for detail—regimental numbers, how many tanks were battleworthy, what reinforcements and supplies were available, and so forth—was quite astonishing.

He poured out masses of figures and ordered various troop movements, referring only to the map. The situation was serious. The front lay approximately along the Hungarian 1938 frontier, apart from a few places where the Russians had broken in. Even my own experience prompted some unspoken questions: Were the divisions mentioned still battleworthy? What about their guns and transport? How many more guns and tanks had they lost since the last reports came in?

"There will be no great decisions to-day," I heard some staff officers whisper. I had forgotten that in this milieu men thought only in terms of big units such as corps and armies, and that it was here that the critical decisions were taken.

When the Luftwaffe representative made his report, the atmosphere became strained. Adolf Hitler seemed to lose patience and the old note of complaint crept into his voice as he asked the speaker to be more precise. The once idolized Luftwaffe appeared to be out of favour. The number of aircraft said to be employed did not sound convincing. The Führer cut short the recital with a wave of the hand and turned away. General Jodl nodded to me to leave the room. Other sectors of the front were now on the agenda.

I stayed, talking in an ante-room with some junior staff officers. An orderly offered us a glass of vermouth. We discussed the eastern front. At that time the revolt of the Polish Underground in Warsaw was in full swing. The fighting there must be terrible. The position south of Warsaw was even worse and the news very bad. "We cannot possibly tell the Führer the truth," remarked one of the officers. "It's got to be ironed out somehow."

Three days later I happened to be present when other fronts were being discussed and was not asked to leave the room. An officer spoke frankly about the critical situation on the Polish front. Adolf Hitler jumped up and shouted at him: "Why wasn't I told about this before?" He flung his pencils down on the map table and some of them fell on the floor. He railed against Jodl, OKH and the Luftwaffe. No one stirred or said a word and I myself shrank back behind the others.

Almost as alarming was the way in which he suddenly recovered his self-control and quietly addressed a number of technical questions to another officer. "Are reserves still available? Cannot an ammunition train get there in time? Is there a heavy pioneer unit near by?" It was in that fashion that the work of patching up the front and filling holes was commenced.

In the course of that afternoon I ran into Hanna Reitsch. We were glad to meet again. She told me that she had come with Colonel-General von Greim, showed me her quarters and asked me to visit them that evening.

After the evening conference (it was nearly midnight), I groped my way in the darkness to the building she had mentioned. In a big room, which was both living and sleeping quarters, Hanna Reitsch introduced me to Colonel-General Ritter von Greim. His white hair, carefully parted, surmounted a pleasant face and clear-cut features. I noticed the *Pour le Mérite* order of the first war under his Knight's Cross. We were soon engaged in a serious and animated discussion, the theme of which was the war and the Luftwaffe. I was astonished at the energy and enterprise of which the General still showed himself capable. Before long he was telling me of the real meaning of his presence at FHQ: Reichsmarschall Hermann Göring was to relinquish command of the Luftwaffe, and von Greim was to be appointed his successor. But the matter had not yet been finalized. Göring still wished to keep the general policy of the Luftwaffe in his own hands. Von Greim did not agree. The Führer had not yet given his decision.

Two whole nights I spent talking with these two outstanding personalities, both of whom were idealists in the best sense of that word. Though no novelty, it amazed me to hear how bitterly the handling of the Luftwaffe, and above all Göring himself, were criticized by von Greim. "The Luftwaffe has been resting on the laurels it deservedly won in 1939 and 1940," he said. "It has not been thinking of the future. Göring himself used the words 'we have the best, fastest and bravest air force in the world, and it can win the war by itself!'"

I do not recollect all the details of our long conversations, but one of his criticisms remains in my memory. He said that the new jet fighters were in action, though years too late. Perhaps they would help us to beat off the continuous air attacks on German cities and enable us to recover mastery of the air, at least partially. It was pertinent to enquire whether these jet fighters could not have been available long before. Production could have started in 1942. Was this another chapter of German history to which the words "too late" could be applied?

Unfortunately, Colonel-General von Greim was not then appointed head of the Luftwaffe. It was only at the end of 1944, when Berlin lay in ruins, that he took over that office. He was seriously wounded flying over the capital, then completely isolated, with his faithful companion Hanna Reitsch, and a fortnight later was captured by the Americans at Kitzbühl. There the allies tried to compel him to talk against his superior, Göring. This was one of the reasons for his suicide. A man of honour took his knowledge of Göring's responsibility towards the German people with him to the grave.

At the conference on the third day, I was told to remain behind. The Führer had also asked Keitel, Jodl, Ribbentrop and Himmler not to go. We sat at the same round table in the corner. Hitler gave a short dissertation on the situation in the south-east. He said that the front on the Hungarian border had just been stabilized and must be maintained there at all costs. In the vast bulge there were more than a million German troops, who would be lost for good if there was a sudden collapse. "We have received secret reports," he said, "that the head of the Hungarian state, Admiral Horthy, is attempting to get in touch with our enemies with a view to a separate peace. It would mean the loss of our armies. He is approaching both the western powers and the Russians. He is even prepared to throw himself on the mercy of the Kremlin.

"You, Skorzeny," he continued, "must be prepared to seize the Citadel of Budapest by force, if he betrays his alliance with us. The General Staff is thinking of a *coup de main* with parachute or glider troops. The command of the whole operation in that city has been entrusted to the new Corps Commander, General Kleemann. You are under his orders for this affair, but must push ahead at once with your preparations, as the Corps staff is still being got together."

It was in these words that Adolf Hitler put his audacious plan before his little audience. He continued: "To make it easier for you to cope with any difficulties in getting your force together, you will receive from me written orders and wide powers." Colonel-General Jodl then read out a list of the units placed under my orders. It included one parachute battalion from the Luftwaffe, parachute battalion No. 600 of the Waffen SS, and one motorized infantry battalion formed from members of the Officer Cadet Training School at Wiener-Neustadt. Two sections of gliders had been notified and given movement orders. "An aircraft from the FHQ transportation pool will be placed at your disposal for the duration of the operation," added General Jodl.

Adolf Hitler went on to discuss with Ribbentrop the reports just received from the German Embassy in Budapest, which were to the effect that the situation was very strained and the Hungarian government was showing itself far from well disposed towards its axis partner.

The written order was handed over to me after it had been signed and the party went their different ways. With the words "I rely on you and your men", the Führer left the room.

I remained behind alone and when I read what was written on the paper, I was more than amazed at the possibilities it offered. It was a sheet of so-called state paper, with an eagle and swastika in gold at the top left-hand corner and underneath the words "Der Führer und Reichskanzler" in old-fashioned script. This document (which was lost during the troubles of 1945, or to be more accurate, stolen with the rest of my belongings) was more or less in these terms:

"Sturmbannführer Skorzeny is carrying out a personal and highly confidential order of the highest importance. I order all political and military authorities everywhere to give him all the help he needs and comply with his wishes."

At the foot was the signature—by now a very shaky signature—of the head of the German state. I may say that I had to produce the document on only one rather unimportant occasion.

After reading my orders—it was already 2 a.m.—I still had work to do. Two days previously I had taken the precaution of warning the "Mitte" commando, formerly SS infantry battalion 502, to be ready for action. I knew that, even at this late hour, Captain von Foelkersam would still be expecting a call from me, so I promptly got through to Friedenthal. "Hallo, Foelkersam. I've just received an important new assignment! Get out your pencil and write down: The 1st company at full strength will emplane at Gatow airfield at 8 a.m. to-day. Treble ammunition supply and don't forget explosives for four pioneer detachments. Emergency rations for six days. Lieutenant Hunke will be in command. Our destination is known to the commander of Ju Flight 52. I'm leaving here by air as early as possible and will land before ten at the aerodrome of the Heinkel works at Oranienburg. Meet me there. Two hours

later you, Radl and Ostafel will fly on with me. Any questions?
Password 'take it easy!' as before."

Having got things going at Friedenthal, I decided on "panzerfaust" as the code word for the new operation. Then I recollected
that I had not informed Friedenthal accordingly and made good
the omission by telegraph.

Then I remembered that I had gliders at my disposal, and also
parachute troops. But how could the General Staff be thinking
of parachute or glider landings on the Citadel? I knew my Budapest pretty well.

The only possible landing-place in the city was the big open space
known as the "Field of Blood". But if the Hungarians were
hostile, this area would be completely commanded from the Citadel,
not to mention the other three sides, and our fellows would be shot
to pieces before they could assemble. I should not be able to put
down more than a handful of special troops there, and then only
if the situation at the time permitted.

Following our flight to Vienna, Foelkersam, Ostafel and I drove
on straight to Wiener-Neustadt from Aspern. Radl was to contact
the Intelligence Headquarters as further news might have come
through. In Wiener-Neustadt we reported at the old "Kriegsakademie", which had traditions going back to the time of Maria
Theresa. In the lofty corridors the portraits of former comman-
dants gazed down upon us. The commandant in office, Colonel
H., had been told of our coming. When I explained what was
afoot, he was most anxious to lead the battalion himself, and I had
some trouble in convincing him that, in view of his seniority, it
would hardly be appropriate. But he refused to be denied the
opportunity of participating as a freelance.

Then the battalion commander selected, a major, and the company commanders were called in. They were all old-front fighters,
who had been transferred as instructors to the Akademie. Meanwhile, all the suitable cadets had been assembled in the court. There
were nearly a thousand of them. When I passed down the ranks to
familiarize myself with my new command, I could almost have
jumped for joy. Germany would find it hard to produce such a
hand-picked selection, I thought. Battalions of that calibre were
almost non-existent. I felt proud to be leading such men and something of my feelings must have been betrayed in the short speech I
made to them: "You have, no doubt, heard my name from your

officers and many of you will remember the Italian affair. But don't think that I'm merely taking you on another adventure. It will be a serious and perhaps bloody business and the stake is high. You and I will do our duty together, and as we believe in our cause we will do what we set out to do and thereby serve our country and our people."

The SS parachute battalion had also arrived in the vicinity of Vienna, and both officers and men made a good impression. I had a feeling, however, that I must keep them well in hand, as they seemed only too prone to act on their own—a procedure which could well endanger the success of the whole expedition! What shape it would take I then had no idea. I could not even tell how the situation in Hungary would develop.

After arriving in Budapest it was three days before we had settled the motorization and equipment problems, and then I felt it was time I had a look round the city myself. The papers for a certain " Dr. Wolff ", a gentlemen of about my size, were soon produced. I slipped into comfortable civilian clothes, an acquaintance gave me an introduction to a friend in the city and I was ready to start.

The friend, a business man, gave us the sort of welcome of which only Hungarians are capable. His hospitality extended to placing his whole house, and the butler and cook, at my disposal. I almost blush to say that I had never lived so luxuriously as in these three weeks—and in the fifth year of the war too! Our host would have been positively insulted if we had not done full justice to his menus.

My Corps Commander had also arrived in Budapest. He had his work cut out to get together an effective staff and train his troops to the requisite standard. I lent him Foelkersam and Ostafel to work with the Corps staff. The first thing was to devise a plan to alert all the troops in and around the city, so that they would be ready for action at any moment. It was essential that all railways, stations, post-offices and other transport and communication centres should always be in German hands.

Our Intelligence had ascertained that Niklas von Horthy, the son of the head of the state, had had a secret meeting with some delegates from Tito, with a view to getting in touch with the Russian High Command and opening negotiations for a separate peace. FHQ had obviously been accurately informed on the matter. The fact that Tito should be used seemed to me quite incomprehensible. How was it possible for the Protector of Hungary to seek the good offices of her mortal enemy, Yugoslavia? What sort of fate could he expect for himself and his country?

I suggested to the top men of our Intelligence Service that an attempt should be made to introduce one of our agents into the negotiations. In this we were successful. A Croat managed to be well received, both by the Yugoslav delegates and Niklas von Horthy himself, and to win the confidence of both parties, and we thus learned that there was to be a meeting with old Horthy himself, one night in the immediate future. This was a shock, as it was not in our interests that the head of the state should be personally involved in the affair. But I felt that this was a headache for the Intelligence people and the Security Police. I had plenty of troubles of my own.

Every time I visited the Citadel, ostensibly to see the Air Attaché, German Ambassador or Corps Commander, I became more and more worried as to how we should tackle this natural fortress. Though my original instructions on the point were not too clear, I could not see how we could prevent the defection of the Hungarian government by anything less than an operation against the whole government quarter and the Citadel. Any such action must be preceded by some hostile act against Germany. It could only be a swift answer to such an act.

Foelkersam was therefore instructed to make a most careful study of all available plans of the city and supplement his knowledge with minute inspection of the streets and buildings. The result of his labours was full of surprises. There was a labyrinth of passages under the Citadel—a nasty " snag " for us.

The " alert " plan, which had now been worked out, provided that I and the detachment under my command should effect a military occupation of the Citadel. I had abandoned the idea of a glider or parachute landing altogether.

It was now time for my troops to come to Budapest. The GOC Corps insisted that there should be no further delay. They left Vienna about the beginning of October, and took up their quarters in the suburbs.

In the first week of October, SS Obergruppenführer Bach-Zelevski also came to Budapest. He had been sent by the FHQ to take charge of all proceedings in the city. Having come from

Warsaw, where he had just put down the rising of the Polish Underground, he took care to let us know at our conferences that he was a "strong man". He told us he was determined to be as ruthless as he had been in Warsaw. He had even brought a 65 cm. mortar with him, a weapon which had only been brought into play twice before—at the sieges of Sebastopol and Warsaw.

I considered his methods unnecessarily brutal, and said that we would attain our ends better and quicker in other and less objectionable ways. "Operation Panzerfaust" could succeed without the help of the famous mortar. Many of the officers seemed impressed by Bach-Zelevski's intervention and almost afraid of him, but I disregarded his bad manners, stuck to my point of view and got it accepted.

I could not understand why fifteen or twenty officers should be present at conferences when the alert plan was discussed. It seemed to me that the Hungarian government was bound to hear of them and act accordingly. We received a very alarming report from our Intelligence that General M., commanding the Hungarian army in the Carpathians, was personally engaged in direct negotiations with the Russians. Of course that information was transmitted to FHQ, but it issued no definite orders as to what counter-measures should be taken. Conference followed conference.

On the night of the 10th October, there was a meeting between Horthy junior and the Yugoslav delegates. The German police were warned in advance, but took no action. The next meeting was to take place on Sunday, the 15th, in the vicinity of the Danube quay. Just before the 15th, FHQ sent General Wenck to Budapest with orders to take command if necessary and issue such orders as he thought fit. The Security Police were determined to take action at the first opportunity and arrest the Protector's son and the Yugoslav delegates. The code-word "Mouse" was chosen for this operation, owing to Niklas's nickname, "Nicky", being mistaken for Micky. The association with "Micky Mouse" was obvious.

The adoption of this plan by the police was based on the supposition that the Protector, to avoid the public exposure of his son, would mend his ways and abandon the plan for a separate peace.

General Winkelman had asked me to have a company of my men ready for that afternoon. He said that he knew that Niklas von Horthy's previous meetings had been guarded by Honved troops.

If he was right, I could see that my men were considered in the light of a counterblast. I agreed on condition that I myself should decide how and when they should intervene.

On the Saturday, I received an urgent telegram from Berlin, ordering me, to my sorrow, to send Radl back to Berlin. He was very annoyed, but of course complied.

The 15th October was a bright Sunday. The streets were empty at the time appointed for the rendezvous. My company was in a side street in covered trucks. Captain von Foelkersam kept me in touch with them, as obviously I could not show myself in uniform that day. If I was to appear on the stage, so to speak, I must be inconspicuous. My driver and another man, both Luftwaffe personnel, were taking the air on a seat in the little garden which occupied most of the square. I drove up in my own car shortly before the meeting began. When I entered the square, I noticed a Hungarian military lorry and a private car, which was presumably Horthy's, stationed in front of the building of which we had been told. It took me no time to make up my mind and park my own car right in the path of these vehicles, so that they could not get away in a hurry.

The floor above the offices in this building had been occupied the day before by policemen, who had taken lodgings near by. Others were to enter it from the street about 10.10 p.m., and make the arrests.

Three Honved officers were sitting in the covered lorry, but could not be seen from the street. Two others were lounging on benches in the gardens. I was standing by my car, pretending to be fiddling with the engine, when the curtain rose on the drama.

The first German policeman had hardly entered the building when there was a burst of machine-pistol fire from the lorry, and the second fell to the ground with a wound in the stomach. The two other Hungarian officers came running out of the gardens, firing their revolvers. I had just time to take cover behind my car when its open door was drilled. Things were getting really hot! Honved soldiers appeared at the windows and on the balconies of houses. The moment the first shots rang out, my driver and his companion rushed up to me, assuming that I had been hit. The driver was shot through the thigh, but could still walk. I gave the agreed signal to my detachment, and we three defended ourselves with our weapons as best we could against the rain of fire from the enemy. It was a most uncomfortable situation, though it only lasted a few minutes.

By then my car was not much more than a sieve. Bullets ricocheting from walls passed unpleasantly near and we could only put our noses out of cover for long enough to have pot shots at the enemy and keep them at least 10 to 15 metres away.

Then I heard my men running out of the side street in our direction. Foelkersam had taken the situation in at a glance and posted the first section at the corner of the square, while the others swept through the gardens and began firing at the house-fronts. My first assailants now withdrew to the shelter of a nearby house, which was occupied by Hungarians in some strength. I observed that these men were lining up for an assault and quick thinking inspired us to hurl a number of grenades in the doorway, thereby bringing down the door and some marble slabs, which temporarily blocked the entrance.

With that the fighting ceased. It may have lasted five minutes.

Our policemen now came down from the upper floor, bringing four prisoners with them. The two Hungarians, "Micky Mouse" and his comrade Bornemisza, were bundled into one of our trucks. To conceal their identity, our fellows had tried to roll them up in carpets, with only partial success, I observed, noting the effort required to get the refractory prisoners into the vehicle.

The lorry moved off and my company withdrew. I was anxious to avoid further scuffles, which were only too likely when the enemy recovered from his surprise. Fortunately, our retirement passed without further incident.

Some instinct prompted me to follow the truck. Another car and driver were available for me. Barely a hundred metres from the square, under the Elizabeth bridge, I saw three Honved companies approaching at the double. If they got any nearer, they could easily find themselves involved in a mix-up with my men—an eventuality I was determined to prevent at all costs. Time must be gained somehow, but bluff was my only resource. I told my driver to pull up, and ran towards the officer who appeared to be in command. "Halt your men quick!" I yelled. "There's a hell of a mix-up going on up there! No one knows what's happening! You'd better find out for yourself first!"

The trick came off. The troops halted and the officer seemed undecided what to do. It was lucky for me that he knew some

German, as otherwise he might not have understood me. The short pause was vital from my point of view. By now, my own men must have got away in their trucks. "I must get on!" I called to the Hungarian officer, jumped into my car and made for the aerodrome. When I arrived, the two Hungarians were in a plane, and two minutes later they were on their way to Vienna.

My next destination was Corps Headquarters, in a hotel at the top of a hill. Here I met General Wenck. We were all wondering what would happen now. It was known that the Hungarians had been taking military precautions at the Citadel for some days. The garrison had been reinforced and it was said that some of the streets had been mined.

About midday, a call came through from the German Embassy, lodged in a small palace on the Citadel. The Military Attaché told us that the Citadel was now being officially occupied by Honved troops, and the gates and roads were closed to traffic. He had tried to get away himself, but had been turned back. Shortly afterwards, the telephone wires must have been cut, as we could not get through. The German establishments, of which there were several, were practically isolated.

Just before 2 o'clock, we were told to stand by for a special announcement on the Hungarian wireless. A message from the Regent, Admiral Horthy, came through: "Hungary has concluded a separate peace with Russia!" Now we knew where we were. Our counter-measures must be carried out at once.

Orders for the execution of "Operation Panzerfaust" were also issued. I thought them premature, and asked that it should be postponed for a few hours, and that the immediate reply to the Hungarian action should be to draw a cordon of German troops round the Citadel. This job was assigned to the 22nd SS Division. The occupation by German troops of the railway stations and other important buildings passed off without incident in the afternoon.

A General was dispatched to the Hungarian GHQ at the front. Unfortunately, he arrived too late. General M. and some of his officers and secretaries had already gone over to the Russians. It surprised us greatly that his action, and the Hungarian wireless announcement, did not have such a serious effect on the Hungarian troops as might have been expected. Generally speaking, they remained where they were and few of the officers followed the example of their commander-in-chief. But it was essential that there should be no delay in preventing the Hungarian War Ministry from following up with an order to capitulate.

At a conference late in the afternoon, it was decided that " Operation Panzerfaust " should be carried out early in the morning of the 16th. The slight postponement suited me well, as I could put it to good use. I fixed on 6 a.m. for zero-hour, as I considered surprise essential and the early hours were best from that point of view. Foelkersam and I pored for hours over the plan of the Citadel which we had made, and our ideas of the coming action began to assume definite shape.

I projected a concentric assault, which should yet have a focal point in the centre, which I intended to be a detachment approaching from Vienna Street. The factor of surprise would be of greatest effect at that point. I hoped to rush the Vienna gate with little resistance and without too much noise, and suddenly emerge in the square facing the Citadel. A rapid decision should follow automatically. If we could quickly force our way into the presumed centre of the Hungarian resistance, the action would soon be over, with a minimum of casualties on both sides.

We then instructed our units in their specific tasks. We had been allotted one company of Panther and one of Goliath tanks. Incidentally, these little Goliath tanks were a recent addition to German armament. They were radio-controlled, low, handy affairs, with caterpillar tracks and a big explosive charge in the bows. They could prove very useful in breaking down any barricades or gates.

The battalion of the Wiener-Neustadt Kriegsakademie was to attack through the gardens on the southern slope of the Citadel, no small undertaking, as we knew that these gardens had been converted into a complex of trenches, machine-gun emplacements and anti-aircraft gun positions. Its function was to beat down resistance and facilitate the occupation of the castle.

A platoon of the " Mitte " battalion, reinforced by two Panthers, would attack the western side with the object of forcing one of the entrances at the back, while a platoon of the 600 SS Parachute battalion made its way into the chain-bridge tunnel passing under the Citadel, cleared out the subterranean passages and reached the Ministries of War and Home Affairs above. The rest of the " Mitte " unit, the bulk of the SS Parachute battalion, six Panthers and the Goliath company, were to be available for my *coup de main*. The Luftwaffe parachute battalion would be kept in reserve for emergencies.

The orders for the individual assignments were carefully worked out, and about midnight my troops were in position behind the cordon drawn by the 22nd Division.

The streets had worn their usual appearance all day, as the civil population did not seem to have noticed the activities of either the Hungarian or German troops. The coffee-houses were full as ever, and did not empty until a very late hour. The news from the stations was equally reassuring; supply trains were coming from Germany and passing through to the front in the ordinary way.

Just after midnight, a high-ranking officer of the Hungarian War Ministry presented himself at Corps Headquarters. He had come by some route unknown to us, and said that he was authorized by his Minister to negotiate. We replied that there could be no negotiations until the Regent's proclamation was withdrawn, and also that it was an unfriendly act to hold the members of the embassy and other German organizations prisoner in the Citadel. At my suggestion, the Hungarians were given until 6 a.m. to decide whether they would remove the mines and barricades in Vienna Street leading to the German Embassy. That time was fixed with a view to my design for a surprise attack on the Citadel with a minimum of bloodshed.

About 3 a.m., I went to my command-post at the foot of the Citadel and summoned all my officers. The night was very dark and we had to use our torches when examining our sketch-plans. There were a few details to be cleared up, though my officers had worked hard and familiarized themselves thoroughly with the ground. My second-in-command produced some coffee, which was very welcome on such a nerve-racking occasion.

Meanwhile, I had made my final decision on the procedure to be adopted. We must simply march up the hill to the Citadel and do our best to give the impression that nothing unusual was afoot. The men must stay in their trucks. I knew that my order to that effect was taking a big risk, as they would be defenceless for the first few moments if the convoy was attacked, but I had no option if I wanted a quick end to any scuffle. I informed my battalion commanders of my plans and assured them that if it succeeded they could count on speedy help from the Citadel.

I assembled my column and told the officers that as soon as the

Vienna Gate had been passed it must split in two and proceed at full speed by two parallel roads to the Citadel square. The company and platoon commanders were given strict instructions as to the use of their arms. They were not to reply to casual shots in their direction, and must do everything in their power to arrive at the rendezvous without firing themselves. The watchword must be: "The Hungarians are not our enemies".

Just before 5.30 a.m., when it was beginning to get light, I took my place in my truck at the head of the column. Behind me, I had two Panthers, followed by a platoon of the Goliath company, and the rest of the unit in their trucks. Automatics were set at safety. Most of the men had slumped in their seats and were enjoying a quiet nap. They had the hardened warriors' gift of snatching a bit of sleep when a really tough job lay ahead.

I took the precaution of sending my second-in-command to Corps Headquarters, to ascertain whether there had been any change in the situation, but the answer was in the negative, so zero-hour was adhered to.

In my truck I had Foelkersam and Ostafel, as well as five NCO's who had been in the Gran Sasso show. I considered them my personal assault group. Each was armed with a machine-pistol, a few hand-grenades, and the new *panzerfaust* (bazooka). We were wondering what the Hungarian tanks in the Citadel would do. If necessary our tanks and *panzerfausts* would have to look after them.

At one minute before 6 o'clock, I waved my arm as the signal to switch on. Then I stood up in my truck and pointed upwards several times, whereupon we started off, rather slowly, as it was uphill. I could only hope that none of our vehicles struck a mine, which would have blocked our advance and upset our plan. The Vienna Gate emerged out of the half-light—the way was open! A few Hungarian soldiers stared curiously at us. We were soon at the top. "Gradually accelerate," I whispered to my driver.

On our right was a Honved barracks. "Nasty if we get fired on from the flank," murmured Foelkersam at my side. There were two machine-guns behind sandbags in front of the barracks, but nothing happened. No sound could be heard but the rumble of the Panthers behind.

I chose the side-street on the right in which the German Embassy was situated. We could now travel at a good pace without losing the rest of the column. The tanks were doing a good 35 to 40 kilo-metres to the hour, and at length the Citadel was not more than a thousand metres away and a substantial part of our task had been accomplished.

Now the great detached mass of the War Ministry appeared to the left, and we heard the distant sound of two heavy explosions. Our men must have forced their way through the tunnel. The critical moment was at hand. We were past the War Ministry and in the square in a flash. Three Hungarian tanks faced us, but as we drew level the leading one tilted its gun skywards as a signal that they would not fire.

A barricade of stones had been placed in front of the gate of the Citadel. I told my driver to draw aside and signalled to the leading Panther to charge it. We left our truck and ran behind, while the barricade collapsed under the weight of the thirty-ton monster, which continued its irresistible thrust. Levelling its long gun-barrel at the centre of the courtyard, it found itself faced with a battery of six anti-tank guns.

We leaped over the debris of the barricade and burst through the shattered gate. A colonel of the guard got out his revolver to stop us, but Foelkersam knocked it out of his hand. On our right was what appeared to be the main entrance, and we took it at the run, almost colliding with a Honved officer, whom I ordered to lead us straight to the Commandant. He immediately complied, and at his side we rushed up the broad staircase, not failing to notice the elegant red carpet.

On reaching the first floor we turned left into a corridor, and I left one of my men behind to cover us. The officer pointed to a door and we went into a small ante-room where a table had been drawn up to the open window and a man was lying on it firing a machine-gun into the courtyard. Holzer, a short, stocky NCO, clasped the gun in his arms and flung it out of the window. The gunner was so surprised that he fell off the table.

I saw a door on my right, knocked and walked straight in. A Honved Major-General got up and came towards me. "Are you the Commandant?" I asked. "You must surrender the Citadel at once! If you don't, you will be responsible for any bloodshed. You must decide immediately!" As we could hear shots outside, including bursts of machine-gun fire, I added: "You can see that any resistance is hopeless. I have already occupied the Citadel."

I was speaking the truth, as I was quite certain that the "Mitte" battalion, led by the redoubtable Lieutenant Hunke, was just behind me and must have seized all the strategic points.

The Hungarian Major-General was not long in making up his mind: "I surrender the Citadel and will order the cease-fire at once." We shook hands and soon arranged that a Hungarian officer and one of ours should inform the troops fighting in the Citadel gardens of the cease-fire. After ten minutes had passed, no noise of battle could be heard.

Accompanied, at my request, by two Hungarian majors to serve as interpreters, I went along the corridor to have a look round. We came to the rooms adjoining the Regent's reception room. I was astonished to find that he was not there and learned that he had left shortly before six o'clock. It transpired later that he had been escorted by General Pfeffer-Wildenbruch, of the Waffen SS, to the latter's residence on the Citadel hill. His family had previously taken refuge with the Papal Nuncio. The presence of Horthy would have made no difference to our plans, which were not concerned with him personally, but confined to controlling the seat of government.

While we were looking out of the window over the so-called "Meadow of Blood", a few bullets whistled past. Hunke subsequently explained that it had proved impossible to notify the cease-fire to some of the Hungarian posts on the Danube side of the Citadel gardens. Two rounds from a *panzerfaust* soon convinced them that it would be wiser to abandon resistance.

The whole operation had not taken more than half an hour. Peace returned to the city and the citizens in the vicinity could turn over and go to sleep again. I rang up Corps Headquarters on a special line and could almost hear the sigh of relief at the other end. Apparently they had considered the success of my *coup* as somewhat problematic.

Shortly afterwards, the reports came in from the War Ministry (where alone, there had been a short, sharp action), and the Ministry for Home Affairs, and one by one the commanders of the different groups turned up to relate their experiences. Our casualties had been agreeably low, not more than four killed and about twelve wounded. The only serious fighting had been in the gardens. I asked the Commandant about the Hungarian casualties and was told that they amounted to three killed and fifteen wounded. It was a great satisfaction that the operation had not resulted in serious losses on both sides.

We made the Hungarian other ranks surrender their arms and stack them in the courtyard, but I allowed all officers to retain their revolvers and then invited them to meet me in one of the assembly rooms of the building. I made a short speech, reminding them that there had been no war between Germany and Hungary for centuries and that we had always been loyal allies. I went on to say that even now there was no reason for strife. What everyone wanted was a new Europe, but that could only come into being if Germany was saved.

My Austrian accent certainly reinforced the impression made by my words, to judge by the warmth with which each of the Hungarian officers shook hands with me. In the afternoon they marched back to their barracks with their men and next day took the oath of allegiance to the new government at the War Ministry.

Corps HQ had ordered that I and my troops should remain in occupation of the Citadel until further orders. In the evening, I gave a dinner to all my officers in one of the salons. My guests included the commandant of the Kriegsakademie at Wiener-Neustadt, who was highly delighted that his " eagles ", as he called his cadets, had given such a good account of themselves.

The head of the new Hungarian government came to pay his respects and thank me on its behalf. I replied that I was thankful that the action had been so brief and damage to the splendid buildings had been avoided. I shuddered to think what a mess the 65 cm. mortar of ruthless Herr Bach-Zelevski would have made of them. We agreed that there should be a state funeral for the Hungarian and German dead, the arrangements being left to the government. I welcomed the idea as calculated to put an end to any ill-feeling between the two nations.

I was again reminded of the good old days by my next visitor, an old gentleman wearing an antiquated Austrian field-marshal's uniform. " Servus. Servus! " were his opening words. " I've heard you are a Viennese! Very glad to hear it! So it was you who did the Mussolini business! Splendid! Splendid! " Foelker-sam whispered that our visitor was the Hapsburg Archduke Frederick. I offered him a chair and enquired what I could do for him. " Oh, yes," he said. " There was something I wanted to ask you. I keep my horses in the stables. Can they remain there? "

"Of course, Your Highness," I replied. "Nothing has changed."

In the evening, an order arrived from FHQ that next day, the 18th October, I was to conduct the Regent, as the Führer's guest, in a special train to Schloss Hirschberg, near Weilheim, in Upper Bavaria. I should be responsible for the safety of the train. I chose one company of the "Mitte" battalion to escort it, and arranged that my private plane, which was at the Budapest aerodrome, should wait for me at Riem airfield, near Munich, because I wanted to get back as soon as possible to attend the state funeral.

Next day, I went to General Pfeffer-Wildenbruch's headquarters, and was formally presented to the Regent. I told him I was in charge of the train and learned that we should have his family and two Hungarian generals, Brunsvik and Vattay, with us as well.

As soon as possible, I flew back to Budapest from Munich. I had let my company, which had travelled on the train with its wounded, go on to Friedenthal. I was just in time for the funeral ceremony on the 20th, for which the Citadel provided a fine stage. One German and one Hungarian company did the honours. The seven coffins were draped in the flags of Hungary and Germany. The German dead were subsequently brought home for burial.

I did not see Admiral Horthy again until after the war, when we were both prisoners of the Americans in the Palace of Justice at Nuremburg. He was then occupying the first cell of the ground-floor of the so-called "Witness Wing". When I was transferred from solitary confinement to those more agreeable quarters—it was towards the end of November, 1945—Horthy objected at first, but after a few days' hesitation, the U.S. prison commander, Colonel Andrus, authorized the move. On the suggestion of Field-Marshal Kesselring, the doyen of the prisoners, Horthy agreed to meet me, and we had a pleasant conversation for more than two hours, at the end of which we were good friends and I had learned a great deal. I had been able to satisfy him that "Operation Panzerfaust" was not directed against him personally and he told me that his policy towards Germany had always been friendly, but had been thwarted by difficulties which became insurmountable towards the end of the war. The conversation brought home to me the truth of the old saying, that one must always hear both sides of a question.

On the 20th October, Foelkersam, Ostafel and I were back in our plane and flying straight to Berlin, where a mass of work awaited us which had accumulated during our five weeks' absence. But the moment we landed I was handed an order to report to FHQ the following day. The crew of the aircraft were only too glad of the breather.

CHAPTER XII

NEXT DAY I was summoned to the Führer's bunker. Foelkersam had to wait in the ante-room, as Hitler wanted to see me alone. The passage into the bunker was like the entrance to a fort, and there was nothing but artificial light. Hitler gave me his usual friendly reception and seemed in better form than on the previous occasion. Coming forward with outstretched hands, he burst out: "Well done, Skorzeny! I've promoted you to Obersturmbannführer (Lieutenant-Colonel) with effect from the 16th October, and awarded you the German Cross in gold. No doubt you want decorations for your men, too. You have only to speak to my aide-de-camp, Günsch. It's all arranged. Now tell me all about it." He drew me into a corner, where there was nothing but two armchairs, a table and a standard lamp.

I gave him the whole story of "Operation Mouse", the ultimatum, and our *coup* at the Citadel. He was particularly interested in the work of the Goliath company and my speech to the Hungarian officers, and laughed out loud when I told him of the Archduke's visit. When he suddenly became serious again, I thought it was time to go and got up, but he stopped me. "Don't go, Skorzeny," he said. "I have perhaps the most important job in your life for you. So far very few people know of the preparations for a secret plan in which you have a great part to play. In December, Germany will start a great offensive, which may well decide her fate."

During the next few hours he gave me a detailed picture of the projected operation in the west, which is now known to military history as the "Ardennes offensive", or the "Battle of the Bulge".

He said that in this time of uninterrupted retreats and continuous loss of ground on both fronts, the German leaders had not been able to consider anything beyond keeping our foes at bay. Allied propaganda, especially in the west, concentrated on representing Germany as a " stinking corpse ", merely awaiting burial in their own good time. " They cannot or will not see that Germany is fighting and bleeding for Europe, and barring Asia's path to the west," said Hitler, with mounting fury.

Continuing, he explained that England and America were tired of the war, and if the " corpse " rose from the dead and dealt them a resounding blow, pressure from their own people and the demonstrated falsity of their propaganda would make them ready for an armistice with Germany. Then he would concentrate all our forces in the east and in a few months remove the threat from that quarter for ever. Germany's historic destiny was to hold the fort against Asia.

A small number of General Staff officers had been busy for some weeks with the preliminaries to a great offensive. It involved planning on an immense scale and everything must be treated as top secret. Even during the wide sweep of the Allies from Normandy to the German frontier, his thoughts had been occupied with the problem of how we could wring the initiative from them by some great counter-stroke, which would frustrate or hold up their plans. He appreciated that the unfavourable position everywhere had so far made it impossible. But now the western front had been stabilized for about three weeks, thanks either to the enemy's supply difficulties, or the deterioration of their equipment—which was perhaps, over-specialized—after four months' continuous fighting.

" It was their practically unchallenged air superiority which enabled them to succeed with their invasion," said Hitler, continuing his monologue. " But now the German Command could expect that the weather in the autumn and early winter would hamper air activity, at least temporarily, and our offensive must be timed accordingly. Besides," he added, " we shall produce 2,000 of our new rocket-planes, which have been held in reserve for this occasion."

An unexpected offensive would also delay the appearance of a considerable number of new French divisions. The seventy Anglo-American divisions were not enough for a front 700 kilometres long. It must be possible to concentrate a superior force at some weak point and break through before the French reinforcements were in the line. The decision as to where to strike was open for weeks. Five alternatives had been considered: (1) Holland, and a westward thrust from Venlo to Antwerp; (2) an offensive from northern Luxemburg, first north-west and then north, combined with a secondary thrust from the region north of Aachen; (3) a Luxemburg operation, with the main thrusts from central Luxemburg and Metz respectively, meeting somewhere round Longwy; (4) two thrusts from Metz and Baccarat, meeting at Nancy and (5) an "Alsace" operation, with two thrusts east of Epinal and Mompelgard respectively and meeting in the vicinity of Vesoul.

The advantages and disadvantages of these various alternatives had been carefully considered and the three last rejected. The operation "Holland" appeared very attractive, but was distinctly risky. Ultimately the offensive from northern Luxemburg, with the supplementary offensive from Aachen, had been selected and worked out.

"I am telling you all this so that you can consider your part in it and realize that nothing has been forgotten," Adolf Hitler continued.

I found it far from easy to follow his indications and explanations on the map, as strategic planning was no part of my training. He went on to say that the offensive could not be contemplated unless stability could be maintained for some weeks on the rest of the front, and that in the French campaign in 1940 a break-through had been achieved in the same area and the experiences in that campaign were a valuable basis for the present calculations of the General Staff.

"One of the most important tasks in this offensive will be entrusted to you and the units under your command, which will have to go ahead and seize one or more of the bridges over the Meuse between Liège and Namur," said Hitler. "You will have to wear British and American uniforms. The enemy has already done us a great deal of damage by the use of our uniforms in various commando operations. Only a few days ago I received a report that the use of our uniforms by an American force had played no inconsiderable part when they captured Aachen, the first German town in the west to fall into their hands. Moreover, small detachments in enemy uniforms can cause the greatest confusion among the Allies by giving false orders and upsetting their communications with a view to sending bodies of troops in the wrong direction.

Your preparations must be complete by the 2nd December, and you can settle all the details with Colonel-General Jodl.

"I know you will do your best. Of course, the most important thing of all is the strictest secrecy! So far, very few people know about our plan. To help you in keeping your troops in complete ignorance, you can mislead them by allowing it to be known that the German High Command is expecting a big enemy attack in the Cologne-Bonn area this year, and all these preparations are for the purpose of defeating it."

I saw some objections to what was proposed and felt it was my duty to give expression to them. "Mein Führer, the short time available will make necessary a great deal of improvisation. What is to be done about the other commando projects? I cannot manage them all together!"

As the Führer did not answer at once, I continued with this theme and referred to the fact that the attack on Fort Eben Emael in 1940, for instance, had taken more than six months to prepare.

The Führer let me finish and then replied: "I know that the time is very, very short, but you must do all that is humanly possible. I am giving you a deputy for this new job during the time of preparation, so that you need be at the front only when it is actually in progress, but I forbid you to pass beyond the front line in person. In no circumstances must you let yourself be taken prisoner!"

Thereupon the Führer got up and accompanied me to the little Operations Room in the bunker, to the left of the entrance, where Foelkersam was waiting for me. Here I was introduced to Colonel-General Guderian, who was then Chief of the General Staff. I, in turn, presented Foelkersam to the Führer, and we were both amazed when the latter reminded him of the commando operation in Russia in which the latter had won his Knight's Cross.

A few hours later we were received by Colonel-General Jodl, who referred us to the map and gave various details of the projected offensive designed to reach Antwerp from a base between Aachen and Luxemburg. Such a stroke would isolate the British Army Group and the American forces fighting round Aachen. It would have flank protection from the south by a line passing through Luxemburg-Namur-Louvain-Mechlin, and on the north by a line passing through Eupen-Liège-Laengeren-Hasselt-The Albert Canal.

Under favourable conditions Antwerp should be reached seven

days after the offensive began. The ultimate aim of the whole operation was the destruction of all enemy forces north of the line Antwerp-Brussels.

The forces employed were to form an Army Group under Field-Marshal Model, and comprise the 6th SS Armoured Army, under the command of General Sepp Dietrich, of the Waffen SS, on the right, the 5th Armoured Army under General von Manteuffel, in the centre, and the 7th Army on the left. After a short, but most intensive, artillery bombardment (I involuntarily recalled the 6,000 guns of which the Führer had spoken a few hours before), the armies would break through at several points which were considered favourable from a tactical point of view.

After enlarging upon the individual tasks of the three Armies, Jodl continued: "The Führer has ordered that you, Skorzeny, shall carry out your special task in the operations area of the 6th Armoured Army. For that purpose I have no doubt, you would like to see how we think the position should have developed forty-eight hours after the attack begins."

With these words he spread out another map with various markings on it, from which we gathered that it was assumed that at that stage the attack on the line Eupen-Verviers-Liège would have started and it had been found possible to establish two bridgeheads over the Meuse.

The General went off after giving us a short time in which to prepare a list of the personnel and material we thought we should require and also the plan of what I proposed to do. I must settle further details with the staff officers concerned.

I had an important discussion with a colonel of General Winter's staff about the international-law aspects of our proposed activities. He said that small commandos certainly ran a great risk of being treated as spies if they were captured and brought before a court-martial, but as regards the larger units of my force, international law only forbade the use of arms by anyone when wearing the enemy uniform. He therefore recommended that my men should wear German uniform under the American or British uniform and take off the latter before actually opening fire. I need hardly add that I welcomed such advice, coming from an expert.

A little later, I heard that Headquarters proposed to issue an order throughout the army that all English-speaking soldiers and officers should report for a special operation, with the idea that they should

join my force. This order must be regarded as the perfect military
"bloomer" from the secrecy point of view, and it is
amazing to think that it was perpetrated by the top men of the
German Army.

A few days later, I received at Friedenthal a copy of the order
and I nearly fell out of my chair. It was signed by one of the most
senior officers of Headquarters, and it had at the top, the words
"Secret Commando Operations". The most important passage
was this:

"All units must, before the . . . October, send in the names of
all English-speaking officers and men who are prepared to voluntarily apply for transfer, for a special operation, to the formation
commanded by Obersturmbannführer Skorzeny, in Friedenthal,
near Berlin".

And this order was actually being distributed to all units of the
Wehrmacht, both at home and at the front!

It could be assumed that many of the divisions issued copies to
their regiments and battalions, bearing the legend "Secret Commando Operations".

No wonder I almost had a fit, for I knew that the enemy Intelligence could not fail to hear about it and, in fact, I learned after the
war that the American Secret Service knew all about it within eight
days. What seems incredible to me is that the Americans did not
draw any inferences or apparently take any precautionary measures.

In my opinion, this piece of folly meant the end of our particular
enterprise, even before it had begun, and I immediately dictated a
"violent protest" to FHQ, and "humbly" put forward my opinion
that it would be better to call off the whole thing. Then I found
that between the authority to which I appealed, i.e., Jodl or the
Führer himself, there was a most formidable obstacle, which was
calmly called "Official Channels", and which there was no means
of side-tracking. "Official Channels" meant an approach through
SS-Obergruppenführer Feglein, subsequently Adolf Hitler's brother-
in-law. From him I received the answer that the affair was admittedly incredible and incomprehensible, but for that very reason the
Führer must know nothing about it. Our programme must be
adhered to.

A few days later, I had an opportunity to mention the matter to
the Reichsführer, but the only answer I got was: "It's idiotic, but it
has been done. We cannot hold up your operation now."

My day and night work on our programme planning was interrupted for an afternoon by a summons to the Reichsführer's new headquarters near Hohenlychen, which was a modest hutted camp in a birch wood. After waiting a short time, his aide-de-camp took me into his room. On entering I noticed that Dr. Kaltenbrunner, Schellenberg and Obergruppenführer Prützmann were also present. When we were all seated at a round table, Himmler told us why he had called for us. He said that the National Movement, known as the "Werwolf", the existence of which had been the subject of newspaper and wireless comment for weeks, must be properly organized, as hitherto individual SS and police chiefs in various districts had been organizing solely in accordance with their own ideas and temperaments. Incidentally, Himmler turned to me and said: "The 'Werwolf' should really be part of your job, Skorzeny, but I think you have enough to do already." I heartily agreed with him.

As always when we met, Himmler asked about the position and progress with special weapons for the Luftwaffe and Navy. When I told him that we were examining the possibility of firing the V1 from a submarine he shot out of his chair, walked to a globe by the side of his desk and fired the question at me: "Could we bombard New York with it?" I replied that it was theoretically possible if our technicians could construct a firing platform on a big supply submarine. Himmler, a man of swift and often spontaneous decisions, cut me short: "I'll go and discuss it at once with the Führer and Admiral Dönitz. New York must be bombed with the V1 in the near future. You must leave no stone unturned, Skorzeny, to get the thing going as soon as possible."

I was not expecting this sudden reaction from Himmler, and on various grounds was far from convinced that his decision was right. I waited to see what the others would do as they were my seniors in rank and had the right to speak first. But Prützmann seemed uninterested and Dr. Kaltenbrunner kept his expression of something which was neither approval nor dissent very much under control, and looked at his subordinate Schellenberg, who was chiefly concerned as head of the Intelligence Service. The latter simply nodded all the time and had no need to say the usual "Jawohl, Reichsführer".

So it was left to me to speak up, and when the Reichsführer ceased walking up and down and looked hard at me, I said:

"Reichsführer, I should like to make some observations for your consideration." And I went on to refer at some length to the inaccuracy of the V1 and the devices we were working on to improve it. I also mentioned the fact that our Luftwaffe would have no control over the areas from which the V1s would be fired.

As I was talking, I watched the reactions of the others. Himmler continued walking up and down and seemed to be listening somewhat impatiently. He kept stopping by the globe and looking hard at us. I did not know him well enough to appreciate exactly what his expression meant. Dr. Kaltenbrunner several times nodded at me and I gathered that he was encouraging me to go on, but Schellenberg, not to my surprise, shook his head at me as a signal to stop. Prützmann did not raise his head from his papers.

Suddenly Himmler interrupted: "Here is a great chance— a really great chance—of a turning-point in the war. America shall really *feel* the war for the first time. They think they are out of reach and Roosevelt imagines that they can fight this war against Germany with their money and their industries and a few soldiers. The shock of such an attack would be enormous. They'd never face war in their own country. I have a very poor opinion of the moral stamina of the Americans; it will collapse under such a novel and unexpected strain."

I had no objections to an air war against American cities, fully justified by the increasingly violent air bombardment of our own towns, but I thought that Himmler was quite wrong about the effect on the American people and waited for a favourable opportunity to continue: "I believe, Reichsführer, that it is very possible that the effect will be quite the opposite. The U.S. government is always drumming into the nation that 'America is threatened by Germany'. The threat will become a reality if New York is bombarded with the V1. I attach considerable importance to the Anglo-Saxon strain in the Americans. The British have taught us that their morale rises to great heights when they are directly threatened."

Now Himmler listened more attentively and I took the opportunity to enlarge on the necessary technical developments which were in progress but not completed. At length Dr. Kaltenbrunner intervened to say that he also saw objections to the adoption of the scheme at the moment. We must wait for certain technical devices to be perfected. Eventually, Himmler seemed to be impressed by our arguments. He did not expressly withdraw his previous order but told me to keep him regularly informed of the progress of the new developments. But finally events on the battlefield moved faster than many of the technical developments anticipated in Germany and the V1 was never employed against U.S.A. territory.

CHAPTER XIII

In the next few months I had little time for special weapons or underground movements, as the preparations for the forthcoming offensive were far more important and, naturally, came first. When I was not occupied with the actual organization and training of my battle-group at Grafenwohr, the training area assigned to us, I had to be at Friedenthal, where we were working out all the details of the operation.

We christened our operation "Greif", after a mythical bird.

My force was to consist of an armoured brigade, which was numbered 150, and the basis of our plan was the time-table laid down for the great offensive, which contemplated that there would be a clean break through on the first day, and that by the second day the Meuse would have been reached and crossed. We were thus fully justified in thinking that the enemy troops would be in disorderly flight on the first day.

My colleagues and I fully appreciated that we should have to rely on improvisation. In a bare five weeks (the offensive was due to open at the beginning of December) a brand new formation could not be got together and moulded into a compact unit, particularly if it was to be employed in a special operation. We realized we were being asked the impossible, but we had stressed the point to the Führer when the plan was first mooted and so our consciences were clear.

As we had to prepare for all eventualities, we fixed our gaze on three targets, the Meuse bridges at Engis, Amay and Huy. The 6th Armoured Army battle area allotted to us was divided into three strips, each converging on one of the bridges. Armoured Brigade

150 was accordingly divided into three battle-groups, which we called X, Y and Z.

Even the term "brigade" was a bluff, because, in answer to our application to the Quartermaster, we were told that it was out of the question for us to have enough captured American or British tanks for one section, let alone a whole regiment. It was far from pleasant to embark on such an enterprise with such a deficit in the most important item.

We proposed to constitute Armoured Brigade 150 as follows:

2 tank companies with 10 tanks each.

3 reconnaissance companies each with 10 scout cars.

3 motorized infantry battalions, each with two rifle and one heavy machine-gun company.

1 light anti-aircraft company.

2 tank defence companies.

1 mortar section.

1 Intelligence company.

1 brigade staff, to be kept as small as possible.

3 battalion staffs, ditto.

1 commando company (to carry out the second part of the brigade's task).

To economize in men, we dispensed with almost all the usual auxiliary services. Our total strength was to be 3,300 men.

We had also to make out comprehensive lists of the captured weapons, ammunition, motor transport, equipment and uniforms we should require.

When I saw Colonel-General Jodl on the 26th October, and asked his approval of the composition of our brigade and our list of requirements, I again emphasized the short time at our disposal, and that in my opinion "Operation Greif" could only succeed if it was begun the first night after the offensive started and made the fullest use of the enemy's surprise and disarray. It was vital to us that the front-line troops should reach their objectives and, in particular, have passed the Hoher Venn ridge at all points. I added that air photographs of the three bridges we were to take were indispensable.

The composition of our brigade was approved and we were promised unlimited support from Headquarters.

At a later meeting with General Burgdorf I asked for the loan of three battalion commanders with front-line experience, of whom one should represent me as brigade C.O. during the period in which the formation was being got together. Of the three allocated, Lieutenant-Colonel Hardieck was a splendid officer, but had never led this sort of operation before. The same could be said of Lieutenant-Colonel W. and Captain Sch., but the enthusiasm with which they entered into their new duties made me certain that somehow, everything would be all right. I did not forget that I myself had had no previous experience of leading an attack in borrowed plumage.

On my representing to General Burgdorf that in four weeks I could not be expected to convert volunteers drawn from all branches of the services into a self-contained and compact formation and needed a few regular units to give them stiffening, he replied by letting me have two Luftwaffe parachute battalions, one Army tank company and one Communications company. With these I expanded my two companies of commandos and my parachute battalion.

When the first hundred volunteers reported at Friedenthal a week later, the future of "Greif" looked blacker than ever. We employed a number of language experts who divided them into categories, according to their knowledge of English. After a couple of weeks, the result was terrifying. Category one, comprising men speaking perfectly and with some notion of American slang, was ten strong and most of them were sailors, who also figured largely in category two. The latter comprised men speaking perfectly, but with no knowledge of American slang. There were thirty to forty of them. The third category consisted of between 120 and 150 men who spoke English fairly well, and the fourth, about 200 strong, of those who had learned a little English at school. The rest could just about say "yes". In practice it meant that we might just as well mingle with the fleeing Americans and pretend to be too flurried and overcome to speak.

It was even worse with material. We soon realized that we should never get the number of American tanks we wanted. On the day before the offensive started we were the proud possessors of exactly two Shermans, one of which became useless through transmission troubles when we were assembling in the Eifel region. The Inspector of Armoured Forces in Berlin gave us twelve German "Panthers" in substitution for the missing American ones, and we camouflaged their guns and turrets to make them look like

Shermans. All I can say is that they could only deceive very young American troops, seeing them at night from very far away.

We also received ten English and American scout cars from the captured stocks. We might have been worried as to what use to make of the English specimens, if they had not solved the problem for us by breaking down on the training ground. So we were left four American scout cars and had to make up the difference with German ones. About thirty jeeps also turned up, by dribs and drabs, in Grafenwohr.

The position with motor transport was not much better. In the final result we had perhaps fifteen genuine American trucks available and had to make good the deficiency with German Fords. The only common feature of these vehicles was that they were all painted green, like American military vehicles.

In the matter of weapons we were yet worse off. We had only fifty per cent of the U.S. rifles we needed. There was no ammunition for the American anti-tank guns and mortars. When a few railway wagons arrived with a supply of ammunition they blew up, owing to faulty stowing, with the result that we were compelled to make do with German weapons. There were only enough American arms for the commando company.

But the most fantastic position of all was in respect of clothing, to which, of course, we had to attach the utmost importance. We started off by receiving a consignment of miscellaneous articles, which on closer examination turned out to be parts of British uniforms. Then we were sent a lot of overcoats, which were practically useless, because we knew that the Americans only wore so-called "field-jackets" in the line. When the head of the Prisoner of War Section sent us a supply of these jackets, it was observed that they were adorned with the triangle peculiar to prisoners and the consignment had to be returned. It was an eloquent comment on the way the business was handled that the commander of the brigade—myself—got nothing but an American army pullover in my size. There was an outburst of fury from Hitler against various gentlemen in the Quartermaster's department who were responsible for equipping us. Not that this "pressure at the top" did us much good!

Meanwhile, Lieutenant-Colonel Hardieck was getting very worried at the training centre. For security reasons, it was proclaimed a closed area, and even postal communications were forbidden. In these circumstances the wildest rumours began to circulate as to what was the object of all the preparations, and where and when the special force would be employed. It was also known that I should be commanding the brigade later and this naturally led to the conclusion that something like the Italian affair was afoot. Hardieck took the strongest possible measures against rumour-mongering, but in vain. Security was seriously imperilled. When he told me of his plight, I asked him to come up to Friedenthal for a talk.

What he told Foelkersam and me made our hair stand on end. There was no limit to the imagination of the men. Some were saying that the whole armoured brigade was to rush straight across France to liberate the beleaguered garrison of Brest, which was still bravely defending itself. Others thought that our destination was Lorient, not Brest, and professed to know exactly how we should fight our way into the fortress. Dozens of stories were flying round and each version had its advocates, who were not to be shaken in their belief. We were certain that enemy Intelligence must know something about all this, particularly as the unfortunate order from Headquarters must be assumed to have put it on our track.

We had to decide what we should do. Pains and penalties alone can never solve such problems and we must find some other solution. After ripe consideration, we found that the simplest was the best. So far only we three knew the truth, and we decided to let the rumours increase and multiply, while apparently doing our best to suppress them. We calculated that enemy Intelligence would simply not know what to make of the medley of lurid and conflicting information which reached their ears.

Meanwhile, we pressed on with training at Grafenwohr. Only the best men were picked for our brigade. The rest would prove a useful reserve if, contrary to expectation, we were called on to assist in forcing a passage for my armoured groups.

When we realized, in the middle of November, that the camouflage outfit of the brigade would be very far from complete, we were forced to consider certain changes in our plans. In the absence of camouflage for everybody we must try to obtain the same result by expedients, cunning and, above all, bluff. The latter would not help us, however, unless the enemy was completely surprised, and

his troops bolted in panic, so we must insist on our condition precedent, viz., that our troops must reach their objective on the first
day. My three battle-groups should then go ahead of the attacking
columns and try to concentrate in the vicinity of the bridges. A
reconnaissance party, in American uniforms, must find out and
report the position at the bridges themselves, and when all this had
been successfully accomplished, there would be a good chance that
a surprise attack, openly carried-out, would succeed, particularly
if the enemy had not recovered from his panic.

We naturally devoted special attention to the commando company (which was charged with the execution of the second part of
our task), causing alarm, confusion and despondency in the enemy
ranks. None of the volunteers selected for this unit had ever had
any experience in that line. There were no trained spies or saboteurs among them. In the few weeks at our disposal we could
hardly hope to teach them their job properly.

They knew the perils of their mission and that a man caught
fighting in enemy uniform could be executed as a spy. They were
clearly animated by the most glowing patriotism. In these circumstances, it was incumbent upon us to use them sparingly. It was
difficult to say in advance exactly what they would have to do, and
we must leave them as much as possible to their own initiative.
They would be the eyes of the troops behind them. They could also
make themselves exceedingly useful by increasing the confusion
among the enemy by circulating false information, such as highly
exaggerated reports of the initial successes of the German Army.
They could even send enemy columns in wrong directions by
removing signposts, and they could cut telephone lines and blow up
ammunition dumps.

It was about the 20th November, 1944, that I saw my troops at
Grafenwohr for the first and last time before the start. In the
morning I watched some of the exercises and inspected the equipment of the three battle-groups. It was far more defective than I
had feared, and Foelkersam spent a lot of time making notes of the
most pressing requirements. Headquarters would again be far from
pleased with my next report!

In the afternoon I had a long talk with the CO's of the battle-
groups. I told them that the real task of the brigade would be to
seize and hold one or more bridges behind the enemy's line, though
I was careful to add that this was on the assumption that an expected

Allied offensive would materialize. We anticipated that "pockets" would develop, and the bridges within the "pockets" would be of outstanding importance.

After the conference, N., a lieutenant in the Commando Company, turned up with a request for a private talk with me. When he came in, he wore a perfectly serious expression.

"Sir, I believe I know the real objective of the brigade," he said.

Of course I was very curious to know what was coming. Had either of the two other officers in the know let the cat out of the bag? Was the whole enterprise in peril? Before I had time to pursue this line of thought Lieutenant N. continued, obviously very pleased with the effect of his opening words.

"The brigade is to go straight to Paris and capture Allied Headquarters!"

"Indeed! Indeed! Hmm!"

It was quite enough for this keen officer, who pleaded urgently to be allowed to help, saying that he had lived a long time in France, knew Paris very well and spoke French fluently. He swore I could rely on him and he would not breathe a word to anyone.

"Yes, have you ever stopped to think how we could pull it off? Would it not be rather a risky business?" I asked him.

"It's perfectly possible," the proud inventor of the new plan assured me. "You will, no doubt, have made your own plans already, sir, but I too have given the matter some thought and arrived at the following solution."

He went on to give me all the details of his plan, which was that only the men who could speak English perfectly should be dressed in enemy uniform, and they should appear to be escorts for a prisoner-of-war convoy. The convoys would be distributed in several columns and meet at some suitable point in Paris. The German tanks could be taken along and their presence explained away by a statement that they had been captured and were to be exhibited at Allied Headquarters.

Ultimately I said to him: "Well, go and think it all over very carefully and work out the details. We'll have a further talk—but mind you, keep as silent as the grave."

The future was to show that the grave was far from silent. The Café de la Paix in Paris—which I had mentioned to him—figured prominently as the mysterious assembly point. The Allied security services concentrated their defence measures at that point for months!

In November, 1944, I went to the western front with a view to obtaining better support on the vital equipment question, and also clearing up a few tactical points in connection with our proposed operation. I had talks at the headquarters of General Rundstedt, Commander-in-Chief, West, at Siegenhain, and had several conferences with the Chief-of-Staff and his Ia. I had heard from other sources that Rundstedt favoured an operation on a smaller scale in the region of Aachen. None the less, I was given valuable information about the position at the front and the enemy order of battle. I produced the plan for "Operation Greif", which had been approved by Headquarters, but his reactions were disappointing.

I also called at the headquarters of Field-Marshal Model, who was in charge of the projected offensive, and made the acquaintance of General Krebs, his Chief-of-Staff, who was working at top pressure on the preparations. It struck me that General Krebs was fully convinced that the operation would be a complete success. I remembered Hitler's words, when he was outlining his plan to me: "Skorzeny, this will be *the* decisive battle of the war," and conjectured that General Krebs also had heard something of the kind and was taking it very seriously.

Once again I was promised full backing for our enterprise, and there is no doubt that it was perfectly genuine. The General approved my plans for it and offered various suggestions for the employment of my battalion "South-west", in little raids immediately before the opening of the big offensive.

We, too, had been considering the possibility of interfering with the "pipe-lines", the arteries of the American armies, dependent as they were on an abundant supply of fuel. These "pipe-lines" had been laid, one from Bologne and the other from Le Havre, and ran right up the front. They were a masterpiece of American ingenuity. The idea was to organize and drop little groups of saboteurs behind the enemy lines with a view to blowing up the more important sections. Unfortunately, the very short time at our disposal made it impossible to choose our agents carefully. At that stage of the war, Frenchmen willing to work for the Germans had become very hard to find.

The staff of the 6th SS Armoured Army was then quartered east of Rheims. Its Ic (quartermaster-general), who was an old friend

of mine, asked me to contribute a jeep-team to the head of each
armoured column to serve as scouts for the divisions, and promised
me some jeeps, which actually should have been handed over before.
Though I knew that even now they were keeping some back, I felt
a certain amount of sympathy with the front-line troops, knowing
that there was a woeful shortage of motor vehicles. I was also given
some enemy intelligence which was of interest to us.

D-day had been postponed from the 1st December to the 10th,
and then to the 16th, as concentration had not been effected in time
and the material of the newly completed divisions had not all
arrived. To me it was a sign that Germany's last reserves in men
and arms had been scraped together for this offensive. This impression was confirmed at the "situation conference" in Adolf
Hitler's presence, to which I was summoned three times. I felt
quite clearly that Colonel-General Guderian grudged every tank and
battalion which was taken away from his hard-fighting eastern front
for the new operation in the west.

When it came to my turn to recite my perpetual complaints about
the failure to give me what we needed, my task was far from easy,
but there could be no burking the truth if I was to give a correct
picture of the supply position of my armoured brigade. What I
said could be compressed into a few words: "We are having to
improvise from A to Z, but we will do all that is possible."

Adolf Hitler listened quietly while I spoke and then addressed
endless questions to the officers concerned, but he always got the
same answer: "We have done all that is possible already. We will
issue another order. . . ."

One afternoon, at the beginning of December, a meeting took
place in the Führer's room on the first floor of the Reichskanzlei
in Berlin, a room which was considerably smaller than that in the
"Wolf's Den" in East Prussia. We all had to stand huddled
together and the only persons permitted to be present were the military chiefs and the officer actually making the report. Captain
Foelkersam was with me as usual, and we had agreed that this time
I should speak with no uncertain voice about the failure to supply
us with air photographs of the three bridges.

Reichsmarschall Hermann Göring, who was present on this occasion, had just made his report on the air situation. He said that
the numerical superiority of the American air force could no longer
be overcome by even the supreme courage of our airmen. Hitler

seemed to know that already, as he hardly took the trouble to listen. Then I heard a figure which struck me:

"Two hundred and fifty rocket-fighters would be available for the Ardennes offensive."

I could hardly believe my ears. Was that all that was left of the original figure, which the Führer had given me on the 22nd October when he said: "Two thousand rocket-fighters will give us command of the air during the offensive."

But Hitler seemed to take no notice. He had apparently written off the Luftwaffe.

At that time I did not understand all this, as the Führer seemed to be far happier and fitter than he had been in September and October. The thought of a last chance, this great offensive, appeared to have revived even the worn-out Adolf Hitler.

When it came to my turn to speak, I mentioned the air photographs which I had been promised weeks before. Hitler rose in fury and reproached the Reichsmarschall in the most violent terms. I was in a most painful position, as a lieutenant-colonel is not usually present when a Reichsmarschall is being "carpeted".

Eventually Göring promised to supply a rocket-fighter, equipped with a camera to obtain the photographs we required. It appeared that ordinary reconnaissance from the air had been impossible for weeks, so overwhelming was the enemy's superiority.

The sequel to the Reichsmarschall's order came to hand a few days later in the shape of photographs of the bridges at Huy and Amoy (we never received the third). These showed the anti-aircraft gun positions quite clearly. I almost jumped for joy when I observed that there were no signs of any special preparations for defence of the river crossings. No unpleasant surprises need be anticipated.

The Führer surprised me by saying at the end of the conference: "Skorzeny, I have one private and personal order for you. Once more I absolutely forbid you to go behind the enemy's lines yourself. You must direct the 'Operation Greif' by wireless. I have made the commander of the 6th SS Armoured Army personally responsible that this order is obeyed. You must stay at his battle headquarters. Whatever happens, you must not be taken prisoner. I have other tasks in store for you."

How could I tell my comrades I would not be with them? Captain von Foelkersam fully understood my dismay, though he regarded the Führer's word as law. "Soup's never hotter than when it's first made," he said in his dry, Balt way. "Wait a bit!" I decided to inform my battle-group commander of this order, though it was far from easy. I would like to have told him at the same time that I should not be missing at any critical moment, but would find my way to the front somehow, and was quite sure that the Army Commander would not blame me.

My adjutant, Karl Radl, had often complained that I always took Foelkersam to the Führer's conferences, so when opportunity occurred, I took him with me. When I did so, he was lucky. On the ground-floor of the much-bombed left wing of the Reichskanzlei, I was able to introduce him to Reichsmarschall Göring, who had his offices there. I was greatly relieved to find that the latter bore me no ill-will for what had happened on the previous occasion, when I had been responsible for the Führer's reproaches. He told me that when the offensive started it was intended to drop a parachute battalion at Mount Rigi, the dominating feature of a ridge west of Monschau, with a view to its seizing and holding an important crossroads and thereby hampering the enemy in bringing up reinforcements from the north. I must discuss the matter with its commander (who had been with us in Italy) as it was possible that one of my jeep commandos might be in the vicinity and must be preserved from death at the hands of their own countrymen.

I had hardly paid my respects to the Führer in the operations room on the first floor when I heard someone breathing heavily behind me. Radl had skilfully managed to slide up unnoticed by the other officers. Hitler stared at him and I seized the opportunity: "Mein Führer, may I present to you Hauptsturmführer Karl Radl, my old adjutant and colleague, who was with us in Italy," I said, pushing my mightily surprised friend forward. Adolf Hitler shook hands and then turned to the map again. "May I have the report on the western situation."

The really cheerful feature of the position at that moment was that the concentration of our forces had apparently passed unobserved by the enemy, or its significance had not been appreciated if it had been observed. The front was quiet and lightly held. It looked as if the Americans were settling down for the winter. The weather forecast for D-day, now fixed for the 16th December, was favourable —overcast skies and low cloud. It meant that the enemy's air superiority would be cancelled out. I was personally delighted to hear that no excessive cold was prognosticated, as my men were only equipped for a short operation and had no special winter clothing or other gear, it being essential to save all the space we could.

On the 8th December, the last trains left Grafenwohr and my brigade was transferred to the Wahn area, where we received a few more jeeps. Although my mechanics worked on them furiously till the very last moment, all were not ready in time.

Captain von Foelkersam then worked out the orders for our move to the Blankenheim Forest during the night of the 13th.

On the march there we were already made aware that in some respects the men's training had not been all that it should have been, while some of our transport broke down. Throughout the night all the roads in the vicinity were thronged with marching columns. We struck our first camp in the extensive wooded area south-east of Blankenheim. The air was cold and damp and the ground quite wet, but most of our fellows had passed a winter in Russia and did not find the conditions too bad.

I was familiar with the region, as on the previous day I had attended a meeting at Field-Marshal Model's headquarters, when the final orders were issued to all Corps and Divisional commanders. The question of supply was the main consideration. Towards the end of the conference Field-Marshal Model asked me to give the generals a short description and explanation of "Greif", as it was essential that commanding officers should know all about it, if withdrawing teams of my commando company were not to be taken for enemy formations and fired at. We accordingly agreed on recognition signals. By day, my men would take off their helmets and hold them up and at night fire Verey lights.

Unfortunately some of the divisions communicated this arrangement to their battalions in writing, and on the first day a battalion commander was taken prisoner with the order in his pocket. But as it said nothing about our objective, but only showed that detachments under my command would be wearing enemy uniform, it only added to the confusion prevailing among enemy Intelligence, since they already believed that many commandos were at work behind their lines.

On the 14th December, I had officially taken over command of the Armoured Brigade 150, and was sitting in a forester's cottage talking to the commanders of my three battle-groups. Two of them had just learned that our activities were to be part and parcel of an offensive on the grand scale. They had both seen plenty of front-line service and would certainly prove capable of coping with the trickiest situation. I stressed the vital importance of keeping in close and constant touch. If we did so, we should arrive at the right decisions and could not fail.

We were to be employed in the battle area of the 1st SS Armoured Corps. The northern battle-group, placed under the orders of young Colonel Peiper, commanding the 1st SS Armoured Regiment, was set the task of crossing the Meuse between Liège and Huy. Peiper had already issued the orders for his formation. They were short and to the point. At zero-hour on the 16th December, his armoured group would attack on the Losheim-Losheim Graben sector and break down any enemy resistance. First objective, the seizing and holding of the Meuse bridges south of Liège. Flank protection, or developments on either side of the assault front, must be disregarded and full use made of the speed of the tanks to reach the river.

The supply of fuel for the armoured division was so restricted that it would only suffice to reach the Meuse if the advance was effected without serious fighting. We too had to perform pro-digies of calculation to distribute petrol in such a way that none of our vehicles would run short. We should get no more, whatever happened. As my detachments could not allow themselves to be involved in even a minor scuffle, I had reasonable grounds for be-lieving that our supply would take us to the river.

The enemy front was still quiet and he appeared to have no knowledge of our night movements. During the day, nothing was allowed to move on the roads which might indicate that two armoured armies had concentrated in a very small area. In the night of the 15th, the armoured columns moved up to just behind the front, their approach being concealed by fog, which we regarded as a favourable augury for the whole offensive.

I had arranged with the Army Staff that for the start of the action I would join the battle station of the 1st Corps at Schmittheim, and take with me my wireless gear and staff of four officers—Ia, orderly, wireless and Q.

Before daylight on the 16th, all troop movements had been com-pleted and all vehicles again concealed in the woods. Reports of the three battle-groups soon began to come in to my five wireless posts. These groups had taken up their stations behind the armoured formations.

CHAPTER XIV

A THUNDEROUS roar from thousands of guns announced the opening of the preliminary bombardment of the enemy positions, at 5 a.m., Saturday, 16th December. It was short, the range was lengthened and the German infantry leapt to the attack. The third Parachute Division was dropped in the area assigned for the break-through of the Peiper battle-group.

The earliest reports arrived just before seven and they were not too favourable, although they could obviously take a turn for the better at any moment. Apparently the artillery bombardment had had no great effect on the enemy positions at Losheimer Graben, the Americans were defending themselves particularly stoutly and the attack was progressing but slowly. Up to midday, the only news was of violent fighting, without any considerable gain of ground. The intended collapse of the whole front had not been achieved.

I do not know why the armoured divisions had not already been sent in. All they had done was to go forward to what was the start-line that morning.

I had sent my Ia (Chief Staff Officer) to see the commanders of my three battle-groups and try to get the wireless communications to function properly. Groups X and Y had just reported that he had contacted them when my signals officer came rushing up with a message: "Lieutenant-Colonel Hardieck has been killed!"

By good fortune, my Ia was on his way to his battle-group and could take over the command at once. To me, this meant the loss of my best staff officer, but I knew that I could do him no greater service and that he would make a fine job of it. We soon received his message: "I have taken over command of Group X."

The 16th December passed without a decisive success on the front of the 6th Armoured Army, and even by midday it was clear that the armoured divisions would have to be sent in to effect a decisive break-through. I drove to Losheim to get a clearer picture of the situation. The roads were simply crammed with vehicles of every kind and, in practice, all officers had to walk beside their cars in order to help in keeping the traffic flowing. By the time I reached Losheim I must have walked at least ten kilometres.

I was now faced with a critical decision, as it was already plain that the day's objectives had not been attained. The logical inference was that I must call off " Operation Greif ", something which was entirely against the grain, after all our tremendous preparations. I was not in the habit of abandoning my purpose so easily! I reflected that success was still possible if the armoured divisions went in that night and decided to wait another twenty-four hours. If the Hohe Venn had then been passed, the attacking wave would probably reach the Meuse and the seizing of the bridges by my men could be decisive.

From the men of the commando company I chose three teams whom I considered most suitable for the task of spreading rumours. Most were sailors who spoke English well and therefore had more self-confidence. I sent them off southwards with orders to look for a gap in the enemy front, find their way through and carry out their purpose. I stressed the importance of reconnoitring the three roads selected for the approach by our three battle-groups.

When I returned to Schmittheim I came across the first American prisoners of war. There were about a hundred of them, and one could see at first sight that they were in splendid physical condition. They had been captured in the first assault, many of them before they had had time to leave their billets. Apparently quite pleased with life, they were leaning up against a wall, smoking cigarettes and chewing gum.

Just before midnight on the 16th, Peiper's armoured group and another to the south entered the fray. We should get no news before the early hours, and this time I took advantage of the interval to snatch a few hours' rest, sleeping fully dressed on a mattress laid on the floor of my room. Would the weather remain in our favour next day?

By five o'clock, I was back at the battle station. The first news came in almost at once: "Housfeld has been taken despite strong enemy resistance! " Things seemed to be moving. The southern armoured group also reported good news; it had made progress in a westerly direction.

We had arranged to advance the Corps command post to the vicinity of Manderfeld. I had the team informed that I was on my way to the commando company at Losheim and started off. If possible, the conditions on the roads were even worse than the day before. The endless columns of vehicles could only advance a metre at a time; the confusion was hopeless. I went back to Schmittheim and made my way to Dahlem by side roads, which were only just passable. There was nothing for it but to get out and proceed slowly on foot towards Stadtkyll. In the narrow winding valley approaching the town the traffic was held up altogether by a huge Luftwaffe transporter, probably ten metres long, which had become wedged into the other traffic. Some thirty men were engaged in trying to get it clear.

I was curious to see what it was carrying and greatly surprised to find a quantity of V1 parts. Apparently this was the result of a premature order given on the assumption that the front would be much further forward on the first day. It looked as if someone had forgotten to cancel this order.

Radical treatment was called for and I did not hesitate. I made all the occupants of the other vehicles get out and before long a hundred hands were busy in tipping the contents of the transporter into the lake, after which the lumbering vehicle followed them down the slope. In a quarter of an hour the road was open again.

I had given up the idea of going by the main road, as I felt certain that progress would be faster by the little Kerschenbach-Stormont road, which ran parallel. On our way we passed several uncleared minefields, which we treated with the greatest respect, remembering the fate of Lieutenant-Colonel Hardieck.

On the road from Prüm to Losheim, we observed the effect of the opening barrage on the deserted American headquarters. There could not have been much resistance here. Three battered and burnt Sherman tanks were lying, still smoking, by the roadside.

In the evening there was a great council-of-war at Corps Headquarters at Manderfeld. Colonel-General Sepp Dietrich was present. The northern tank group had made headway after violent fighting, captured Bullingen and had a hard battle for Engelsdorf, which was only taken in the evening. An attack on Stavelot was in progress and meeting with strong enemy resistance.

The news from the other battle-fronts was not much more
favourable. It was true that surprise had been complete, but the
idea of a sweep to the Meuse in a single rush, and the enemy retiring
further without fighting, had to be abandoned. There was no
question of the panic flight which alone would have given "Operation Greif" a chance. Nor could we anticipate that the Meuse
could be reached in our battle sector on the next day, or even the
day after that. The enemy was already bringing up reserves and
throwing them into the fight.

After ripe consideration, I reported to Army Headquarters my
suggestion to renounce our original intentions, and received its
approval. Appropriate instructions were issued to the battle-groups
and they were told to stay where they were and await further orders.
As my brigade was still in the battle area, I put it under the orders
of the first Armoured Corps, for use as ordinary infantry, and asked
for some employment suitable to our capacity.

The advance of Peiper's battle-group was at an end by the 18th.
At Troisponts, which had been taken at eleven o'clock in the morning, the bridges had been blown up. La Gleize and Staumont were
also taken in the course of the afternoon. All the messages which
came through reported shortages of ammunition and fuel, and without these essential supplies further progress was impossible. During
the night we managed to get a few petrol lorries forward, but they
were simply a drop in a bucket.

Next day, a fresh source of anxiety appeared. Almost the whole
of the northern flank of the offensive was exposed and, from
Malmédy in particular, the enemy could deliver a dangerous
southerly thrust with fresh reserves. I was asked whether I could
avert that menace by an attack on that town.

Having regard to the immediate position of my battle-groups, I
could only say that we could not be ready before the morning of
the 21st. In the early hours of the 19th, I issued wireless orders
to my formation to concentrate in the vicinity of Engelsdorf. In
that village I reported to the headquarters of the 1st SS Armoured
Division and discussed the situation with the Ia.

Artillery support being out of the question, we decided to make
a surprise attack from two sides on Malmédy, at dawn on the 21st.
Our objective would be the heights on the north of the town, where
we would establish a position and be prepared to beat off counter-
attacks. It meant that the approaches to Engelsdorf by the two

roads coming in from the north would have to be guarded by detachments of nine men each. A most uncomfortable and indeed impossible position!

When my commando teams reported on the 19th, that on the previous day Malmédy had apparently been lightly held by the enemy, I hoped that our attack would succeed even in the absence of heavy artillery. My ten surviving tanks—the rest were temporarily out of action as the result of damage—would have to suffice.

The leader of this team, an elderly naval captain, provided us with a remarkable example of an honest report. He said that he had not really intended to get into the enemy lines, but had lost his way. "At sea nothing would have happened to me," he said. He was wearing the uniform of a German officer. Before he knew where he was, he was among the first houses of a small town. There were only a few inhabitants about and they asked him whether the Germans were coming. When he learned that he was actually in Malmédy, and that it was still held by the Americans, he made a smart rightabout turn and got back safely to Engelsdorf. "So we got off with nothing worse than a fright," he remarked, adding: "We had more luck than sense!" What was significant to me was that no special defence measures had been taken in the town.

Since the second day of the offensive no more teams had been sent out, and I regarded the special task of the commando company also as at an end. Of the nine teams originally despatched, probably somewhere between six and eight had really got behind the enemy lines. It may sound odd that, even to-day I cannot give the exact figure, but I was honest enough to have my doubts about the reports I received. One can well understand that some of these young soldiers were too ashamed to admit that when faced with their *real* trial—the penetration of enemy-held territory—their courage and resolution had left them.

The actual facts are that two teams were certainly captured and five others put in reports so clear and unambiguous (and confirmed by subsequent investigation) that there could not be the slightest doubt that they had done what they said they had done. In the two remaining cases their reports seemed to me exaggerated.

I should like to refer to some of their exploits.

One team reported that on the first day of the offensive they had actually got through the shattered front and reached the Meuse at Huy, where they made themselves comfortable in the vicinity of a road junction and quietly observed the enemy's movements. The team leader, who spoke excellent English, had frequently walked down to the road "to see for himself what was going on". After a few hours a tank regiment had passed by and its unsuspecting commander had asked him for news. The team leader had retained his presence of mind and doled out a lot of misleading information.

On the way back, this same team had torn up a newly-laid telephone cable and removed signposts for the use of various American supply units. The men were also able to give an excellent description of the confusion prevailing behind the American front on the first day. After twenty-four hours they were back in our lines in the area of the 5th Armoured Army, to which they rendered the first account of their doings, and a little later they rejoined us at Losheim. The report sounded incredible until it was confirmed next day by the Intelligence section employed in checking on enemy wireless transmissions. During the next few days, the latter broadcast several times that the American Command were searching for one of their own tank regiments!

Another team had also got into the American back areas and soon reached the Meuse without meeting any opposition. It reported that the Allies had taken no special security measures at the Meuse bridges. On its way out and back it had paid proper attention to the three roads leading to the front, laying mines, felling trees and distributing false warning notices. We were able to satisfy ourselves that these roads were not used by American supply columns, at any rate for a short time.

Another team had a little adventure which showed us how receptive the Americans then were to rumours. On the 16th December, it arrived at a village (probably Poteaux) south-west of Engelsdorf, where two American companies were organized for defence, having established road blocks and machine-gun nests, etc. It was for our men to get a shock when they were addressed by an American officer who wanted to know something about the situation at the front.

After the team-leader—who was wearing the uniform of an American sergeant—had recovered his first surprise, he invented an excellent story for the benefit of this officer. The fright betrayed in the faces of the men was probably attributed to the alleged previous scuffle with German troops. The team-leader solemnly assured him that the "Krauts" (American nickname for Germans) had passed the village on both sides, so that it was virtually isolated. The American must have swallowed this story, as he soon gave an order to withdraw, but not without sending a scouting detachment with our team. Fortunately, its instructions were confined to pointing out the open road to the west.

Another team had discovered an ammunition dump on its way to the Meuse, and had been able to hang about until it grew dark. Two skilfully laid charges had destroyed a substantial part of the dump. This team had also been lucky enough to come across a big telephone cable, which had been torn up at three widely separated points.

On its return, however, good fortune deserted it. After two days behind the enemy lines it ran into American troops which were engaged in an attack on Chevron, to which the leading tanks of the northern armoured group had penetrated. In the half-light the team had made a smart attempt to break through in their jeep. An officer was fatally wounded by a shot, but his three comrades joined up with the Peiper group, and on Christmas Eve the survivors of that formation reached the German front at Wanne, east of Salm.

The success of these few adventures greatly exceeded my expectations. They must have started a real spy mania in the American back areas, and in their excessive zeal they roped in as "prisoners" a large number of their own men!

In August, 1945, at the Interrogation camp at Oberursel, I was told the following story by an American captain: He had been himself arrested by the Military Police at the end of December, 1944, and it had taken a considerable time for him to clear himself of being a German spy and a member of my band. Admittedly, he had been partly to blame for his misfortune. In the advance across France he had found a German officer's pack and helped himself to a pair of German officer's boots, which fitted him. It was these boots which had prompted a smart M.P. to draw the inference, an inference not easy to counter straight away, that he had a German spy before him. The officer was arrested and handled far from gently. He assured me that he would never forget the week he passed as a suspected German spy.

In the Law Courts prison in Nuremburg an American sergeant also told me that in December of 1944, he and two of his friends had been arrested near the Meuse. They had been unlucky enough to find a German camouflage tunic and leave it in their jeep, where it was found by an inquisitive M.P. To make matters worse one of their number was a German-American, and spoke with a foreign accent. They were held prisoner for more than ten days and even confronted with four men of 150 Armoured Brigade. According to this sergeant, this hunt for German spies continued until January, 1945.

The work of the American counter-espionage service was made more difficult by the fact that many German soldiers were captured wearing American "field jackets" (a sort of windcheater), which some GI's had left behind. Their reason for doing so was that it was an outstandingly practical garment for December, when the weather alternates between frost and thaw. There was no comparison between the quality of German and American clothing in the fifth year of the war. But the wearing of this windcheater was quite enough to arouse suspicion that its wearer was a member of the 150 Armoured Brigade.

In the subsequent trial of my nine officers and myself, it was lucky for us that not one member of the battle-groups (not the commando company) was wearing such dress when he was captured. Otherwise our conviction would have been a certainty.

CHAPTER XV

As a result of the interrogation of many American prisoners, we found out that we had made a small but fundamental mistake when organizing the commando company. It may well have led to the capture of two of our teams. With economy ever present to our minds, we Germans never thought that the Americans would not fully man their jeeps as we did. We had assumed that these vehicles would carry the full complement of four, and constituted our jeep teams accordingly, and we only later learned that this was considered unusual and suspicious, because in the U.S. Army, suffering from no shortage of motor transport, the jeep crew comprised three.

The end of my experiences during the Ardennes offensive can be soon told. In the afternoon of the 20th December, battle-group Y, of Captain Sch., arrived at Engelsdorf and took up quarters on the main road leading to Malmédy. Captain Foelkersam was already back, though his group was still on the way and could not be with us before night. The position of Lieutenant-Colonel W.'s group was unknown. It was still too far away, and with conditions on the roads getting worse all the time we did not know whether it could arrive in time. I could only treat it as a distant and doubtful reserve. Its absence meant a reduction of our fighting powers, but the fact had to be faced.

Engelsdorf was under heavy artillery fire. I had set up my head-quarters in a villa a little way out of the village on the road to Belle-vaux. It was on the reverse side of a slope, so that the shells could be expected to pass harmlessly over it. At any rate they scarcely disturbed our discussions.

I had set daybreak for zero-hour. Captain Sch. was to attack from the south-east and Foelkersam from the south-west. The plan was to overrun the first lines and if possible get right into the town. But only the smaller part of my force must let itself be tied up there, as the main body was to pass through the town and seize the roads on the ridge to the north.

Foelkersam's group did not arrive until late that night, as they had been held up by a barrage at the exit from Engelsdorf. They were lucky to escape with a few casualties. Shortly before 5 a.m., I received the report that they were all "set" and the two com-manders left.

Just when the attack was about to begin I heard heavy gunfire from the north. The right wing of the attack had run into a violent barrage and been held up. Captain Sch. then decided to break off the attack and withdraw to the start line. When I got the news, I ordered a defence line to be established four kilometres north of Engelsdorf, as an infantry counter-attack could be antici-pated. In any case, the right wing must stand fast if the left were to succeed.

For a long time I had no news of the latter and the only evidence of what was going on was the sound of battle and vehicles bringing back the wounded. When it was light, I went ahead to a ridge from which I could see, not the whole of Malmédy, but a substan-tial portion of the road system on its western side. I had a good view of six of our tanks engaged in a hopeless struggle with a

superior force of the enemy, while trying to protect the left flank
of the attack.

Soon afterwards the first infantry arrived, and I learned that they
had run up against well held and strong defences, which could not
be overrun without artillery support. Our tanks were fighting a
hopeless action in order to cover the retreat. I gave orders that the
unit should reform behind the crest with a view to a counter-attack.

By the afternoon, we had established a frail defence line about ten
kilometres long. Our "heaviest" weapons were medium mortars.
To deceive the enemy as to our strength, I had ordered several
reconnaissances to be carried out. The American artillery fire had
greatly increased and was concentrated on the valley, the village of
Engelsdorf and the roads leading to it.

Towards evening I went to Divisional Headquarters to report.
The Ia had parked his wheeled "office" in the garden of the hotel.
I had not quite reached the entrance, some thirty paces away, when
a familiar sound made me take a flying leap into the house. The
ensuing bang was eloquent enough. From the truck, which had
received a direct hit, we pulled the wounded Ia, who had been
remarkably lucky, as a splinter the size of a short pencil had penetrated his back without reaching any vital organ.

We waited for the next salvo and jumped into our armoured car,
which was parked against a wall for cover. It was a pitch dark
night and we could hardly see anything in the murk, so we
groped our way along, keeping to the middle of the road. We had
just passed the bridge when three shells landed quite near. I felt
a blow on the forehead and jumped out of the car into the ditch
at the side of the road. A truck came rumbling along and ran into
my car, which was not showing any lights.

Then I felt something warm running down my face and got a
terrible shock when I put up my hand and discovered a bleeding
piece of flesh hanging down over my right eye. After a few
minutes we were back at Divisional Headquarters, where we gave
the staff quite a shock. With my undamaged left eye I had a look
at myself in a mirror. It was not a pretty sight! But when my
driver discovered two pairs of related holes in my trouser leg, and I
found the corresponding bruises on my thigh, I realized how amazingly lucky I had been and the thought restored my spirits completely.

My luck continued at the dressing-station, as one of the four operating tables was available though the doctors had been working for days without stopping. To keep my head clear I refused the more powerful anesthetics, but only felt pain when the doctors were removing splinters and experienced nothing worse than discomfort when I was being sewed up.

The doctors insisted that I must be sent off to hospital, but it was out of the question, as the situation was far too serious. I knew myself better than they did and that I was pretty tough. I told them that I would return to the line on my own responsibility.

Next day I went straight to Corps Headquarters and again asked for some heavy artillery. Then I went on to my old command post, taking the precaution of having with me Lieutenant-Colonel W. (whose group was in reserve) to act as my deputy in case I proved incapable. It is extraordinary how a wound in the eye can handicap a man. I found it quite hard to find my way about, and so spent most of the time in the house. But nothing stopped us from carefully planning the battery sites for the guns we had been promised, and I arranged that several American gun positions should be reconnoitred. We were glad to think that we should soon be able to reply to the enemy's drumfire. At night V1s passed overhead on their way to Liège.

On the 24th December, I set out to visit the 6th Armoured Army HQ at Meyrode, to press for delivery of the artillery which had been promised. The journey was most uncomfortable. The improvement in the weather left the skies open to enemy air activity, and more than once we had to stop and take refuge in ditches or fling ourselves flat on our faces when we were going crosscountry because the roads were blocked.

It was while lying on my face, after leaving Nieder-Emmels, that I started shivering fits. My wound had been suppurating during the last few days and I naturally associated the two things. Lieutenant G. insisted on my retiring to a lonely farmhouse near by.

There we found several soldiers sitting round a table and warming themselves. They gave me some hot tea, but the shivering continued as violently as before—even when I was put to bed. Yet within a few hours I had so far recovered as to be able to "go home", home being my command post.

On the 24th December, the commander of the long-awaited artillery turned up as a sort of Christmas present. Before he had time to say a word, I had him examining our maps and was pointing out the targets and the gun positions I had fixed. I did not notice his hesitation and confusion at first, but when I got up and asked him to go straight to his post and let me know at once when he was ready to fire, he found his tongue: "I must inform you, sir, that I have only sixteen rounds for the whole battalion, and for the moment there is no prospect of my getting any more."

I was simply speechless. What use was artillery without ammunition? This incident was, perhaps, characteristic of many parts of the front during the Ardennes offensive. It is not for me to say why supply broke down. The cause may have been the appalling conditions on the roads, the shortage of petrol for transport, the enemy's superiority in the air or the fact that enough of the material required did not exist and could not be produced at home.

Christmas Eve was hardly a cheerful occasion. The enemy artillery never let up for a moment, and every second we expected the infantry assault which could hardly fail to succeed, as we knew that our positions were but lightly held. Nor was that the end of our worries. Even rations were coming up only fitfully to our brigade, and we were still woefully short of winter clothing.

My young orderly officer went off to find a Christmas tree. He was away a considerable time before returning with the top of a lofty pine and a single candle. With these we endeavoured to create a seasonable atmosphere. Our cook, an old sailor from the commando company, a real Hamburg "smutje", produced a tough joint from the dead cow. The most pleasant surprise was a bottle of wine per man, which had been presented by the local priest.

On Christmas Day I made a call on Foelkersam at his command post which, as usual, was right forward, barely 300 metres behind the front line. On my way there I was frequently flat on my face, as shells of every calibre simply would not leave us alone.

In the early dawn, one of his returning assault detachments had surprised and captured an American scouting party. The latter was carrying a portable wireless apparatus, the "walky-talky". We appropriated this and one of our fellows, who could speak English, carried on a conversation for hours without the American end finding out what had happened. It was only when an urgent order to return was given that we allowed a genuine American NCO to answer, and what he said was: "I'm now off to Germany."

On the 28th December we were relieved by an infantry division, to which the task of covering the vital flank was assigned. The anticipated infantry assault did not materialize, perhaps because the enemy had been misled about our numbers by the audacity of our raids. Our brigade went into temporary rest billets at Schirbach, east of St. Vith. Before long it was to be dissolved.

During that period, a round robin from Army Headquarters, with a remarkable query, was brought to our notice: there must be an immediate enquiry whether anyone knew anything about the shooting of some American prisoners of war. The result of the investigation must be reported by a certain date. The reason for the query was an announcement on the Calais broadcast that on the 17th December, a number of American soldiers had been shot at the cross-roads south-east of Malmédy. 150 Brigade reported that nothing was known of the alleged incident, and we forgot all about the affair, as the enemy's propaganda methods were familiar enough. In any event, we considered that such a crime was quite unthinkable in the German Army.

CHAPTER XVI

O N   T H E 31st December, 1944, I was summoned to report at FHQ, which was then in the west, at Ziegenhain. It was a little hutted camp in the middle of a wood on the slope of a hill. To my surprise the morale of the officer who met me was not as bad as might have been expected in view of the failure of the last offensive.

Adolf Hitler received me the same morning in a small conference room. When he saw my head bandage he enquired about my wound and sent me to his personal doctor, Stumpfecker, for an immediate report. The doctor was consumed with rage when he removed the bandage and saw the suppurating wound and inflamed eye. He said I should have gone to hospital long before. Now the damage was done and my sight was seriously threatened.

I had a great deal of difficulty in convincing the good man that I had an excellent constitution and had to submit to drastic handling, lying for hours on an operating table while the wound was cleaned and treated with infra-red rays. I was also given a series of injections to counteract the suppuration. The whole business was most unpleasant, but ultimately it saved my eye, though the doctor was not exactly encouraging when we parted: "I can't yet say whether the injections will do any good. The next two months will show. If you find the sight of your right eye getting weaker in that time, it will mean that the optical nerve is already affected and it can't be saved." In fact it healed up well.

"We are now going to start a great offensive in the south-east," said Hitler when I saw him that afternoon. His attitude seemed to me very puzzling and I wondered whether he was deceiving himself or was under the influence of Professor Morell's injections. Dr. Morell had been able to acquire almost unlimited power over him. Many other doctors, Rudolf Brandt and Hasselbach, for instance, had long been greatly concerned about his health. Dr. Brandt told me that Morell relied on continuous stimulating injections, a treatment which he, Brandt, regarded as harmful in the long run. Purely by chance he had learned one day that for a long time Hitler had been taking a considerable number of stomach pills, which were harmless in themselves. When they were analysed it appeared that they contained traces of arsenic. He knew that Hitler could not continue to take arsenic, even in the minutest quantity, for years without ending up with a serious illness, and had warned him accordingly. But Morell proved the victor.

This was my last long talk with the Führer. Despite my forebodings, I left the room more cheerful than when I entered it. Field-Marshal Keitel, who was my host, looked much more concerned. I declined an invitation to spend New Year's Eve at FHQ, left the same evening and heard the bells of Cologne ring the New Year in. Early next morning I was back with my brigade.

When the 150th Armoured Brigade was dissolved at the beginning of January, most of the volunteers remained with my commando formations. It says a great deal for the morale of the German Army at this juncture that more volunteers applied for special service than could be accepted.

At the beginning of 1945 it was clear to my staff officers and myself that we were entering the very last phase of the war, so when the Russians started their great offensive early in January and obtained great successes it was certain that a decision in the east would precede one in the west. The dispositions of the German military chiefs also showed that they intended to employ what was left of Germany's defensive strength in the east.

In the afternoon of the 30th January, I was sitting at my desk at Friedenthal when a telephone call came through from the head-quarters of Himmler, who had just been appointed commander of Army Group Vistula. It was an urgent order to the following effect: my commando formations must leave to-day with all avail-able units, proceed direct to Schwedt on the Oder and establish a bridgehead east of the river. The bridgehead must be extensive enough to form a base for a subsequent offensive thrust. On their way the formation must relieve the little town of Freienwalde, which had fallen into Russian hands.

I checked this order word by word. Even the last sentence was not a mistake! I find myself still wondering how Army Group Vistula could relieve a town "in passing", so to speak. My officers and I stared at each other. Another lightning job for us! The necessary orders were immediately issued to the "Mitte" battalion, the parachute battalion at Neustrelitz and the "North-west" bat-talion, which was only one company strong. It was then 5 o'clock, and I summoned my battalion commanders for 11. How we were to get away "to-day" was far from clear.

The question of transport was a great worry, but I got all the transport officers working at top speed and the nearby depot agreed to work all night and also help us out with their own vehicles. At headquarters there was furious activity. With my new Operations officer, Captain Hunke, I worked out the orders for the recon-naissance and march. We calculated that if all went well we could get away by 5 a.m.

Shortly before eight o'clock I was in Schwedt, where the recon-naissance parties were waiting for me by the Oder Bridge. They were ordered to reconnoitre as far as Königsberg in the Neumark, so that I should know what lay ahead of the bridgehead. Then I sought out the commandant of Schwedt, a colonel who had lost a leg and told me that he had to take morphia from time to time to deaden the pain.

A call to Army Group soon cleared up the position as to command in the town. The colonel and a small staff were wanted elsewhere, and he would be leaving on the 1st February. Three depot batta-lions and a pioneer battalion would also come under my orders in Schwedt, but I must have no fancy ideas about their efficiency, as they were mainly elderly invalids, all the good men having been sent to the front-line long before.

Before these battalions arrived I wanted to have a good look at the bridgehead. The bridge itself, almost a kilometre long, spanned the river and the Oder Canal, between which were some flooded meadows with a causeway. The river was frozen, but the ice would bear, a very unpleasant feature if the Russians arrived. The first job of the pioneer battalion would be to blow up the ice. We could also ask for some ice-breakers from Stettin. If we could then manage to open the sluices and flood the area between the river and the canal, we should have a good barrier against surprise Russian attacks across the river.

By the time I got back to barracks, my plan was decided. An efficient collecting centre must be organized to gather in all the stragglers now drifting in, whom we should use to convert the depot battalions into battleworthy formations. I could only hope that the Russians would give us time.

In the afternoon I had a long talk with the pioneer major. We sketched out on the map the boundaries of our bridgehead, which was to have a radius of six kilometres, and follow the lie of the ground, itself hilly and good for defence. We constructed an outer ring and when that was ready a small inner ring, drawing our man-power from a labour battalion and the male population of the town and its immediate vicinity. Plenty of country carts were available, and the pioneer battalion supplied the skilled direction and the foremen.

I sent my parachute battalion to hold a position east of Königsberg and fight a delaying action if necessary. The Königsberg militia battalion, led by its NSDAP commander, was placed in support. The " Mitte " battalion occupied the inner defence line with a view to holding the reduced bridgehead at all costs if the Russians broke through by surprise.

During the next few days everyone worked feverishly on strengthening the field works. The civilians knew they were defending their homes and all of us had a great opportunity to see what we really meant by a united nation. In a few days we were ready to proceed with the construction of the inner line, and the final touches could be left to the soldiers.

I had advised the civilian population of Königsberg, through their burgomaster, to evacuate the town and arranged with the burgomaster of Schwedt to find homes there for all the evacuees. We could not take the responsibility of leaving civilians in areas liable to be fought over.

A militia battalion from Hamburg arrived unexpectedly in Königsberg. Nearly all the men were fine specimens and full of enthusiasm, as far as I could judge. I knew I could not value the fighting efficiency of the militia battalions very highly, but I needed every man who could fire a gun and the weapons and equipment of the Hamburg lot, at any rate, were excellent—thanks to the defence commissioner, Kaufmann, in that city. The Königsberg battalion were worse off.

We reconnoitred strenuously from the start to ascertain where the enemy was and from what direction he might come, and as early as the 1st February, Russian troop movements near and south of Bad Schönfliess were reported. If their patrols were small they were attacked, usually successfully and with hardly any casualties. Our men profited by their excellent training in every way.

By the 3rd February we were able to put a full strength battalion on each flank. I reserved the two centre sectors for my own two battalions, as I anticipated that the main attack would come from the direction of Königsberg.

A Luftwaffe lieutenant-colonel reported to us with the information that he had been ordered to form a battle-unit out of all stray airmen. In the course of a week, he produced three companies as well as useful equipment from Luftwaffe stocks.

FHQ had sent its own wireless party to Schwedt to keep us in direct touch with them. Apparently they attached particular importance to this part of the front. We were thus able to give them completely reliable news about enemy movements in our sector.

Instead of the artillery we had asked for, the Schwedt Battle Group received from Army Group three Luftwaffe anti-aircraft sections. They came from different regiments, and there were other bureaucratic complications, so that it was only after a long talk with the Luftwaffe general attached to the Corps that the command tangle was sorted out and I was able to convert the mobile batteries into field artillery, and settle their battle stations in the bridgehead. The remaining batteries had gun positions made for them on the western bank of the Oder, and were used as heavy artillery. They needed a lot of training, but fortunately Army Group had also sent us an artillery officer who did wonders with them in a few days.

One day a Corps general arrived and told us that we had a naval division in the defence line on the western bank of the Oder to the south of us, and that our battle-group had been converted into the Schwedt Division, and both divisions were to form his new corps.

This general approved my orders to date and told me to carry on as before. The only order he gave was that the divisional boundaries must be defined. What particularly pleased him was the security measures enforced in our sector, for soon after he left me he came back, the sentries having refused to let him leave the bridgehead because he was unknown to them.

One day I received a secret and extremely urgent order from FHQ to the effect that two trucks loaded with incredibly important state documents had been abandoned in a forest east of Bad Schönfliess through the mistake of an official. In no circumstances must they be allowed to fall into enemy hands. Aircraft had been sent out to destroy these trucks, but had not been able to find them. The Schwedt Division must not fail to recover possession of the forest and bring the documents away or destroy them.

Some preliminary questions were necessary and I then learned that the vital papers were not state documents, but party documents of the NSDAP party (Nazi party) emanating from Bormann's office. I insisted that the official who knew exactly where they were to be found should go with us. In any case we should have to reconnoitre to ascertain whether an attack could have any chance of success. I was not prepared to take a vast risk with my troops for the sake of some documents and the reputation of a party official. I needed my men for more important occasions.

Eventually, I decided to see what I could do myself. I took my dog and four men who had been with me in Italy. My Ia, Captain Hunke, and four other men made up the party.

Cautiously picking our way on foot towards the town of Bad Schönfliess, we told our drivers to follow us later. Not a sound came from the first houses and we soon reached the medieval gateway. On the right there was a road leading to the station. Two civilians were lying dead close by. At length a man peered out from a window and then sidled out of his house, apparently unable to believe that he was seeing German troops. He told us in great agitation that Russian troops had been in the town for two days.

They had their headquarters and a number of tanks at the station, and had got the railway going again, so that troops and supplies were arriving continuously.

I decided that we would check this report ourselves. Three men were told off to try to sneak to the station through the town, while another party approached it by the road from the town gates. When they returned they reported that they had seen not less than fifty tanks by the station and that the Russian troops were encamped south and east of the town.

Now we knew enough. Any attempt to reach the forest and the two trucks through the screen of Russian troops had no possible chance of success. Besides, I was certain that the Russians must have found them.

Two young women, with children at the breast, had stayed behind with us. Neither had uttered a sound, but their eyes pleaded with us to take them along so we let them sit on the floor of the scout-car and drove away.

That same evening, the Russians attacked Königsberg with about 40 tanks and several battalions. The parachute company beat off the first attack, though suffering heavy losses, but towards midnight the enemy, attacking from north and south, made their way into the town. There was fierce fighting from house to house and more than ten enemy tanks were destroyed by bazookas. Our troops gave way step by step and towards morning were able to disengage and withdraw into the bridgehead. This first action had shown that even the newly-formed units could fight as a formation. They improved every day.

When I returned to Schwedt from my command post I was amazed to find the commander of the Königsberg militia battalion (and local NSDAP leader) waiting for me. He burst out: "All is lost at Königsberg!" As I learned that he had been waiting to see me since the previous evening, it meant that he had simply run away and left his men to fight without him. In military language he had been guilty of cowardice and desertion. I had the man arrested and brought before a divisional court-martial. The case was so clear that there could be no doubt about the outcome, and he was condemned to death.

I had a long talk with the legal officer, who told me that there was a regulation providing that senior party leaders could only be tried by a party court. I anticipated that the Third Reich would produce one of the usual red herrings and was not disappointed, as Gauleiter Sturz appeared on the scene next day. At first he overwhelmed me with reproaches, but when I put the simple question, whether desertion by party functionaries went unpunished, he laid down his arms and had to admit that I had acted in strict accordance with the law.

By the 5th February, we had abandoned all the outposts with the exception of the village of Nipperwiese, and the Russians were attacking the bridgehead every day. We had nothing comparable to the Russian tanks, which often got right up to our lines and had to be knocked out with bazookas. We heard from prisoners that our opponents were a Russian Guard Armoured Corps, which was equipped with improved T-34s and American tanks supplied under Lend-Lease.

The battle raged back and forth day after day. Attack alternated with counter-attack. One day two Russian tanks got within a few hundred metres of the bridge before they were knocked out. The infantry following was driven off almost single-handed by my sharpshooter platoon. On another occasion two tanks got near enough to fire at Schwedt Castle, but were then laid out by the commander of that sector personally with his bazooka. Such examples by officers worked wonders with the troops. All my earlier fears proved groundless. The men fought and behaved superbly.

One day the Luftwaffe company holding the last post in Nipperwiese was compelled to fall back and I gave this news in my evening report to Corps. Next morning—in the middle of a violent Russian attack on Grabow—a wireless message came through Corps: "Has the officer commanding at Nipperwiese already been court-martialled or shot?" I could hardly suppress my rage as I drafted the reply: "The officer has not been shot and will not be court-martialled!" Then I drove to Grabow in the bridgehead to join the parachute battalion there.

Violent fighting was in progress. Our front line in this sector was frequently lost and had to be restored by counter-attacks, which cost us heavy losses. The Russians always returned to the attack with fresh tanks and battalions.

In these circumstances I soon forgot the morning's message, and we were sitting in the cellar of a cottage when a telephone call came through from my headquarters and I was told that I had to report at Army Group at 4 o'clock. My immediate reaction was that

Corps, who did not like me, had probably repeated my ill-chosen words verbatim to Army Group. I was in trouble again!

But at the moment there were more important things to think about. The Russians had broken through on the left of the road and were threatening to force their way into Grabow itself.

On the other side of the road, tanks were attacking. Two anti-tank guns were quickly brought up and assisted an anti-aircraft detachment to beat them off. Our men crept up, like Indians, their tank-busters in their hands. Here and there a column of smoke showed that another tank had succumbed.

The ground on the left of the road had to be recovered yard by yard. The obstinacy of the Russians was amazing and few of them got back to their lines.

When I returned to my headquarters it was nearly dark. I glanced at my watch. Six o'clock! I had already kept the Reichsführer Himmler waiting two hours!

It was 20.30 when I arrived at his headquarters at Prenzlau. Most of the officers treated me as if I were a disgraced criminal, and Himmler's ADC told me that I was wanted in connection with the telephone message in the morning and said that the Reichsführer was in a rage over my belated appearance. "You can really expect something this time," were his parting words when I left.

I was soon called back and, entering the familiar room, presented myself. Himmler hardly acknowledged my presence and simply shouted at me. I caught the words "impudence", "disobedience", "degrade", "court-martial". I just stood stiff as a rod and waited for a chance to speak.

While Himmler was railing at me, he had been striding backwards and forwards. When he stopped for a moment opposite me, I took a deep breath and told him the Nipperwiese story in a few words. "The officer withdrew to the bridgehead on orders from me," I said, and went on to give vent to all the resentment that had been accumulating inside me for days: "The Schwedt Division got a whole lot of silly orders from Corps, but nothing at all in the way of supplies," was my parting shot. I was amazed not to be interrupted.

"But you've kept me waiting four hours!" the Reichsführer resumed. I explained that I could not leave my post during the fighting. His anger suddenly melted away and his mood changed. While I was telling him about the bridgehead he listened attentively and followed me on the map. When I said that I urgently needed tanks, I was promised an armoured-gun detachment. It was much more than I expected, but I was careful not to say so.

The Reichsführer even invited me to dinner, and put his hand on my shoulder when we left the room together. I can still see the astonished faces of the officers who were waiting for the return of a "cashiered Skorzeny".

During dinner, the conversation was all about failure and defeatism in many quarters, and treachery in our own ranks—about which I had learned something at Schwedt. Our signal units had overheard talks between enemy tanks and recognized some of the voices as German, thus proving that there was truth in the rumours about the "Seydlitz Army".

When dinner was over and Himmler got up to go I slipped in a question: "So far we have only discussed negative things, Reichsführer. You probably know much more than I do. How can we win the war now?"

I shall never forget his answer: "Believe me, Skorzeny, we'll win the war yet!"

As he gave no reason for his optimism, I could only bow myself out. The calculations made at GHQ relied on too many unknown quantities. Hitler was always preaching his belief that even the Russian reservoir must give out some day. That miscalculation accounted for the offensive in Pomerania in February, which was launched too soon. The flank thrust, which was to strike the enemy a deadly blow, came up against strong Russian reserves which, according to his reckoning, did not exist.

We had several striking successes with the new tank detachment when it arrived. On one occasion we rubbed out a flame-thrower detachment and on another we captured the village of Hanseberg, which was outside the bridgehead. The booty, in the shape of mine-throwers, anti-tank guns and machine-guns, was so great that Corps would hardly believe our figures. Unfortunately, these admirable reinforcements were taken away again after ten days. Yet we still took the offensive whenever we could and achieved considerable success.

Reichsmarschall Hermann Göring was extremely interested in what was happening at the bridgehead as his estate, Karinhall, lay just west of Schwedt. It was usually about two o'clock at night when we got our last call from Karinhall enquiring about the situation.

When I was asked one day whether there was anything I wanted, I promptly replied that reinforcements were always needed.

The very next day we received a newly-formed battalion of the "Hermann Göring" Division. It consisted of fine, upstanding young men, and was commanded by a major who had the Oak Leaves to his Knight's Cross. He immediately asked that his unit should be allotted a sector of the line, but when I enquired about his infantry experiences it turned out that until quite recently he had been a fighter pilot. Most of his men were in the same boat, and, as it would have been a crime to use them as a unit under such circumstances, I brushed aside the major's protests and broke the battalion up into small groups, which I sent as reinforcements to my best units. When I reconstituted the battalion a fortnight later, the airman was very grateful. His men had not suffered heavily, and had become useful front-line fighters as a result of their short, but hard experience.

The severity of the fighting increased from day to day, and conditions were made worse by the cold and damp weather, which made very heavy demands on the men's powers of resistance. As a large number of men had been incorporated in newly-formed battalions, which had been tied down to one area for weeks, it was quite remarkable that we had no more than six or seven cases of desertion during the whole period. I need hardly say that they were court-martialled. If I remember rightly, four death sentences for desertion were pronounced by our court-martial, and these were carried out after confirmation by Corps. Otherwise there were no signs of relaxed discipline and, in the opinion of experienced commanding officers, our formation fought as well as divisions which had been constituted as such for years.

One day a Cossack company reported under the command of a colonel. It carried out several audacious night operations. A Rumanian regiment was also sent to us and its men fought quite as well as the Germans. In our commandos we had Norwegians, Danes, Dutchman, Belgians and French, and it could almost be said that we were a European division.

There was an alarm one day when the Russians in the semi-darkness had succeeded in overrunning our main position along the Königsberg road. A few hours later they captured the village of Grabow and were barely three kilometres from the Oder. Our counter-attack with the storm company and part of the pioneer battalion was beaten off and it was only the third flank attack which enabled us to reach the village again. It had to be recovered house by house. Burning tanks and houses lit up the fog, and every wall and hedge was the scene of a desperate struggle. It was nearly dark when the position was completely restored.

When I reached the newly recovered cellar, which had been the command post of the parachute battalion, the telephone was, by some miracle, still intact. I called up Divisional Headquarters to report the conclusion of the fighting and was informed that Field-Marshal Göring had been waiting for me for hours. I said I would come at once.

I found Hermann Göring in an open car, surrounded by soldiers, and noted that he had no ribbons on his grey uniform. After I had reported the situation he insisted on going to the bridgehead at once. I readily agreed, but some of his officers were not enthusiastic. " It must be your responsibility," a general said to me.

Just behind Niederkrönig I halted the two cars. The road ahead could be seen by the Russians, and I could not risk exposing the Reichsmarschall to artillery fire, so we walked together along the trenches to the burning village. We often fell flat side by side when a shell came too close.

We caught sight of a burning Russian tank on the road with an 8·8 Luftwaffe gun close by. " You've made a fine job of that," said Göring, pointing to the tank, shook hands with the gun crew and gave them schnapps and cigarettes. A few hundred metres further on there was an anti-tank gun. Its crew stood smartly to attention. " I suppose you're grumbling because *you* didn't bag it," was his remark to them. The NCO retorted: " Begging your pardon, Herr Reichsmarschall, but we hit it twice." Göring laughed and produced some small gifts for them also.

When we reached the village he followed the course of the action closely. He was particularly interested in the tanks, and it was a good thing that we had not yet blown them up, as we usually did. He also crept into the command post and distributed presents. To my Ia, a box of the most expensive cigars. It was dark by now and I sent for the cars. We separated by the bridge at Schwedt.

The Russians had got the airfield at Königsberg going again, but we did our best to make them uncomfortable with our long-range 10·5 anti-aircraft guns. We had an observer on the church-tower in Hohenkronig, and he reported all aircraft landings by telephone.

Our well-aimed shots at the runway probably caused many a crash. On the other hand, we were often made unpleasantly aware of the efficiency of the excellent Russian fighter-planes.

An English broadcast about this time amused us greatly. "The well-known SS Obersturmbannführer Skorzeny, who carried out the Mussolini rescue, has now been promoted to major-general, and entrusted with the defence of Berlin, thus becoming the most powerful man in the German capital." There was the usual sting in the tail: "He has already made a start with the liquidation of doubtful elements among the civil population of the northern districts of Berlin."

I found out later that this was not such a bad shot, as about that time the idea of employing me in some way in the defence of Berlin was mooted in the Chancellery. The mention of my name may have been the origin of the broadcast. But how did the news get to England so soon?

On the 28th February, 1945, I unexpectedly received an order to return to Berlin, with an intimation that it was the wish of FHQ. My effort to take some of my formations with me was defeated, and I thought that the two battalions and the special units were lost to me for ever. I had to hand over the division to its new commanding officer within twenty-four hours.

CHAPTER XVII

IN BERLIN I was all at sea at first, as I had long lost all taste for staff work at a desk and, in any case, it was made much more difficult by the fact that most of my staff had been sent off to Hof in Bavaria. Supply and transport difficulties had increased enormously, and even the best organization could not make good the continuous damage done to the railways by allied air attack. Trains had to make detours and arrived very late.

On the 7th March, there was a catastrophe on the western front, as the Americans seized the Rhine bridge at Remagen. In the days following, we made many attempts to destroy the bridge from the air, but without success. In the evening I was summoned to FHQ in the Chancellery, and General Jodl gave me the job of getting my frogmen to work. Aircraft to bring them from Vienna had already been arranged.

For the first time, I made my acceptance of an assignment conditional. At this time of the year the temperature of the Rhine was about zero. Moreover the American bridgehead already extended for nearly ten kilometres upstream, so I said that I saw extremely little prospect of success, but would rush my best men to the spot and leave it to them to decide whether they would take the risk.

Lieutenant S. was the commander of the "Danube" Commando, and he decided to make the virtually hopeless attempt. It was days before the necessary torpedo mines could be brought to the Rhine from the North Sea coast. Several of the convoys were attacked from the air and prevented from proceeding further. When everything was ready, the enemy's bridgehead already extended sixteen kilometres upstream.

It was a very frosty night when the men entered the water, which was itself so cold that many of them vanished for good. The surface was swept by searchlights and before long they came under fire and suffered casualties. Great must have been their dismay to find, before they reached the bridge, that the Americans had already built several pontoon bridges. Nevertheless, some of the charges were attached to the pontoon bridges, though only the few survivors could say whether the necessary precision could be attained with frozen fingers, and those few survivors crept, half-dead, out of the water and found themselves prisoners. Some damage was done by the explosion of these charges.

It must have been about the end of March when I happened to be in the great corridor of the Chancellery as Adolf Hitler emerged from the conference room. I was horrified to see what a tired and bowed old man he had become. When he saw me, he came forward and put out his hands: "Skorzeny, I want to thank you and your men for all you have done on the eastern front. For days on end there was no good news except from your bridgehead. I have awarded you the Oak Leaves to the Knight's Cross, and will give it you personally in a few days."

A few days later, on the 31st March, I received the order to transfer my staff to the so-called "Alpine Fortress", where I was to wait for further orders. As the inevitable end of the war was at hand,

I could only assume that FHQ would also be transferred there with a view to the fight to the death.

I tried to obtain the release from the eastern front of any of my men with experience of mountain warfare and, after long negotiations, the commander of the " Mitte " battalion and 250 of his men were allowed to join me. So I had to start from the beginning again with two companies.

While the preparations for the transfer were in progress, I received a further order to travel by way of Colonel-General Schörner's headquarters in Silesia, where I was to discuss with his staff the chance of employing my battalion "Ost 11 ".

On the 10th April, I arrived there in time to congratulate Schörner on his promotion to Field-Marshal. Even on so short an acquaintance, I could understand why he was hated for his ruthlessness by some, but admired for his determination by others. Two commando attacks on two important road bridges behind the enemy front were considered and approved. In the week following, they were successfully carried out.

I first heard from a staff officer of Schörner's HQ of the critical situation in Vienna. I rushed south in a neckbreaking drive, and it was just beginning to get dark when I crossed Florisdorf bridge and entered the city. Distant gunfire could be heard and smoke was rising from some buildings which were on fire. I drove as fast as I could to Corps Headquarters at the former War Ministry building on the Stubenring. The whole place was in darkness, and a sentry informed me that the command-post had been transferred to the Hofburg. I found officers working in a cellar when I got there, and learned that enemy troops had reached the suburbs in many places but were being held, for the moment at any rate.

I decided to pay a hasty visit to my own factory at Meidling. When I reached the Matzleinsdorf ring-road I could hear heavy fighting in progress on my left. The road was blocked at this point. I got out and suddenly two shadows, Viennese policemen wearing battle helmets and carrying tommy-guns, emerged from the murk. " We are the garrison of this road block," they said with grim humour. " The Russians have occupied the Sudbahn area and are said to be surrounded there."

Eventually, I managed to find my way to my own works at Meidling and get into my old office across the yard. I left my men behind in the truck. The noise of battle was so near that we had to be extremely careful. On the upper floor, I found my partner and his woman secretary. They told me that there had already been some looting of public buildings, and for some incomprehensible reason the authorities had forbidden the citizens to leave the city by car. (Judging by what I had seen, this decree had not been universally obeyed.) What surprised me even more was that the municipal food stocks had not already been distributed to the civil population. It was plain that the administration would shortly cease to function altogether.

Returning to the Hofburg, I met the ADC of the Gauleiter, Baldur von Schirach, and reported what I had seen and heard. He seemed to find it impossible to believe. "According to the reports, the front is still firm everywhere," he said, and then took me in to his chief office.

When I entered the room it struck me that it was too elegant for a command post in a besieged city, especially as he was also Defence Commissioner. I repeated what I had said to his ADC, adding: "I haven't seen a single German soldier! The road blocks are unmanned! The Russians can walk in whenever they like!" His answer was: "Impossible!"

I suggested to Schirach that he should drive round to see for himself, or send someone to report to him. But his thoughts were further afield. On his battle map he saw divisions hastening down from the north, and others closing the trap from the west. He was liberating Vienna with a plan, which bore a strong resemblance to the relief of the city in the famous campaign of 1683. In those days Prince Starhemberg had been the saviour of the capital. There was something spectral about this strategic dissertation by the map, by candlelight in a deep cellar of the old imperial palace! Was he not fighting with ghost divisions? I knew that no troops were available. When I left, the parting words of the former Youth Leader of Germany were: "Here will I fight and die!"

About 5 a.m. on the 11th April, we were back on Florisdorf bridge. I had a last look round. A vision of fires and the thunder of guns, with some defence-post firing at something—such was my farewell to Vienna! Something inside me seemed to collapse and during the next few days my old spirits deserted me.

We reached Upper Austria through the Waldviertel, where the roads were not so crowded, and I put through a message to FHQ: "In my opinion Vienna will be lost to-morrow morning. A disorderly withdrawal must be prevented by using the police to appoint definite exits."

I ordered the surviving commandos, south-east and south-west, to join me in the Alpine Fortress in which I was, of course, extremely interested. It was certain that for weeks we had been working on defences in the foothills of this region, but I could not help wondering whether the necessary supplies of food and war material had been accumulated. Could weapons and munitions be produced without factories? Was it not too late to start on all this now? I had imagined from all I had heard in Berlin that the necessary preparations had been completed long before. Yet there seemed to be no single, all-embracing plan, and every Gauleiter and Defence Commissioner appeared to be concerned only with his own area. Where was the top authority which could co-ordinate all the individual efforts and direct them to a common aim?

On the 20th April, the Order of the Day was worded "Berlin will remain German and Vienna will be German again". It was the very day on which the first Russian shells began to rain down on Berlin. To those in the know it was the tolling of the bell. Goebbels' call to the nation on this day, the Führer's birthday, will always haunt me: "Loyalty is the courage to face destiny!"

What would our fate, the fate of Europe, be? Was the total defeat of Germany, an event approaching every hour, the real answer? Was there no other solution to the perennial problem of the discord of Europe? No doubt, the war had been decided. But who would win the peace?

On the 30th April, the radio announced the death of Adolf Hitler. I called the remaining officers and men of my staff together and gave them the news. I felt that they expected more than the bare fact, and considered what I should add. My short address ended with the words: "The Führer is dead. Long live Germany!"

When the new government was announced, it emerged that Admiral Dönitz was its head, and his last order was—armistice, with effect from the 6th May. No further troop movements were permitted. I had already decided to take a few of my closest staff to a spot in the mountains, and the rest of my men were given a strict order to hide and wait till they received further instructions from me.

CHAPTER XVIII

O N T H E evening of the 6th May, we were occupying a mountain hut near Radstadt. Lieutenant-Colonel W., Radl, Hunke, and three men were with me. These first days of peace amidst the sun and snow of the mountains would have been like a pleasant leave if we had not been so worried about our future. I was attracted by the idea of escaping abroad and also of suicide. It would have been quite easy for me to get away in a Ju 88 from some aerodrome, but that would mean good-bye to everyone and everything—home, family and comrades. As for suicide, many have felt that it was the only way out, but I considered it my duty to stand by my men and share their fate. I had done nothing wrong and had nothing to fear from our former enemies. From our reflections during those days one conclusion clearly emerged—the day of narrow nationalism and national states was over. All of us, friends and enemies alike, must aim higher and think as Europeans, without any sacrifice of our ideals. We felt that the European idea must grow out of the existing chaos and it could well be that those most qualified to foster it were the soldiers who had really been inspired by glowing love of their own country.

On May 15th, I sent a message to an American unit asking that a car should be available at 10 a.m. Surprisingly, the car was waiting and we reported to the orderly-room of the nearest American unit. The sergeant was extremely busy, as the unit had just received fresh orders to move on elsewhere, so he sent us on to Salzburg. The driver, a Texan if I remember rightly, was very sentimental. He stopped at an inn and proposed that we should have a bottle of wine. I went in with him and paid. When we resumed our journey he produced the bottle, had a drink and then handed it to us, with the remark: "Drink, you guys, to-night you will hang." Hunke had one reply: "Take it easy." Radl and I laughed.

In Salzburg our GI could not find the division, despite all the signposts, but eventually we were brought before a major who arranged that a lieutenant should escort us to St. Johann in Pongau and get movement orders and transport from the local German *kom-*

mandatur, after which we must collect our formation in the vicinity of Radstadt.

When the movement order was written out, the general refused to sign it and sent us to an American battalion in Werfen. I suspected something tricky and told Hunke to remain behind and look for the promised transport. I said that Radl and I would go to Werfen, and if we were not back in three hours Hunke was to get in touch with our split units himself. It would mean that we were being prevented from returning and the arrangement that we should assemble them had been cancelled. In that case every man must decide for himself whether to surrender or try to make his way back home.

In Werfen I was ushered into a big dining-room and placed at a table opposite two American officers and an interpreter. Referring to a map, I showed where my troops were and again asked that the movement order should be signed. Three doors leading into the hall and the window in one wall were suddenly opened, and I saw the barrels of machine-guns pointing directly at me. Then the interpreter asked for my revolver. After I had been carefully searched I was taken outside, where a fair-sized convoy had assembled. At its head was an armoured car, with its gun pointing at the car immediately behind which was obviously destined for me. Then came two jeeps and, last of all, another armoured car with its gun pointing forward.

Radl and the ensign stood aside, and I think we all turned a little pale. Nodding in the direction of the convoy, I remarked: "Too much of an honour for us!" and stepped into the car. An officer seated himself immediately in front of me—a silly arrangement, I thought, having regard to the possibility of the gun being fired at me. Next to me was a grim-faced GI, who kept his tommy-gun levelled at my stomach. As I knew the model, I was aware that it was not at safety, and the man kept his finger on the trigger.

My comrades took their places behind in separate jeeps and then we started off. It was already rather late and darkness was falling, and by the time we reached Salzburg it was quite dark. We were taken to the villa quarter and I was immediately struck by the unwonted spectacle of lighted rooms and windows wide open. The blackout was a thing of the past.

We were taken into a garden. I lit a cigarette and, while I was wondering what was coming next, several shadows jumped out on us from behind and before we knew what was happening our hands were tied behind our backs. Then I was taken up to the first floor.

In a room looking out on the garden two officers and an interpreter were seated at a table. There was a row of chairs in front of the window, and these were occupied by three reporters in uniform, but without badges of rank. Behind them movie-cameras were installed. On each side of me was a GI with his tommy-gun levelled at my navel. Everyone stared at me as if I had been a wild animal. I was almost blinded by the flashlights. I had not realized that the interrogation was about to begin.

Before a captain could put his first question I had made a protest both against the handcuffs and the loss of my watch. After some talks on the telephone my hands were released and my watch returned. The captain was about to open the proceedings when I asked him to wait a minute and, to the general astonishment, got up and walked to the window. I still wonder why I did not get a bullet in the back. I called out to my comrades in the darkness below: "Are you still handcuffed?"

"Yes, and it's a damned shame!" replied Radl.

I turned round and addressed the room.

"My protest goes for my comrades, too. I won't say a word until you release them!"

I remained standing at the window until Radl called up: "It's all right now. Many thanks!"

After a few personal questions, the officer said suddenly: "Didn't you try to murder General Eisenhower?" I believe I smiled as I answered: "No. If I had received orders to attack Allied Headquarters in any shape or form, I should have planned accordingly, and if I had tried to carry out my plan, it would probably have succeeded."

The reporters diligently took down every word.

Then the captain turned to the Mussolini episode. His questions simply tumbled out, so that it was hard to keep pace with my answers. He was particularly interested in the glider operation and why the Italians had not fired at us. When I answered that our arrangements covered that eventuality, all the officers and reporters shook their heads.

"In 1940," I added, "our parachutists carried out the well-known attack on Fort Eben Emael. It was three minutes before the surprised Belgian garrison fired a shot. I felt certain I could rely on a similar interval in Italy, particularly as no one would expect a landing from the air on such rocky ground. Of that interval we made full use."

Eventually, I rejoined my comrades in the garden and our hands were again secured. Once more I repeated my protest, but without my earlier success. With the barrels of two tommy-guns in my back, I was hustled out into the street and taken with my comrades to a guardroom, which had apparently been a bedroom of an inn.

At about nine in the morning I was escorted to a room on the upper floor, where an American major was waiting for me. This time reporters were absent. He wanted to start questioning straight away, but I made it clear that I had certain preliminary requirements. First, I asked for the removal of the handcuffs, as otherwise I would not answer. This request was granted. Then a cup of hot coffee and a piece of bread were produced unsolicited and the conversation began. The questions were on the same lines as on the previous day and ended up with the enquiry whether Hitler was still alive. The usual headshake followed my answer in the negative.

When they took me below again, I rejoined my comrades. They had been allowed to wash. Photographers were standing about and made excellent use of their time, perhaps because three generals were there to accompany us. Then a civilian emerged from the house, a most comical apparition. He was wearing light-blue pyjamas under a mackintosh, slippers on his bare feet and a Tyrolese trilby on his round head. It was the German minister, Dr. Ley. Even under such depressing circumstances, I could not help smiling.

Then a transport column appeared, headed this time merely by a jeep, with a machine-gun mounted on it. A senior officer made a sketch in the sand for the benefit of the officers and men around him, and seemed to be explaining something. We three prisoners seized the chance to exchange a few words and Radl suddenly whispered: "They're taking us somewhere to shoot us!"

I must admit that, seen from a distance, the drawing in the sand justified that conclusion.

"We must try to get away," Radl whispered further. "Better

be shot escaping than otherwise. They'll turn off the road into a wood somewhere and that'll be the moment."

I nodded agreement. Of course I did not like the idea of ending up as a "shot-while-trying-to-escape", but it would be better than simply being led like a calf to the slaughter.

I was put in the first truck, so order of rank was apparently disregarded, as I had Radl and P., each in a jeep, immediately behind me, followed by Dr. Ley and the three generals bringing up the rear. The captain got into the front seat and I again had a GI each side of me, with his tommy-gun levelled at my stomach and his finger on the trigger.

The day was oppressively hot. At one moment, we got out and sat on the grass by the roadside. We had never turned off the road, so that so far our suspicions had proved to be unfounded. While I was lying in the grass and nibbling at a piece of chocolate sticking out of Radl's pocket I tried to turn my hands in the handcuffs. I had read somewhere in Edgar Wallace that practised criminals, when being handcuffed, had turned their wrists slightly and this enabled them to slip them off afterwards. I had followed that advice that morning, with the result that I now succeeded in slipping the left handcuff down as far as the bottom of my fingers. It was a valuable lesson in the importance of reading detective fiction.

In the afternoon we arrived in Augsburg and were brought before several senior American officers, one of whom was Colonel Sheen. After another protest, my handcuffs were removed.

Towards the end of the interrogation a new dodge was employed to introduce an old question. Colonel Sheen suddenly asked: "We know for certain that you were in Berlin at the end of April. What were you doing there?"

I could only answer that I had left Berlin at the end of March and never returned.

The major flashed out: "But Radl has admitted it!"

"In that case bring him in, so that I can tell him to his face that he's a liar. He was with me the whole time and we were in Austria!" For a time no one spoke.

"But, Colonel Skorzeny, we know that you brought Adolf Hitler out of Berlin. Where did you take him?" pressed Colonel Sheen.

To this surprise attack, I had my answer ready: "In the first place, Adolf Hitler *is* dead, Colonel Sheen. Secondly, I wouldn't be here if I had brought him away. I should have stayed with him and not surrendered voluntarily." Colonel Sheen seemed satisfied with my reply.

But the real surprise of the day was to come. We were taken to another and larger room, in which the whole American CIC staff seemed to have assembled to witness the performance. I had to do a number of gymnastic exercises naked in order to expose every part of my body to the most minute examination. But, though defamed as the prince of saboteurs, I had neither secret weapons nor any other prohibited weapons about me. All I could show was some hard-earned scars, about which I was, of course, closely questioned.

Then my clothes were returned and we drove off in a car to the town gaol, where we were put into separate cells. I knew that in the morning my treatment was to be brought before higher authority, an authority no less than Allied Headquarters itself—the higher, the better from my point of view—my old optimism returned and I slept soundly and dreamlessly the whole night through.

Among other questions put to me next day, was whether I had not listened to Allied broadcasts and why we had never accepted the truth of the statements made. "Look," I said to Colonel Sheen, "if I had taken your Intelligence reports seriously the Mussolini rescue would never have taken place at all. Do you remember that on the 11th September, 1943, you broadcast the news that Mussolini had arrived in Africa as an Allied prisoner on an Italian warship? A trifling calculation showed me that the news could not be true. On the 12th September, Mussolini was still in Italy and that evening he was flying to Germany a free man."

CHAPTER XIX

WE WERE now sent on to Wiesbaden and this time our escort was nothing like so strong as previously. The convoy comprised merely two jeeps. Apparently Colonel Sheen's promise did not apply to the escort officer who, despite our protest, had us handcuffed again.

In the evening we arrived at Bodelschwingstrasse, in Wiesbaden. After the mass of GIs and others had had a good look at us I went into what was to be my home for the next few weeks, a wooden hut, which was one of five in a row. Once more I had to undress and perform various exercises, but this time I did not get my uniform back, though it had been most carefully searched. I was given a stiff, ill-fitting, prison suit, and then the door was closed.

I dropped on to a field-bed—there was a second against the other wall, separated from mine by a folding table—and was soon lost in thought about what the next few days would bring.

It was hot and damp in this wooden cage, the windows of which, naturally enough, would not open. Pillows were not allowed, and I was most uncomfortable, but one can get used to anything and eventually I fell asleep. After some time, the door opened again and someone came in and dropped on the other bed, but it was too dark for me to see who it was and in any event I was too sleepy to be inquisitive.

On awakening I had a big surprise. The newcomer was none other than SS Obergruppenführer Dr. Kaltenbrunner, head of the German Security Police. As I could not imagine that we had been put together for humanitarian reasons, or merely because we were both Austrians, I tried to think of some other explanation. It was not hard to find. I assumed that there would be sharp ears at telephone receivers connected with concealed microphones in the room. When I looked out of the window and saw a number of wires lying on the ground, my suspicions were confirmed.

When Dr. Kaltenbrunner awoke, it was his turn to be surprised. No doubt the listeners at the receiver heard our greeting, and the not exactly cheerful reminiscences of our first days as prisoners which we exchanged. Although we had no more state secrets to discuss, either then or later, I can give a useful tip; if you scrape the floor hard in a small, wooden room, you can produce very loud and unpleasant covering noises in a microphone!

I shared this hut with Dr. Kaltenbrunner for about five days. He told me that he had been interrogated in unimpeachable fashion by a history professor from an English university, and that it had restored his optimism for the future—a feeling which I did not share.

The weeks went by and on the 21st June—I can guarantee the date because I had made a calendar on a scrap of paper, which had miraculously survived the numerous searches—the sergeant called me out of the hut and said I was to go to the adjoining villa, as several officers wanted to talk to me. When I started dressing, the sergeant gave me the well-intentioned advice to stay as I was and tell them about the unbearable heat in my hut. I was never a man to reject good advice.

My appearance must have been highly comical, and yet impressive. I was wearing wooden clogs and pyjamas drenched in sweat, and with the sleeves full of holes. When I walked into the hall of the villa I felt very humiliated on finding myself in the presence of three generals and several other senior officers. But when I stammered out my apologies they showed they had a sense of humour as well as a certain sympathy with my position. They excused my clothes and offered me a drink.

The subject of discussion was certain military aspects of the "Battle of the Bulge". Fresh points of view were exchanged by both sides. I learned for the first time what a surprise that offensive had been to our former enemies, and how near we had got to our objective, the Meuse. Last of all came the old question whether we had not planned an attack on Allied Headquarters, to which I returned the usual negative. I believe that my answer was accepted. For the first time I had a feeling of being engaged in a discussion between soldiers as such, and that there was an atmosphere of understanding such as should prevail even between the conquerors and the conquered.

Next day I was transferred to the town gaol of Wiesbaden, and a little later my two comrades followed.

Solitary confinement was to be my lot.

I had arranged with Radl a special whistle to serve as a recognition signal. When I used it for the first time, I got an immediate answer. As he told me later, my particularly unmelodious whistle was unmistakable. I found out that he was below me to the left on the first floor of the prison. Ensign P. had apparently already been sent to a camp. Radl and I were soon able to inform each other that we were well and not downhearted—which was the main thing. In time, I learned the names of all my companions in misfortune, and we even managed to introduce ourselves.

The concession was made that twice a day I should be allowed out for a walk in one of the big yards. My guards on these occasions were more friendly, and my time in the fresh air often exceeded the regulation quarter of an hour. Of course I was always alone. In one of the courts there was a water tank, a relic of the war, but later on I was forbidden to disport myself in it, on grounds of hygiene.

On the 30th July, a serious start was made with the transfer of most of the Wiesbaden prisoners. It was carried out in accordance with a most complicated plan. The prisoners were divided into separate groups, collected in one room and kept waiting for hours and hours until distributed among the waiting trucks according to another plan. The whole business took four hours. There was an old general, whom I did not know, in the crowd in the waiting-room. I gave him some cigarettes and have seldom seen a happier face. I realized that the old man had much more to put up with in the changed circumstances.

As I was getting into the truck, I whistled our usual signal. When it was answered, I knew that Radl also was in the convoy.

We were taken to a Luftwaffe camp at Oberursel, which was fairly near. The cells, in wooden hutments, were smaller but cleaner than those at Wiesbaden. My door was numbered 94, and to it was pinned a white card with no name, but a red diagonal. I never completely solved the mystery of that diagonal. There were blue, green and parallel red lines on cards on other doors. All I could gather was that a red line probably meant something like "Caution. Dangerous man!"

Once again I was interrogated about the "Battle of the Bulge", and the favourite question, which was always cropping up, was: "Did the 6th SS Armoured Army issue an order that American prisoners were to be shot?" I could only reply once more that I myself had never seen such an order, and did not believe in its existence. To my mind it was inconceivable that any German soldiers could have deliberately committed such a crime, which would have received wide publicity if it were a fact. I also pointed out that about the end of 1944, in reply to a statement made by the Calais radio, the 6th SS Armoured Army issued a questionnaire on the subject to all its units—which did not exactly indicate a bad conscience!

In the weeks following there were four or five additional sessions on the Ardennes offensive, but they were purely military discussions and far more agreeable. From the interrogating officers I learned a lot I did not know about the striking effect of the rumours we had

spread. One of the most remarkable was the arrest of a lot of
Allied officers as alleged members of Armoured Brigade 150.

The 11th August was my particularly lucky day. When the door
of my cell was suddenly opened, there was my friend Radl in the
doorway and finding himself shoved into the room. His surprise
was as great as mine. My second interrogator at Wiesbaden had
been working hard to bring about this meeting, as the interrogations
were said to be concluded.

On the 10th September these pleasant days together suddenly
ended. A guard flung open the door and bawled out: "In five
minutes you have to be ready!" pointed at me, banged the door
and disappeared. It did not take me long to pack, even though in
the course of time I had acquired a second shirt. Outside I re-
newed acquaintance with the inevitable handcuffs and then we drove
to the aerodrome. It was only when I glanced at the other passen-
gers that I realized our destination—Nuremberg!

CHAPTER XX

In the two-engined aircraft I saw many familiar faces—
Admiral Dönitz, Colonel-General Guderian, Oberstgruppenführer
Sepp Dietrich, Minister Seldte (whom I knew only from photographs), Baldur von Schirach, Dr. Kaltenbrunner and others. All
had strained expressions.

From Nuremberg aerodrome we were taken in Red Cross lorries
to the Palace of Justice. A captain had previously removed my
handcuffs, as the precaution must have struck him as ridiculous. At
that time no one thought that many of those who passed through the
portal would never come out again alive.

Colonel Andrus, the Commandant of the prison, received us in
his office. Admiral Dönitz and I were the only officers with
shoulder-straps on our uniforms, and when we heard that all of us
must be regarded as "common prisoners", we rendered each other
the last service of removing those signs of our membership of the
German armed forces.

Cell 31 on the ground floor was allotted to me and I took a good look round through the open spyhole in the door. My first glance took in the door opposite from which Hermann Göring, apparently in very good humour, nodded to me. The organization here was excellent and I benefited from it from the start. After only two days I was transferred to cell 97 on the first floor, where there was more air and a view of tree tops and a patch of sky. The wind often brought the music of a distant sawmill through my window, and an old hurdy-gurdy never stopped playing " The night is stormy and the waves are high ".

On my walks in the prison courtyard I often saw Rudolf Hess, who was always handcuffed to his guard. Staring straight ahead, he hurried past me. Yet he never looked mental to me, but rather a man whose behaviour was a self-imposed mask. Later on I talked to various people who had known Hess in the old days, and was always coming against the question whether he had not made his flight to England on Hitler's instructions and been bound to silence by him.

When the suicide, first of Dr. Ley and then of Dr. Contis, created considerable stir in the prison, we prisoners were treated to a very disagreeable innovation. At night the cell was lit up by a light directed through the spyhole of the door at the prisoner's face, which must always be visible to the guard, which meant that he could not pull the blanket over it. One night a very conscientious guard woke me several times, and even brought the officer on duty to my cell. I was able to convince the latter by a demonstration that I had no wish to hide my face and, if it projected beyond the head of the bed, it was only because I had to use every inch of its length, owing to my exceptional height. After that I was allowed to sleep in peace.

One day I was summoned to a particularly big interrogation-room, where a number of very senior officers, including a general, were waiting for me. Once more I had to give them a most detailed account of the whole Italian affair. When I had finished, the general put some questions which revealed the greatest professional efficiency. Unfortunately, it was only later that I learned that he was Major-General William I. Donovan. During the war he had been chief of the " Office of Strategic Services " so, without knowing it, I had met the officer who performed the same function in the American Army as I did in the German. For a short time he was to preside at the Nuremberg trials; later he resigned from this unpleasant post.

When a Nuremberg prisoner talks about those days he cannot possibly fail to mention a man whom everyone knew, Captain Father Sixtus O'Connor, the Roman Catholic chaplain. His name shows that he was of Irish extraction and his temperament confirmed the fact. At regular intervals he visited all the prisoners, who welcomed his calls, and never confined himself to religious subjects unless the prisoner preferred. His sympathy with the fate of one and all won him many friends and with him one could discuss something else besides the trial and the past.

It would be unfair to write about Nuremberg without referring to the German prison personnel. They were soldiers who were subsequently released as prisoners, and some of whom voluntarily re-engaged as civilians. With very few exceptions, they behaved perfectly correctly, and showed much sympathy towards all the prisoners. Among them were two of my countrymen, and it was quite touching to see how kind they were to me. Their jokes and little presents—forbidden of course—such as a piece of cake or an extra cup of coffee, helped me over many a heavy hour, and I must admit that I was a proud man when I heard the Viennese labourer and the small builder from Lower Austria talking about " our " Skorzeny.

On the 21st November, after two written applications by me, I was suddenly transferred to the so-called Witness Wing. It was a great relief to find myself among other men and be able to talk to them all day long. But I was depressed to discover that many of our " leaders " were neither demigods nor deserving of the description in any real sense. They turned out just to be men—with all the ordinary human failings and weaknesses. We had certainly expected that after the collapse they would at least preserve their dignity and stand up for things they had advocated and practised for years past, so it was a terrible blow to me to find many high Nazi dignitaries proving themselves pitiable weaklings at Nuremberg.

We paid a weekly visit to the shower-baths in the cellars. On my way down there one day, I saw a whole pile of sheets. I wondered whether we were going to enjoy the luxury of bed linen, and after contemplating it covetously for three weeks, took the plunge and snatched three sheets. The same evening I gave away two of them, one to Field-Marshal Blomberg, who had been in bed for several days, and the other to my Austrian countryman, General Glaise-Horstenau, a former minister. Both assured me next morning that they had not slept so well for a very long time. My conscience could not have troubled me much, as I had my sheet with me for the whole three years of my captivity.

At the beginning of May, the Nuremberg phase came to a sudden end with an unexpected order to get ready to move out. My wardrobe was slightly more extensive, because when our uniforms got so worn out that they began to fall off, we had been given discarded tunics and underwear from the U.S. Army. Still, all my worldly possessions went comfortably into two cardboard boxes. Off we went south in a lorry which was a proper cage.

At night we arrived at Dachau and passed straight through to the bunker. Again I found myself in solitary confinement and wondering why. A few days later I was given the explanation by an interrogator. The subject of the investigation was the old favourite, the Ardennes offensive. He wanted to know what Army Commands had been known to me, what the Corps Commander had said, and a lot besides. I told him everything I could remember, but apparently it was not what he wanted.

In the days following, he became more pressing. He gave me the quite superfluous assurance that the Military Court at Dachau had nothing against me, but it would pay me to help him to elucidate the truth. I told him that I also wished the real facts to be ascertained, but I could only tell the truth, which was that I knew nothing whatever of any oral or written orders of the nature they desired, viz., orders to shoot prisoners.

One day he showed me a statement by a major of the 1st Armoured Division, which was said to contain serious charges against me personally. He said that I could keep this document and destroy it if I would help him. To this offer I replied that I would have nothing to do with so serious a matter as tampering with evidence to be given in court and that, in any event, I was not in the least interested in what had been said by the major, whom I did not know.

I was brought back to Nuremberg as suddenly as I had been removed to Dachau, but this time I was taken on a stretcher, as I had had a recurrence of stomach trouble. In my absence Nuremberg had been working at high pressure. The trial of the alleged criminal organizations was on, and the defence wanted some affidavits from me. None of us had any doubts about the outcome of the great trial, but the case of whole organizations being charged with crime was so novel that we had no idea how the charge would be put.

After a few weeks there was a fresh move, and some ninety prisoners were taken away on three big lorries to the camp at Nuremberg-Langwasser. But the relief to be anticipated from the somewhat freer life at a camp was very short-lived as, after two hours, Field-Marshal Kesselring and I were removed in a jeep to the " solitary " cells.

About a week later I was again removed to the Regensburg camp, but solitary confinement was for a very short time, and my stay here did me a lot of good. My comrades treated me with a degree of sympathy which I had not expected. The Austrians in the camp, myself included, were awaiting repatriation. One day about 250 of us were piled into goods wagons and taken to the camp at Darmstadt, where I knew Radl was. Our first journey through a German landscape did us good, and for many of us meant the first chance of a few words with German civilians, mainly railwaymen and travellers.

The hard floor and the rattle of the wagons made sleep impossible for us during the two nights, so we had long talks in which we discussed the choice—Austria or Germany—which would be offered to us at the repatriation centre at Darmstadt. Why could a man not be both a good Austrian *and* a good German? What was the sense of placing another frontier between these brother nations at the very moment when all the hopes for the future depended on the abolition of frontiers throughout Europe? National egoism could only delay, if not thwart, the healing process.

But there was a further consideration, which in the end determined my decision. Most of my comrades had to go through the mill of the German Denazification Court, and I felt I must do the same. The country whose welfare had been my dearest wish, and to which I had dedicated all my enthusiasm, should be the judge as to whether I had ever done it any wrong. I decided to share the bad as well as the good days with my men and to remain in Germany. The words of the national anthem " . . . and most of all in evil times " should mean something more than lip service.

But at first the realization of my decision was hindered by higher powers. We stood for hours in Darmstadt station without receiving orders to march to the nearby camp (where, as I learned subsequently, the slogan "Skorzeny ante portas", spread like wildfire among the prisoners). Meanwhile we had become very hungry, as the journey had taken longer and meant exhaustion of the available rations. At my request, the Red Cross sisters solved our problem for us. They conjured up soup, bread and a little butter. Then there were sudden shouts of "Get in", and we left on another two days' journey back to Regensburg. Our motto might have been "long live immortal bureaucracy!" It appeared that the coming of our train had not been reported to Darmstadt, so it had to be sent back.

The Regensburg days did not last much longer and I soon heard the order, "Get Skorzeny ready". Accompanied by several comrades, I was taken before the American camp commandant. I made a violent protest when I was handcuffed again. Even the captain did not see the necessity for such an order, and spent over an hour on the telephone trying to obtain its withdrawal, but in vain. Next day we arrived at my old gaol in Wiesbaden, which had already been handed over to the German authorities and had only a small "American" section.

I read how the death sentences had been carried out at Nuremberg. Was that the final curtain to the tragedy of Germany, or the end of an act in the struggle for the ideal of a world-embracing justice? But what would be the consequences in the future of the unprecedented condemnation of whole organizations as "criminal"? It is true that the General Staff had not been found to be such an organization. But the very fact that this institution, which every nation possesses and which performs the same functions everywhere, had been in the dock, was something the effect of which could not be foreseen. But the unlimited character of the verdict, which affected millions of men, was equally disturbing. Where would the line be drawn next time?

After a week I was transferred, this time without handcuffs and far more comfortably, to the familiar Interrogation Camp at Oberursel, but before anyone interviewed me I was again on my way to Dachau, where I was condemned to solitary confinement again. I seemed to be completely forgotten.

My health got worse and worse, but the doctor, an interned

Austrian, was unable to procure my removal to the hospital unless I consented to an immediate operation for the removal of the gall-bladder. I had great confidence in him and as he advised me to agree, I was transferred and given a single room. A guard sat by my bedside day and night, though at the time I could hardly crawl. On the 6th December, everything was ready, including the guard, who came into the operation room to see that I did not bolt and take the operating table with me!

Then began a weary period of convalescence. It was weeks before I could really manage to walk. In February, 1947, I was released from hospital and transferred to the so-called " Court Bunker ", a building dating from 1946, and in every respect worse than its Dachau counterpart. The cells were some 2·50 metres long, 1·40 wide and about 2·20 high. They were of concrete throughout and had one small airhole measuring 15 to 60 centimetres. The furniture consisted of two bunks, one above the other. But the worst feature was that boards had been laid in the passage between the cells, and the Polish guards marched up and down on them all night.

I had some compensation in the shape of news from Karl Radl. He had reached Dachau via Wiesbaden and been given a good job in the camp. With a few other of my men, who were known to the American staff as " Skorzeny Boys ", he was looking after the kitchen garden. Thanks to him, a little " green fodder ", as we called it, often came my way by secret routes.

The morale of the more than 350 prisoners at Dachau's " Court Bunker " was frequently below zero. Many of them had been detained for months without being interrogated or knowing what was in store for them. By way of contrast, the women internees kept up their spirit remarkably well, and proved a shining example to the men. They included a number of secretaries, who had no idea why they were imprisoned.

CHAPTER XXI

I<small>T MUST</small> have been some time in March when a lieutenant-colonel had three long and most objective discussions with me about the Ardennes Offensive, and I had the impression that "Operation Greif" was to be subjected to close scrutiny for the last time. As I was absolutely sure that nothing wrong had been done, I was not worried in the least.

When I had signed the last statement I asked the officer for his frank opinion whether any of the activities of 150 Armoured Brigade had been a breach of any of the laws of war, and he replied in the negative and said that the decision of his superiors could be expected in about a month. I marked the approximate date on my wall calendar.

But weeks went by and the date was long past and still no news came. About the middle of July, I was summoned to the office of the bunker commandant and found myself faced by a large number of people, whom I did not know, apart from Colonel R., and the civilian I have previously mentioned. Reporters were standing about with their cameras and it appeared that some important affair was afoot. When eight more German prisoners, members of 150 Armoured Brigade, came in one after another, I knew that we were going to be charged.

I studied their faces. Six of them were wholly unknown to me. Then the colonel began to read the charge and the civilian repeated it in German. I simply could not understand the second count. After the introduction, which spoke of a common plan and a joint conspiracy, came the words: ". . . and ill-treated, tortured and killed American prisoners of war, whose names and numbers are not known, but were not less than one hundred in number."

I hardly listened to the rest of the charge. It was the second accusation which particularly staggered my comrades also. In none of the interrogations during the two years of my captivity had it ever been suggested that I was in any way connected with such an affair, and I was able to satisfy myself that the same was true of the other men charged with me.

The trial began with the presentation of the case against us, and

I waited day after day for the prosecution to produce evidence in support of the second count.

At the end of the case for the prosecution, Colonel R. wanted to withdraw Count 2, but the president of the court expressly pointed out that if that were done this charge could never be made again. It was poor compensation when I was told later that the murder charge was only retained because, without it, there was little chance of obtaining even a trial against us. In 1947 other prosecutions were intended if a murder charge could be incorporated.

After the reading of the charge, we were taken back to the bunker. My "fellow conspirators"—five naval, three army and one Waffen SS officers—and I had a very busy time the next three days. The three officers appointed to defend us, Lieutenant-Colonel Robert D. Durst, Lieutenant-Colonel Donald McClure and Major L. I. Horwitz, grilled us in accordance with all the rule of the art. I was not certain at the time what the idea was, but the explanation came on the last day when Lt.-Col. Durst shook me by the hand and assured me that he was absolutely convinced of our innocence, and he would defend me as if I were his own brother. Subsequently, he told me that, even as defending counsel he had a duty to the court to elucidate the truth, and that was why he had given us such a grilling.

The three American defence counsel were soon joined by three German lawyers, who voluntarily offered to act for us. I had to tell them plainly that they could not look to us for any payment, as we were all poor as mice, and the best we could do was a post-dated bill without any security.

I had a very pleasant surprise a few days later when one of my countrymen, Dr. Peyver Angermann, arrived from Salzburg. He had had himself arrested there so as to be sent in a prisoners' convoy to Dachau. The highest sense of humour was his greatest virtue. "I made enquiries about your reputation before I came," he said as soon as he had shaken hands, "and the answers were excellent."

At the very outset we accused had to make two very important decisions. Lt.-Col. Durst told me that he could not promise success at the trial unless we worked together as a team with a "team-leader", and accordingly he asked that we should agree in writing that he alone should decide how the defence should be conducted, and on other defence counsel should take any step without his approval. He would consult me as "leader" of the accused before making any decision.

This was a tremendous responsibility for me, as it meant that I had the fate, and perhaps the lives, of my comrades on my hands, particularly as Lt.-Col. Durst proposed that, if possible, I alone should go into the witness-box and represent all the defendants. It was only after long and hard reflection, and with the full approval of my comrades, that I made up my mind to shoulder the responsibility.

There were other unhappy moments in the weeks preceding the trial, as one lot of bad news followed the other. At first Colonel Durst was quite satisfied with the composition of the court, though personally I was not too pleased to hear that Lt.-Col. Ellis, who had been the prosecutor in the Malmédy trial, and with whom I had not got on particularly well, was the chief of the "War Crimes Group" at Dachau. A few days later, Colonel Durst came in rather depressed because the composition of the court was being changed. He said that the president would be a Colonel G. It was not very cheering to hear whispers that this officer was familiarly known as "the hanging G". But it was only after considerable hesitation that I agreed to Colonel Durst protesting against the appointment of Colonel G. and some other members of the court of nine, as I thought we should thereby make enemies in certain quarters. But higher issues were at stake. In the end, four or five changes were made, though Colonel G. remained president. The majority of the nine judges were front-line officers and certainly decided in accordance with their convictions.

Colonel Durst took the greatest pains in picking civilians from the War Crimes Group to form a little staff to work under his directions. We only objected to two, one of whom had previously arrested and interrogated one of the defendants, while the other had assisted in the Schwabisch-Hall prosecution of my comrades of the 1st SS Armoured Division.

In the bunker the nine defendants were accommodated three to a cell, and we worked like bees at the preparation of the defence, though we had to wait for the main part of our task until the trial started, as we were not given any incriminating documents beforehand. To accusations in such wide and general terms we could only reply by setting out the exact facts of our actions in the past.

Head of the charge was that we had fought in enemy uniforms.

We knew that it was untrue, but how could we deal with it in the absence of dates and places? The next complaint was that we had stolen equipment and Red Cross parcels from American prisoners. All we knew was that we had received all our miserably inadequate equipment from GHQ, which had ordered us to participate in the offensive. How could we prepare our defence till we knew when, where, how and by whom the alleged misdeeds had been committed?

It struck me as rather odd to find that a vast number of bets were being made on the result of the trial. Quite substantial sums were at risk between the Americans backing the prosecution and the defence respectively. From the start the betting was in our favour and by the end of the trial the odds had risen to ten to one in our favour. The course of the market helped us to fancy our chances.

It was not so easy to get all ten defendants together and weld them into a team. I hardly knew any of them as, curious to relate, no charge was brought against any member of my personal staff. There were conflicting interests among the accused. But I must record how I acquired my best champion in those days.

One defendant, a naval officer, came to me one day and told me the following story. He was the son of a German father and English mother and had always been an opponent of the Third Reich. He had applied for transfer to my brigade only because he was waiting for an opportunity to desert. He had given that information to the authorities after his capture and said that he hated me, though he had only seen me once and there was no ground for his dislike. During captivity his eyes had been opened and his idea of me had been completely changed after he got to know me well. He said that despite his former behaviour I could trust him implicitly and he would prove my best and most loyal friend. He has remained so to this day.

I do not intend within the limits of this book to describe the trial in detail. It began on the 18th August, 1947. During the evidence a U.S. lieutenant said that in the fighting round Stourmont some German soldiers were wearing American field jackets over their German tunics. In cross-examination he honourably admitted that these men, when questioned, said that they belonged to the 1st SS Armoured Division and were not attached to Armoured Brigade 150. In the further course of the trial it appeared that many German soldiers in the west had worn U.S. field jackets they had found to make up for the lack of warmth in their own poor winter clothing.

After the evidence for the prosecution had been given, Colonel Durst asked for the acquittal of all defendants on all the charges, but his application was turned down.

The appearance of the first witness for the defence was the greatest surprise to everyone present, and particularly to the accused. He was Wing-Commander F. Yeo Thomas, who had taken a leading part in the French resistance movement, as a representative of the British Secret Service, and had volunteered to give evidence on our behalf. The statements of this officer gave the court a most comprehensive picture of the courageous deeds performed by the British during the war. Disguise was certainly not barred, and all means were considered fair to obtain the gear required for that purpose! I felt sorry that I could not shake his hand when he said: "Gentlemen, Colonel Skorzeny and his officers have always behaved as gentlemen."

After some other witnesses for the defence, I entered the witness stand, which was in the middle of the room. Colonel Durst let me tell the court, almost entirely in my own way, the whole story of the initiation, preparation and execution of "Operation Greif". I made what I had to say clearer with the help of a vast map of the area which covered almost the whole of one wall. My cross-examination by Colonel R., for the prosecution, was extremely fair and courteous.

The closing speech by Lt.-Col. McClure made the greatest impression. He turned to the judges and said: "Gentlemen, I should have been proud to have men like the accused in any unit I commanded."

A verdict of acquittal for all defendants was pronounced on the 9th September in a courtroom packed to the doors. Before I could shake my defender's hand, the leading advocate for the prosecution came up to me, shook hands and congratulated me on my success. He said I must know that in instituting the proceedings, he had only done his duty and acted on orders. He would have been glad to be spared the job! My reply was no less warm: "In that case, Colonel, you will understand that we Germans were only doing our duty and we also had to obey orders."

For that reason I am sure that it was by some mistake that the press, a few days later, reported that Colonel R. had described me as the "most dangerous man in Europe". Unfortunately, that undeserved attribute was always used when there was a shortage of headings for the fantastic stories about me which are still in circulation.

A few hours after our acquittal, we were together again in the bunker, but no longer in solitary confinement! Even the congratulations of the staff were sincere. Our unfortunate condemned comrades did not grudge us the relief they must surely have seen in our eyes. A few hours later we were transferred to the American camp.

It was a few days before we realized that the bad days were over. My army and navy associates were getting ready for their release. Of the ten defendants, only a man in the Waffen SS and I were still detained, as we were in the so-called " automatic arrest " class. But as hundreds of thousands of others were in the same boat, this restriction on our liberty was bearable. On Friday, the 12th September, I was returned to the bunker as alleged to be guilty of " war crimes ". Colonel Durst was no longer in a position to help me to clear up the obvious mistake, as he was no longer allowed to talk to me. Meanwhile the press had come out with annnouncement: " Colonel Skorzeny, just released, will probably be handed over to Denmark or Czecho-Slovakia." Even the bunker staff did not seem to credit the fresh accusation, as they treated me no differently.

Within a fortnight the whole mystery had been cleared up. There had been no request by Denmark for my extradition. In all probability some overworked official got his facts mixed up. I had promised a Danish officer that I would come and give evidence in his country whenever he required. The explanation of the Czecho-Slovakia business was even simpler, though it took another two weeks of industrious research to find out what had happened. The alleged request was a pure myth. So back I went to the camp and my return was celebrated by as good a dinner as could be turned out with the available stores. But it was a fortnight before St. Bureaucracy, active here as elsewhere, finally struck my name off the list of war criminals.

American Army personnel, from the Camp Commandant downwards, were now all friendly. When a sergeant found that I looked too shabby in my prisoner-of-war get-up, he got the tailor to make me a suit out of German military cloth. Another invited me to coffee and a third gave me books. I had a feeling that I was once more a soldier among soldiers, even though I was still sharing the fate of prisoners of war all over the world.

We had heard a good deal about the work of the American

"Historical Division" at Neustadt an der Lahn, which was engaged in the study of military history, with the assistance of some German officers. One day Radl and I were asked to write a suitable article about our Italian exploit. We two friends were only too glad to be in together at the death of those tragic times, seeing that we had shared the struggles and glories of better days, so we asked to be sent to Neustadt to work under the same conditions as the other officers.

The journey to Neustadt, which we made with other release cases from Dachau, was by "cage" truck. In view of this degrading and now quite unjustified means of transport, we were not sorry to leave Dachau and have no happy memories of it, despite the successful outcome of the trial. To our astonishment we landed in Camp King, the old Interrogation centre at Oberursel, and as it was late at night, were put into single cells. Under a new regulation, clothes and shoes had to be put out in the passage. Next morning Radl and I were transferred to the same cell, but we decided to refuse to work under such conditions for the Historical Division, and communicated our decision to its head, Colonel Potter, who came to see us with some of his officers. He was in full sympathy with our request for better quarters, but it was three days before room was found for us in "Alaska House", which was occupied by three persons.

We had previously been given false names in accordance with certain special rules of the Secret Service. Radl's name was "Baker" and mine "Abel". We arrived at Alaska House at the right moment. Two acquaintances of the Italian days solemnly introduced themselves as X-ray and Zebra. Abel and Baker, we murmured, suppressing a smile. At meals we had the company of a lady, Miss Mildred Gillard, who as "Axis Sally", had broadcast anti-bolshevist propaganda for her American compatriots. The situation was quite painful, though not for us, when five minutes later a fat sergeant called out my real name.

Axis Sally's nerves and health had suffered greatly during her long imprisonment, but though her hair had turned snow-white in that period, she was still an interesting and most approachable person. She helped us to improve our defective English and we passed many a pleasant evening in her room playing bridge and consuming warmed-up breakfast coffee and toast which we made quite professionally, on an electric stove.

Miss Gillard had remained static for more than a year, while the personnel of Alaska House was constantly changing. From her, I learned the fate of many Germans who had been "detained" there for short or long periods. When we were able to borrow a radio, we had almost a luxurious life in our room, particularly as we had brought our own sheets from Dachau.

At Christmas, 1947, Radl and I were given fourteen days' leave on parole. Of course, we played the game and were back punctually on time. It was my first contact with the life of Germany outside the barbed wire. It was the "hunger" winter and conditions were worse than I had ever imagined. Our first call was on Hanna Reitsch, who was living at Oberursel. She introduced me to a Roman Catholic priest, and with this previous enemy, I had a long talk which was to the advantage of both of us, as we parted as men who understood and respected each other.

The American officials of the Military Government to whom I had to report were very kind, but talk with the man in the street showed me how deep were the wounds of war. I was glad that I could look any starveling in the face, as I was myself as poor as a mouse, having lost all I possessed. In the presence of the innumerable cripples, I felt almost ashamed of my sound limbs.

In February, we completed our work for the Historical Division.

The ghost of the dead Hitler still haunted the heads of many. A small commission turned up at Oberursel one day to investigate the story of a Luftwaffe private, who was apparently out of his mind. He had said that he had been employed as a guard at a private aerodrome belonging to Skorzeny near Hohenlychen and, early in May, had seen Hitler and me getting out of a Storch aircraft which I had piloted. I hope this illusion did not cost the good man too long a stay in an asylum.

In February, the papers were full of a new "story". It was reported that one of Skorzeny's officers had said that, on his orders, he had taken Hitler in a Ju 52 from Germany to Denmark and thence to Spain, but that his plane had been shot down over southern France and he had got off with a head wound.

This pretty story cost me another visit to Nuremberg. There it was recognized at once for the rubbish it was.

The occupants of the cells at Nuremberg were far fewer in number than on my previous stay, but they were also far more interesting, being steel, chemical, economic and scientific experts. From long conversations with such men I learned a lot that was of value to me afterwards.

I had two extremely informative and memorable talks about this time with Professor Dr. Kempner, leading for the prosecution in the Schellenberg case, and Captain Musmane, the president of the court. The principal topic was the old theme, "Adolf Hitler", though they may have had some small interest in me personally. I could only tell them, as I had told others, what a great impression the Führer of 1943 made upon me and what a contrast it was to my last picture of him as a sick old man, breaking under the burden of care and no longer walking upright.

I also told Professor Kempner what it was that made me, and probably many others, fight on to the bitter end: "For a man of character, in certain situations, there is only one course he can take. The man who in the same situation sees two courses open to him may be an artist in living, but is hardly entitled to respect." The professor must have understood my standpoint, as when we parted he paid me the greatest compliment I had ever received from a former enemy: "Colonel Skorzeny, in the long run it will be shown that you were right."

After this last Nuremberg intermezzo, Radl and I went together, voluntarily of course, to the internment camp at Darmstadt, to go through the denazification mill. We were not in the least worried, for we knew that we had never done anything against the interests of Germany or the new state of Hesse, and my acquittal by the Allies, against whom we had worked and fought, was a record that we had only done our duty as good Germans. Nor had we anything to fear from two so-called "specific charges" against us, on any proper interpretation of the Nuremberg judgment against the Organizations.

We had now nearly three years of internment behind us, and there is no further need for me to describe internment camp life common to millions of German soldiers. Some camps may have been better and others worse than Darmstadt. Most of the guards and civilians treated me pretty decently. They took such jobs as the only alternative to starvation.

A president for the trial court was soon appointed. He was a former officer and, sympathizing with our position, was prepared to give us a fair and speedy hearing. Unfortunately, our hopes proved illusory. A date was fixed for the hearing in April, 1948, but it was postponed because a higher official had an idea that the Mussolini episode should be charged as a political crime. Incidentally, that idea had never entered the head of even the most ferocious of my opponents at Dachau. There was a second postponement half an hour before the postponed sitting, on the ground that certain documents had not arrived.

When a new prosecutor was appointed, I tried again and asked that as there were only two complaints against me, there should be a preliminary investigation *before* the trial, in accordance with the usual practice. I felt certain that if this request were refused, I could take the point at the trial, and if I did so, there would be criticism of the authorities, which I did not desire. I also said that if the falsity of the sworn statements were established, the deponent should be prosecuted for perjury.

A telegram was sent in my presence to the criminal police at Heidelberg, asking them to make enquiries into one of the complaints which had been lodged by a soldier, who had sworn that I had condemned him to death because he had refused to turn out for some operation. A few weeks later the papers relating to the affair were produced. My name figured in them.

The second charge broke down when Radl was interrogated.

I made one more attempt to have my name formally cleared of everything, but the interrogation was again postponed. My patience was at an end and, at a final talk with the prosecutor on the 25th July, I told him openly that I would leave the camp. I made my intentions equally clear to all and sundry.

During my last night behind barbed wire I pondered long over the years I had passed there. I could feel no hate in me, despite all I had gone through. The honourable foe, who had fought face to face, could be my future friend, but I could never have any truck with the sneaking enemy behind my back.

APPENDIX

Abbreviations and German terms used in the text

KRIPO—Kriminalpolizei — Criminal Police

Ob—Oberbefehlshaber — Commander in Chief

OKH—Oberkommando des Heeres — High Command of the Army

OKW—Oberkommando der Wehrmacht — High Command of the Armed Forces

RSHA—Reichssicherheitshauptamt — Reich Security Main Office

SD—Sicherheitsdienst — Security Service

SS—Schutzstaffeln — Protection Squads

Waffen SS — SS units forming part of the German Armed Forces used only on the fronts

Ritterkreuz — Knight's Cross of the Iron Cross

Eichenlaub zum Ritterkreuz — Oak Leaves to the Knight's Cross of the Iron Cross

Leibstandarte Adolf Hitler — Guard Regiment "Adolf Hitler"

Ia — Chief Staff Officer of a Division

The Commissioned Ranks of the Waffen SS and their Army Equivalents

Untersturmführer	2nd Lieutenant
Obersturmführer	Lieutenant
Hauptsturmführer	Captain
Sturmbannführer	Major
Obersturmbannführer	Lieutenant-Colonel
Standartenführer	Colonel (Oberst)
Oberführer	Brigadier-General
Brigadeführer	Major-General
Gruppenführer	Lieutenant-General
Obergruppenführer	General
Oberstgruppenführer	Colonel-General (General Oberst)